ARSENAL OF DEMOCRACY

Great Lakes Books

*A complete listing of the books in this series
can be found online at wsupress.wayne.edu*

ARSENAL OF DEMOCRACY

The American Automobile Industry
in World War II

Charles K. Hyde

WAYNE STATE UNIVERSITY PRESS
DETROIT

© 2013 by Wayne State University Press, Detroit, Michigan 48201. All rights reserved. No part of this book may be reproduced without formal permission. Manufactured in the United States of America.

17 16 15 14 13   5 4 3 2 1

Library of Congress Cataloging-in-Publication Data

Hyde, Charles K., 1945–
  Arsenal of democracy : the American automobile industry in World War II / Charles K. Hyde.
    pages cm. — (Great Lakes books)
  Includes bibliographical references and index.
  ISBN 978-0-8143-3951-0 (cloth : alk. paper) — ISBN 978-0-8143-3952-7 (ebook)
  1. Automobile industry and trade—United States—History—20th century. 2. Defense industries—United States—History—20th century. 3. World War, 1939–1945—United States. I. Title.
  HD9710.U52H93 2013
  338.4'7629222097309044—dc23
                          2013006167

∞

Designed and typeset by Anna Oler
Composed in Fairfield and Case Study No1

To the memory of Henry C. Hyde (1910–2001), Technical Sergeant, United States Army Signal Corps, Pacific Theater, New Guinea and the Philippine Islands, 1944–45, and for all who served.

Contents

Preface

This book grew indirectly out of my earlier work in automotive industry history, including the histories of the Chrysler Corporation, the Dodge Brothers, Nash Motors, and the Hudson Motor Car Company. In the course of my research on those automakers, I encountered several "snapshots" or "glimpses" of the contributions made by American automobile manufacturers to the astounding production of weapons and materials during World War II. Much has been written about the conversion of American civilian industry into the "arsenal of democracy," which to a great extent enabled U.S. armed forces and those of its allies to achieve victory. This will be more of an inside view of the war effort from the perspective of the automakers than previously possible because it uses internal corporate records that have been largely ignored.

What has inspired me and at the same time has driven me to write this book is a remarkable collection of records from the wartime auto industry. The auto industry trade association at the time of World War II, the Automobile Manufacturers Association (AMA), was formally established in 1934 but had roots extending back to the formation in 1900 of the National Association of Automobile Manufacturers (NAAM). On 30 December 1941, under the leadership of George Romney, the AMA reconstituted itself as the Automotive Council for War Production (ACWP), with the stated goal of coordinating auto industry war work. By the end of the conflict, the ACWP had collected an enormous amount of information about the auto industry during the war. The documentation includes many thousands of photographs taken of war products and war production in auto plants throughout the United States. In the early 1950s the AMA donated the wartime records to the National Automotive History Collection (NAHC), part of the Detroit Public Library.

I wish to thank many individuals who helped me along the way. First and fore-most are the archivists and librarians who assisted my efforts with considerable skill, energy, patience, and good cheer. Paige Plant and Mark Bowden of the NAHC were extremely helpful, as was Barbara Fronczak, who processed the collection of the ACWP. Terry Hoover, chief archivist at the Benson Ford Research Center in Dear-born, Michigan, helped me navigate through the war records of the Ford Motor Company. Gregory Wallace, the director of the General Motors Heritage Center in Sterling Heights, Michigan, and Christo Datini, the center's archivist, were also extremely helpful. David White at the Richard P. Scharchburg Archives at Ketter-ing University in Flint, Michigan, led me to additional General Motors materials relating to war production. Andrew Beckman, archivist at the Studebaker National Museum in South Bend, Indiana, helped me with Studebaker Corporation materi-als. Randy Talbot, Command Historian at the U.S. Army Tank Automotive Com-mand (TACOM) in Warren, Michigan, made TACOM's historical records available to me.

Special thanks to three friends and colleagues for their assistance and encourage-ment. Tom Geniusz made his extensive World War II library available to me. Mike Davis, the author of an earlier pictorial history of the arsenal of democracy and a good friend, made his extensive library and photographic collection available for my use and encouraged me to move forward with this book. Larry D. Lankton, longtime colleague and friend, shared with me his research files compiled quite a few years ago, when he planned to write a book similar to this one. In addition, Buick historian Larry Gustin and Leroy D. Cole shared some of their private research files relating to General Motors with me. Two anonymous readers who reviewed the manuscript for the Wayne State University Press made this book better, and many others have encouraged me to complete this book. Of course, any errors that remain are my sole responsibility.

Abbreviations

ACAD	Automotive Committee for Air Defense
ACWP	Automotive Council for War Production Collection, NAHC
AMA	Automobile Manufacturers Association
ANMB	Army-Navy Munitions Board
BFRC	Benson Ford Research Center, The Henry Ford, Dearborn, Michigan
CCA	Chrysler Corporate Archives, Detroit, Michigan
CIO	Congress of Industrial Organizations
CKH	Author's personal collection
CPFF	Cost-plus-a-fixed-fee (type of contract)
CPPC	Cost-plus-a-percentage-of-cost (type of contract)
DPC	Defense Plant Corporation
FDRL	Franklin D. Roosevelt Presidential Library, Hyde Park, New York
FHA	Federal Housing Authority
GMCMA	General Motors Corporation Media Archives
GMHC	General Motors Heritage Center, Sterling Heights, Michigan
GOCO	Government-owned, contractor-operated
NAHC	National Automotive History Collection, Detroit Public Library, Detroit, Michigan
NDAC	National Defense Advisory Commission
NDMB	National Defense Mediation Board
NDRC	National Defense Research Committee
NWLB	National War Labor Board
OPA	Office of Price Administration
OPACS	Office of Price Administration and Civilian Supply

OPM   Office of Production Management
OWM   Office of War Mobilization
QC   Quartermaster Corps
RFC   Reconstruction Finance Corporation
SA/KU   Richard P. Scharchburg Archives, Kettering University, Flint, Michigan
SM   Buick Gallery and Research Center, Sloan Museum, Flint, Michigan
SPAB   Supply, Priorities and Allocations Board
SWPC   Smaller War Plants Corporation
SWPD   Smaller War Plants Division
TACOM   Tank Automotive Command (U.S. Army) Library, Warren, Michigan
UAW   United Automobile Workers of America
UMW   United Mine Workers of America
WLB   War Labor Board
WPB   War Production Board
WPRL   Walter P. Reuther Library of Labor and Urban Affairs, Wayne State
         University, Detroit, Michigan
WSK   William S. Knudsen Papers, NAHC

Introduction

The story of America's monumental production achievements during World War II, sometimes expressed as the "arsenal of democracy," is a complex, multilayered story that ideally should also include everything that comprised the home front. This book is not intended to be a comprehensive reexamination of all of the economic, social, and political changes that transpired in the United States from the late 1930s through the end of the war and beyond. There is already an extensive historical literature that examines various elements of this larger tale.

General histories of the war effort and the home front include Michael Adams, *The Best War Ever* (1994); Donald Albrecht, *World War II and the American Dream: How Wartime Building Changed a Nation* (1995); Doris Kearns Goodwin, *No Ordinary Time, Franklin and Eleanor Roosevelt: The Home Front in World War II* (1994); Richard R. Lingman, *Don't You Know There's a War On? The American Home Front, 1941–1945* (1970); Alan S. Milward, *War, Economy and Society, 1939–1945* (1977); William L. O'Neill, *A Democracy at War: America's Fight at Home and Abroad in World War II* (1993); Richard Polenberg, *War and Society: The United States, 1941–1945* (1972); and Allan M. Winkler, *Home Front U.S.A.: America during World War II* (2000).

The complex legal and political dimensions of creating and then operating a government-controlled system for planning and managing rearmament and war production is told in detail by Paul A. C. Koistinen in two studies, *Planning War, Pursuing Peace: The Political Economy of American Warfare, 1920–1939* (1998) and *Arsenal of World War II: The Political Economy of American Warfare, 1940–1945* (2004). Michael Carew's *Becoming the Arsenal: The American Industrial Mobilization for World War II, 1938–1942* (2010) emphasizes the continuity of the World War II military-industrial economy with that of World War I.

Published general histories of the military-industrial partnership during the war include Robert Howe Connery, *The Navy and the Industrial Mobilization in World War II* (1951); Keith E. Eiler, *Mobilizing America: Robert P. Patterson and the War Effort, 1940–1945* (1997); Donald M. Nelson, *Arsenal of Democracy: The Story of American War Production* (1946); Francis Walton, *Miracle of World War II: How American Industry Made Victory Possible* (1956); and Gerald T. White, *Billions for Defense: Government Finance by the Defense Plant Corporation During World War II* (1980).

Books that focus on the automobile industry's contributions to the war effort include the Automobile Manufacturers Association, *Freedom's Arsenal: The Story of the Automotive Council for War Production* (1950); Alan Clive, *State of War: Michigan in World War II* (1979); Michael W. R. Davis, *Detroit's Wartime Industry: Arsenal of Democracy* (2007); and V. Dennis Wrynn, *Detroit Goes to War: The American Automobile Industry in World War II* (1993). Labor's role is considered in James B. Attleson, *Labor and the Wartime State: Labor Relations and Law during World War II* (1998); Martin Glaberman, *Wartime Strikes: The Struggle against the No-Strike Pledge in the UAW during World War II* (1980); and Nelson Lichtenstein, *Labor's War at Home: The CIO in World War II* (1982).

This book will not attempt to cover all of the industries that were involved in war production or to include all of the various war products. The focus will be almost entirely on the American automobile industry and its contributions to the war. This study will ignore the production of ships, certainly crucial to the war effort. The history of aircraft production will be examined only in terms of the contributions of the automobile industry to aircraft production. Basic industries such as steel, coal, and copper, other strategic materials, and vital parts of the national infrastructure, including railroads, will not be included. The construction of housing for defense workers and the building of expressways and other highways will be ignored as well. Broad social changes such as the introduction of large numbers of women and African American workers into the workforce will be examined only insofar as these changes impacted the auto industry. The book will also not consider reconversion to peacetime production at the end of the war.

This book will instead focus on the role played by the automobile industry in war production. This industry was arguably the most important contributor to the war effort; it alone accounted for one-fifth of the dollar value of war production nationally. The auto industry produced an enormous quantity of components for virtually all of the military aircraft produced during the war. Aircraft manufacturers could not have completed more than a fraction of their production without the auto industry's involvement. In a broader sense, the auto industry served as a model for the rest of

American wartime industries. Its mass production methods were the envy of other manufacturers, who tried to adopt them for their own war work.

The production miracles achieved during the war were made possible because of several novel, cooperative relationships that developed between the U.S. military services, the leadership of the auto industry, the suppliers to the auto industry, the United Automobile Workers union (UAW), and the federal civilian government, namely the administration of Franklin D. Roosevelt. These relationships began to develop well before the beginning of hostilities. These disparate forces, which normally had conflicting interests and were deeply suspicious of each other, worked cooperatively for the common goal of winning the war. The constantly evolving relationships did not emerge seamlessly or without conflict and struggle.

This study will focus on the development of these working relationships and will evaluate the success of the procurement and production systems that emerged during the war. Other studies of wartime production have acknowledged that an entirely new system to manage war production developed, but none has examined in detail how the system worked in practice. This book will use several detailed case studies of particular war plants and products as a prism to illuminate the functioning of this cooperative system, warts and all. Several scholars have argued that the experiences of World War II laid the foundation for a subsequent set of relationships often dubbed the "military-industrial complex."

Chapter 1 will examine the extensive preparations for wartime production that began modestly with the passage of the federal Educational Orders Act of 1938 but accelerated rapidly well before U.S. entry into the war in December 1941. One focus will be the development of government agencies in Washington to coordinate and jump-start the rearmament efforts. The Roosevelt administration created increasingly powerful agencies to mobilize the economy in preparation for war: the National Defense Advisory Commission (NDAC) on 30 May 1940, the Office of Production Management (OPM) on 7 January 1941, and the Supply, Priorities and Allocations Board (SPAB) on 28 August 1941. The other focus will be the automobile industry's nearly intransigent resistance to taking on defense contracts until Pearl Harbor and how the industry gradually modified its attitude as a result of government incentives and persuasion.

Chapter 2 will examine defense mobilization from Pearl Harbor through the end of the war. President Roosevelt established the War Production Board (WPB) on 16 January 1942 to manage and coordinate the mobilization of the American economy for the war effort, but the conversion of America's industry for war production had already been well under way for nearly two years. The operation of the WPB under Donald Nelson will be critically examined. The government's efforts to supply the manpower needs of the defense industry and simultaneously minimize strikes and other labor unrest will receive some attention. Much of this chapter will evaluate the operation of the procurement and supply system for war goods. The efforts to minimize war profiteering through the renegotiation of war contracts and the treatment of small business will be part of this discussion. The critical role played by the Defense Plant Corporation (DPC) in building defense plants and in providing the defense industry with machine tools will be considered as well.

The remainder of the book will examine particular categories of products on which the automobile industry had a major impact. These will include aircraft engines, aircraft components, and complete aircraft; tanks; trucks and jeeps; guns, shells, and bullets; and miscellaneous war goods. The roles played by workers in war production, particularly female and African American workers, will be the focus of a separate chapter. The book will conclude with an evaluation of the automobile industry's contribution to war production.

ONE

Preparing for War before Pearl Harbor

As war clouds gathered over Europe and Asia in the late 1930s, U.S. military leaders and President Franklin D. Roosevelt began preparations for war, but only haltingly and quietly at first. Nazi Germany annexed Austria in March 1938, and in September of the same year Germany took control of Czechoslovakia's Sudetenland. Hitler swallowed the rest of Czechoslovakia in March 1939 and, along with the Soviet Union, overran Poland in September. Britain and France declared war on Germany on 3 September 1939, marking the onset of World War II. After a six-month calm, called the "Phoney War" by the press, Germany invaded Norway and Denmark on 10 April 1940. Starting on 10 May 1940, Hitler quickly overran the Netherlands, Belgium, and France. In Asia, Japanese military aggression against China, ongoing since July 1937, resulted in the establishment of a Japanese-controlled puppet government on 30 March 1940, controlling most of eastern China.

While these disturbing developments occurred in Europe and Asia, the United States was woefully ill prepared for any significant military action. In August 1940, the United States Regular Army had about 280,000 men and the National Guard from the various states consisted of another 250,000 men. In sharp contrast, the German army had nearly six million men and the Luftwaffe an additional 500,000 in mid-1940. The Japanese, with a much smaller population than the United States, had an army of 2.1 million by 1941. Poland and the Netherlands both had larger armies, as did Francisco Franco's Spain, with a force of 950,000 seasoned troops. In August 1940, Robert P. Patterson assumed the office of assistant secretary of war, responsible for military procurement for the army and Army Air Corps. His comment upon taking office, "the cupboard was nearly bare," accurately described the available stocks of weapons, equipment, and supplies. There were barely enough 1902 vintage Springfield rifles to equip the infantry, and new recruits often had to train with wooden rifles. Artillery consisted of about 5,000 French 75s (75-mm) from World War I. They had wooden "artillery" wheels and were designed to be pulled by horses or mules. The United States had fewer than 400 light tanks, useless against Germany's 3,000 medium and heavy tanks. The cupboard contained only two hundred .37-mm antitank guns. The Army Air Corps had just 2,775 planes, only 300 of which were combat aircraft; the rest were trainers. There were almost no stockpiles of ammunition.[1]

The lack of preparedness is vividly shown by contrasting the weapons and materials on hand in July 1940 with the projected needs of an army of two million men to be created over the next eighteen to twenty-four months. The number of tanks was to grow from a mere 64 in July 1941 to 4,383 by July 1942; the stock of howitzers of several sizes would need to expand from 756 to 4,337; and the supply of .30-caliber M1 rifles had to jump from 46,067 to 341,199 by December 1941. New weapons that were barely part of the arsenal in July 1940 were also produced in large numbers by December 1941, including 85,000 machine guns, 217,000 submachine guns, and 9,518 mortars.[2]

Prior to Pearl Harbor, the American automobile industry had little interest in making defense products. Following a gradual recovery in sales and production in 1935–37 from the depths of the Great Depression, sales in 1938 plummeted to 2 million units from 3.9 million the previous year. The auto industry enjoyed a recovery of sales and profits in 1939–41, with sales reaching 3.8 million units in 1941. The experience at General Motors reflected that of the entire industry. GM's sales in 1937 (1.9 million units) were greater than they had been in 1929 but then plummeted to 1.1 million in 1938. Sales recovered to over 2 million units in 1940 and 2.3 million in 1941. The automakers were not willing to convert existing factory space they were using to earn profits in car and truck manufacturing over to defense production. They did not have the necessary machine tools on hand, and factory space that worked well in making automobiles and automotive components generally was not suitable for making things like tanks and airplanes. Except for the Albert Kahn–designed Ford Motor Company River Rouge complex in Dearborn, Michigan, and a handful of factories built in the late 1930s, most auto plants consisted of multistory reinforced concrete buildings, each containing a thicket of columns supporting the floors above.[3]

The antiwar sentiments of key automotive leaders, along with their distrust of Roosevelt's New Deal administration stemming from their conservative political beliefs, also hindered rearmament. After initially agreeing to make 9,000 Rolls-Royce aircraft engines for the American and British militaries, Henry Ford rejected this arrangement in June 1940. As an Anglophobe, he objected to the contract's provision to send 3,000 engines to the British. He may have had some lingering pacifist sentiments from World War I. Alfred P. Sloan Jr., the CEO of General Motors at the onset of war, was a more vehement opponent of war and of the Roosevelt administration. Sloan believed that American involvement in the European war would damage General Motors by forcing the company to give up its industry-leading, lucrative automobile production and bring a government-controlled economy that would limit GM's independence. He strongly discouraged GM executives, most notably GM president William S. Knudsen, from leaving the automaker for government service. In May 1941, after Hitler had conquered Europe and threatened Britain, Sloan did not view the war as a moral battle between conflicting ideologies but as "really nothing more or less than a conflict between two opposing technocracies."[4]

In trying to prepare the United States for war against the Axis Powers, President Roosevelt also had to overcome the deep-seated beliefs of a majority of Americans that the United States should not get drawn into the European conflict. Labeled "isolationists" and, more specifically, "anti-interventionists," many influential groups and individuals believed in "Fortress America," the notion that the oceans that separate the United States from Europe and Asia would protect Americans from danger. They believed that the United States should remain neutral and avoid taking any action that might draw the country into the conflict. Anti-interventionists controlled Congress until the summer of 1939.[5]

The America First Committee, founded on 4 September 1940, became the most politically powerful force against intervention in the European war right up to Pearl Harbor. Charles Lindbergh, perhaps the most famous American to actively oppose intervention, delivered his first major anti-intervention speech on 15 September 1939 but did not officially join the America First Committee until April 1941. From then until Pearl Harbor, Lindbergh was America First's most popular and controversial speaker. Long an admirer of the Germans and particularly of German air power developed by the Nazis, Lindbergh often seemed like a Nazi spokesman. Father Charles E. Coughlin, who published a weekly tabloid, *Social Justice,* and hosted a weekly radio broadcast that may have reached forty million people, combined his anti-Semitism and pro-Nazi sentiments in opposing intervention.[6]

The widespread anti-interventionist/isolationist/neutralist sentiments became a matter of law. The First Neutrality Act, signed by Roosevelt on 31 August 1935, prohibited U.S. vessels from trading arms with any belligerent. The Second Neutrality Act (29 February 1936) extended the first law but included a prohibition against granting loans in any form to any combatant. The Third Neutrality Act, signed by Roosevelt on 1 May 1937, continued the earlier arms embargo and the prohibition on loans to warring countries but expanded the definition of "war" to include civil wars such as the one in Spain. Recognizing the perilous military situation in which Britain and France found themselves after the Nazi defeat of Poland, Congress substantially modified the earlier acts with the Fourth Neutrality Act, signed by Roosevelt on 4 November 1939. Congress repealed the previous arms embargo and allowed the export of weapons and munitions to belligerents on a "cash and carry" basis only. All materials purchased had to be delivered in foreign vessels, reducing the likelihood that American ships and American lives would be lost. The law in effect prohibited the United States from providing military equipment and supplies on credit.[7]

In promoting the rearmament of the United States in the late 1930s, the Roosevelt administration tried to avoid the mistakes made during World War I in awarding defense contracts. There is a good deal of evidence that some makers of armaments during World War I earned very large if not obscene profits from their government contracts. This war profiteering became a key argument against intervention in the late 1930s. During World War I, arms makers received "cost-plus" contracts, under which they were paid the estimated cost of the product plus a 15 percent fee based on the predetermined price (the "bogey" price), regardless of the actual costs once production began. The Packard Motor Car Company received a "bogey" price of $6,087 for the Liberty engines it produced, which included a profit of $913 per engine. The price was negotiated downward to $5,000 per engine, and Packard in time reduced the cost per engine to less than $3,200, but its profits were based on the higher costs. Packard invested less than $6 million in the plant that made these engines, kept the plant after the war, and still earned profits of $3.75 million on this contract. The Dayton-Wright Aircraft Company invested only $1 million to produce aircraft for the army but earned $6 million in profits.[8]

World War I profiteering was not limited to manufacturers of aircraft and aircraft engines. At the urging of pacifists and anti-business interests, the U.S. Senate established the Special Committee Investigating the Munitions Industry in April 1934, chaired by Senator Gerald P. Nye (R-ND). The committee's investigation of World War I procurement practices lasted two years. Among its many reports, the Nye Committee concluded that the three largest American shipbuilders conspired during World War I, with the help of the Navy Department, to monopolize contracts for new ships, raise prices, and greatly inflate their profits. The passage of the Vinson-

Trammel Act of 1934, which restricted profits on government shipbuilding contracts to 10 percent of costs, was an attempt to alter the behavior of the navy and the shipbuilders. The Unites States Steel Corporation, which had net earnings of less than $82 million in 1914, saw earnings average $256 million per year for 1917 and 1918. The average pre-tax rate of return for the rest of the steel industry jumped from 7.4 percent in 1914 to 28.7 percent in 1917. The Nye Committee documented several other glaring examples, like the Savage Arms Company, which in 1917 earned a 60 percent rate of return on its investment. E. I. du Pont de Nemours and Company, which had a near monopoly on smokeless gunpowder, became an easy target for the Nye Committee. Du Pont's sales jumped elevenfold during the war, dividends paid on common stock skyrocketed from 2.5 percent to 32 percent, and share prices of common stock increased fivefold.[9]

Because of these long-held suspicions of traditional arms manufacturers, the Roosevelt administration proceeded cautiously in issuing the defense contracts needed to rearm the nation. Congress and the administration took one halting baby step toward rearmament with the passage of the Educational Orders Act on 16 June 1938. The act provided for the issuing of no-bid contracts to manufacturers to produce small quantities of products with which they were not familiar. These were "cost-plus" contracts, where the manufacturer could recover all of the costs of production and charge a small profit, typically 5 or 6 percent of the value of the contract. The government would provide all machinery needed for the work. These were "educational orders": the contractor would learn how to make war goods at no risk to the company.

The initial educational orders program provided for $2 million in contracts awarded to six manufacturers to produce gas masks, searchlights, M1 rifles, and recoil mechanisms for anti-aircraft guns, and to work on forging and machining 75-mm shells. After the army discovered it needed at least fifty additional products that had not been manufactured before, Congress appropriated an additional $32.5 million in January 1939 to expand the program. The second round of contracts went to 250 companies. The military services preferred to issue educational order contracts to multiple firms to compare the performance of different contractors in terms of the speed, quality, and cost of production.[10]

The Chrysler Corporation's extensive surviving records offer some insight into the educational orders system of procurement. After refusing to accept an order for 500,000 cases for 75-mm cartridges on the grounds that it lacked manufacturing experience, Chrysler agreed to an educational order for 5,000 cases in March 1940, followed by an order for 10,000 cartridge cases in May 1940, and an additional order for 878,000 cases in late September 1940. At the request of the government,

Chrysler shared its expertise in making cartridge cases with the Motor Products Company, a Detroit supplier to the auto industry. Chrysler signed a dozen educational order contracts in 1940 and 1941, including contracts to complete forging and machining work for 75-mm shells, to manufacture bomb nose fuses, and to assemble recoil mechanisms for three types of artillery. The government did, however, reject eleven proposals Chrysler made for educational orders in 1941 and 1942. The government rejected Chrysler's offer to build incendiary bombs because the company had not subcontracted the required 60 percent of the value of the contract.[11]

An educational order granted to the Saginaw Steering Gear Division of General Motors to manufacture .30-caliber Browning machine guns illustrates how the process worked. In late 1937, an officer from the U.S. Army Detroit Ordnance Office casually discussed the feasibility of Saginaw Steering Gear making these machine guns. Following a visit of all the parties to the Colt Patent Firearms plant in Connecticut in spring 1938, Saginaw Steering Gear agreed in principle to an educational order for 500 machine guns. Upon completing the order, Saginaw Steering Gear would turn over to the government the guns, the machinery used to make them, and all the plans and blueprints. On 15 June 1940, the government finally placed the educational order, which called for the delivery of 280 machine guns by March 1942. Saginaw Steering quickly built a new plant, which was fully equipped and operational in April 1941. By March 1942, Saginaw Steering had delivered 28,728 Browning machine guns to the government and the price per gun fell from $667 in the original contract to $141 after Saginaw Steering Gear improved its production efficiency.[12]

Although the system of educational orders provided a means for introducing manufacturers to the production of unfamiliar military products, this was a very modest program. If the United States was going to prepare for involvement in the war raging in Europe and Asia, a broad national program for coordinating defense production would be needed. Drastically changing circumstances of the European war in May 1940 provided FDR with a rationale for moving to war planning on a national scale.

The National Defense Advisory Commission and Rearmament

Shortly after the Nazi invasion of the Low Countries, President Roosevelt sent a message to Congress on 16 May 1940 asking for additional defense appropriations of nearly $1.2 billion. He called for a program to build 50,000 military aircraft a year. The president repeated these goals in a "fireside chat" on 26 May 1940. Shortly thereafter on 28 May 1940, Roosevelt reactivated the Advisory Commission to the

Council on National Defense, more commonly known as the National Defense Advisory Commission (NDAC). The act of Congress that created the original Advisory Commission on 29 August 1916 to help mobilize the United States for entrance into World War I had remained on the books. The Council on National Defense, as defined in the 1916 statute, consisted of the secretaries of war, navy, interior, agriculture, commerce, and labor. By reactivating this Advisory Commission to direct industrial mobilization for war, Roosevelt maintained civilian oversight but avoided congressional involvement.[13]

President Roosevelt announced the identities and duties of the seven-member Advisory Commission: Edward R. Stettinius Jr., chairman of the board of the United States Steel Corporation, would be in charge of raw materials; Ralph Budd, chairman of the board of the Chicago, Burlington and Quincy Railroad, would take control of transportation; Chester C. Davis, a member of the Federal Reserve Board, would manage agricultural production; Leon Henderson, a member of the Securities and Exchange Commission, would manage price stabilization for raw materials; Sidney Hillman, president of the Amalgamated Clothing Workers of America, would coordinate wartime employment policies; Harriet Elliot, Dean of Women at the University of North Carolina, would focus on consumer affairs; and perhaps most important, William S. Knudsen, president of the General Motors Corporation, would be in charge of the manufacturing of all war products.[14]

William Signius Knudsen (1879–1948) was born in Copenhagen, Denmark, the first of six children and the only son of Knud Peter and Augusta Zoller Knudsen. He completed nine years of public education and was an outstanding student in a demanding education system. After working as an apprentice for a wholesaler who sold hardware, crockery, and toys, Knudsen assembled bicycles and managed the warehouse for a Copenhagen bicycle maker. He migrated to the United States in 1900 and initially worked in a shipyard and later as a boiler repairman for the Erie Railroad. Knudsen's big break came when he took a job at the John R. Keim Mill in Buffalo, New York, in 1902. Keim manufactured bicycles, ball bearings for automobiles, and a wide variety of automobile components. Knudsen quickly moved up the administrative ladder at the Keim Mill and served as general superintendent in 1909–13. Keim won a large contract in 1906 from the Ford Motor Company to manufacture rear axle housings and crankcases. Henry Ford was so pleased with Keim's work that in June 1911 he bought the company (and Knudsen's services).[15]

Following a wildcat strike of Keim workers in Buffalo in September 1912, Henry Ford moved most of Keim's machinery to his Highland Park, Michigan, factory later in the year and Keim's key executives followed in late 1913. Knudsen reluctantly moved to Detroit in 1913 and Ford put him in charge of establishing and managing

Ford's branch assembly plants all over the country, a position he held until 1918, when Ford appointed him production manager for all of Ford's operations. Following a dispute with Henry Ford, Knudsen resigned from the Ford Motor Company at the end of February 1921 and soon began a long tenure with General Motors. Knudsen served as vice president for manufacturing at Chevrolet (1922–24), as general manager of Chevrolet, and as a vice president and director at General Motors (1924–33). Knudsen became president of General Motors in May 1937 and served until resigning his position in May 1940 to work on war production. Commonly called "Big Bill," Knudsen was an imposing figure, six feet three inches tall and weighing well over two hundred pounds.[16]

Bernard Baruch, a member of Roosevelt's "Brain Trust" during the New Deal and a close advisor to FDR, had highly recommended Knudsen to manage war production. Roosevelt called Knudsen in late May 1940 and summoned him to Washington to take a still undefined assignment. Knudsen stopped first in New York to discuss the matter with Alfred P. Sloan, the chairman of General Motors. Sloan vehemently opposed Knudsen's plans to work for the government, but the Danish immigrant was equally adamant, reminding Sloan that he could take a ninety-day leave of absence from General Motors before making a final decision. Knudsen's rationale was simple: "My duty lies in what the President of the United States wants me to do. . . . I came to this country with nothing. It has been good to me. Rightly or wrongly, I feel I must go." In leaving General Motors, he gave up an annual salary (with bonuses) of roughly $300,000. He would not even become one of the many "dollar-a-year men" but worked for no pay.[17]

Knudsen recalled his first meeting with Roosevelt, his cabinet, and the other members of the NDAC on 30 May 1940. Roosevelt outlined the general functions of the NADC and asked his cabinet to cooperate in every way with their work. Roosevelt admitted that the advisory group had no real legal authority other than what he gave them. Knudsen noticed that there was no chair for the commission and at one point asked, "Who is the boss?" The president's response was, "I guess I am." Knudsen sent FDR a letter on 5 June 1940 in which he agreed to serve for only ninety days to start, after which the president would decide whether his work was satisfactory and Knudsen would then serve as long as needed. Knudsen listed all of the securities he owned and promised to make no changes to his holdings while he worked for the government. He wanted to avoid the charges made against the "dollar-a-year men" of profiting from inside knowledge. Knudsen ended the letter with another expression of his patriotism: "I am most happy and grateful that you have made it possible for me to show, in small measure, my gratitude to my country for the opportunity it has given me to acquire home, family, and happiness in abundant measure." Knudsen categorized the war products that needed to be manufactured into six divisions and named one man to head up each division. For example, one division incorporated tanks, trucks, and other vehicles while another included small arms, explosives, and ammunition.[18]

The NDAC lasted for a little more than seven months; it was replaced in January 1941 by the more tightly structured Office of Production Management (OPM). The NDAC had to quickly ramp up military production using civilian industry that needed a lot of assistance and convincing. After starving the American military for decades, in June 1940 Congress agreed to a $1.3 billion appropriation for the navy and a $6 billion spending plan for the army. The latter appropriation included funding for the Army Air Corps, which was part of the army at that time. Knudsen had to ask Roosevelt to remove several legal and bureaucratic barriers that would have made fast and efficient war production nearly impossible.[19]

One barrier was the Vinson-Trammell Act, passed in 1934 to prevent war profiteering by limiting profits on war contracts. The Treasury Department had ruled that these contracts needed to be audited in advance, an unreasonable requirement for manufacturers making unfamiliar products. Another problem was the result of the slow speed at which contracts for war work were issued. The government wanted manufacturers to move ahead with work before actually receiving a contract, but companies were worried about their liability for expenditures if the contract ended up being canceled. They also wanted a "letter of intent" from the government so they could arrange bank financing to start the work. Roosevelt agreed to make these contracts "bankable" and to reimburse all expenses incurred. These barriers were largely removed when Congress passed the Second Revenue Act of October 1940. Knudsen also discovered an Army General Staff rule prohibiting the operation of defense plants within 250 miles of a foreign nation, including Canada and Mexico. He pointed out to General George Marshall that this would rule out production in Detroit, Cleveland, and Buffalo, among other places. The rule was never changed, but Knudsen and others ignored it.[20]

Early in his tenure, Knudsen had many requests from congressmen and senators who wanted defense plants built in their districts. These he politely rejected. Knudsen decided early in his tenure that most contracts for war goods would be awarded to companies with engineering departments because extensive re-engineering of these products was typically required. This meant that most contracts would go to large firms, which brought criticism that smaller firms were unfairly excluded. Knudsen argued that smaller companies would receive plenty of work as subcontractors. Later in the war, rules were put in place guaranteeing that this would be the case.[21]

One of the greatest barriers to getting war production under way was obtaining financing to construct new war plants. The NDAC established a separate committee on 10 July 1940 to address the problem of plant financing. There was general agreement that the government would have to build arsenal-type factories that would make guns, gunpowder, explosives, shells, and other ordnance. These plants could be operated directly by the government or by private companies (for a fee) but would be owned by the government. These were special-purpose plants that would become surplus after the war because they would be unsuitable for the production of goods for civilian use. By the end of the conflict, the War Department, Navy Department, and the Maritime Commission had spent $8.9 billion on military arsenals.

At the urging of the NDAC, Congress amended the federal tax code with provisions in the Second Revenue Act of 1940, passed in October, for accelerated depreciation of defense plants and equipment. Manufacturers had been allowed depreciation rates of 5 percent on buildings and 10 percent for equipment, but the new provisions allowed for a 20 percent annual rate of depreciation on both. These tax incentives helped generate $6.5 billion of private investment in new plants and equipment, with the bulk of the investment concentrated in 1940 and 1941. The same act also suspended the provisions of the Vinson-Trammel Act. Another $8 billion invested in wartime plants and equipment was supplied by the Reconstruction Finance Corporation (RFC) or its subsidiaries, particularly the Defense Plant Corporation (DPC). The government's role in expanding defense production was huge. During World War I, American companies invested about $6 billion in new defense plants and the government financed one-tenth of the total. Investment in defense facilities in World War II ballooned to $25 billion, with government supplying two-thirds of the funding. In 1940, the dollar value of the country's manufacturing plants was less than $50 billion.[22]

Government financing of wartime plants and machinery derived indirectly from powers granted to the RFC, a federal agency created by Congress in January 1932 to provide emergency financial assistance to banks, insurance companies, mortgage companies, and railroads. After June 1934, the RFC could loan funds to any business that was unable to get loans from commercial banks. Congress authorized the RFC to create a half-dozen specialized subsidiaries in the late 1930s to provide funds for disaster relief, rural electrification, and loans for commercial mortgages, among others. One subsidiary was the Federal National Mortgage Association (Fannie Mae), organized in February 1938. President Roosevelt signed legislation on 25 June 1940 authorizing the RFC to loan funds to promote national defense production. The law specifically authorized the RFC to create subsidiary corporations to build and equip war plants and to lease these plants to private corporations. On 22 August 1940, the RFC organized the DPC for this purpose.[23]

Why did the federal government need to become so heavily involved in building defense plants? Most of the expanding defense production required new plants, particularly when the existing automobile factories were still producing cars. Automobile companies such as Ford Motor Company, which had plants large enough to fulfill large war contracts, were simply unwilling to stop automobile production to take on the new work. Most DPC-financed plant construction during the war involved aircraft or tank assembly, which required extremely large buildings rarely found in automobile plants. Financing for most large defense plants was nearly impossible to obtain from the private sector because of the sheer size of the plants and the normal risk-aversion of bankers. The DPC financed nearly $7 billion in new plant and equipment during the war, involving 2,300 projects. The largest twenty-six projects accounted for over $1.5 billion or one-fifth of the total spent. Twenty-three of those were Army Air Force projects ranging in size from the Dodge-Chicago B-29 engine plant ($174 million) to a Boeing assembly plant in Wichita, Kansas ($27 million).[24]

Conservative business organizations such as the Investment Bankers Association and the largest New York financial companies opposed the DPC, fearing government control of all industrial investment. To alleviate these fears, the NDAC announced on 23 August 1940 an alternative means of financing war plant construction: the Emergency Plant Facilities (EPF) Contract. Private defense contractors could build their own plants and the government would then buy them over sixty months and then own the facilities outright. Most contractors, however, needed to borrow the funds for construction from private banks and many of the projects were too large to be financed by a single bank. Arranging financing became a major barrier to this program and the offer made in late January 1941 by New York City's four largest banks to form a consortium to facilitate lending was not well received. By the end of the war, the EPF program financed only $350 million in new defense facilities, in contrast to the DPC's expenditure of nearly $8 billion on defense plants and equipment.[25]

The first DPC lease was issued on 6 September 1940 to the Packard Motor Car Company for machinery needed to make Rolls-Royce aircraft engines for the United States and Britain. The DPC would purchase the needed machinery for $8 million and Packard would pay the DPC a rental fee of $1,500 for every engine it delivered to the U.S. government. Similar leases were drawn up during the next six weeks to provide machinery to the Continental Motors Corporation and to the Baldwin Locomotive Works, both of which were involved in the production of tanks. The DPC also awarded its first contract to provide a manufacturer with land, buildings, and machinery. The DFC agreed to spend $550,000 to build and equip a plant for the W. F. and John Barnes Company of Rockford, Illinois, which made machine tools needed to manufacture machine guns. The DPC's first large lease agreement was with the Wright Aeronautical Corporation on 19 October 1940, in the amount of $57 million. It included monies for land, buildings, and equipment needed for an aircraft engine plant. Wright leased the plant for five years and paid a nominal rent of $1 a year. By the end of 1940, the DPC had negotiated more than thirty leases covering plants and equipment valued at more than $250 million. The lion's share went for aircraft manufacturing facilities, including three plants for the Curtiss-Wright Aircraft Corporation, one for Consolidated Aircraft, and one for North American Aviation. By the end of April 1941, the DPC had over $500 million in lease agreements in place.[26]

Defense contractors leased most of the war plants the DPC built for a fixed fee. Commonly known as GOCO (government-owned, contractor-operated) plants, these facilities were usually leased from the government by the contractor for $1 a year. Government ownership of certain types of plants was needed to get these facilities into operation. Specialized factories that made products such as high explosives, bombs, ordnance chemicals, and gunpowder required highly specialized machinery and equipment that could not be used in any other manufacturing process. Once the war ended, there would be little demand for these products. In addition, the location and layout of these specialized plants made them unusable for the production of civilian products. The giant aircraft plants built during the war would not be needed for the small peacetime production of aircraft. Outright ownership of these facilities by the government was also viewed as a way of assuring standby munitions capacity in the event of another war.[27]

The most daunting rearmament challenge was to increase production of weapons, vehicles, ammunition, and other supplies to meet the needs of the rapidly expanding military services. Roosevelt's May 1940 call for the production of 50,000 military aircraft a year must have seemed like wishful thinking. During the worst Depression years of 1932 and 1933, the industry produced fewer than 1,400 aircraft annually. In 1938, the U.S. aircraft industry made only 3,623 aircraft, including 1,800 for the military and 1,823 for civilian use. The vast majority of these planes were small, one-engine types. In 1938, twelve companies with combined sales of $156,368,000 dominated the industry. Three of these—United Aircraft, Curtiss-Wright, and Douglas—accounted for two-thirds of aircraft sales. Two firms, the Wright Aeronautical Corporation and Pratt & Whitney (United Aircraft), accounted for two-thirds of aircraft engine production.

Although scores of different aircraft were produced, the production runs for any single model were small. Typically aircraft parts and components were manufactured in small "lots" or "batches" and the completed planes were hand-assembled in small batches of 100 units or less. The parts were not interchangeable, so they were hand-fitted together. The aircraft industry generally did not employ the mass-production methods commonly used in the automobile industry, so it was not well positioned to expand production dramatically. Well before the war began, the NDAC began to develop a manufacturing system that would eventually produce the enormous numbers of planes needed. Aircraft production reached 47,873 in 1942, not far from Roosevelt's lofty goal, and leaped to 85,946 planes the following year.[28]

William Knudsen's links to the auto industry and his powers of persuasion helped jump-start aircraft production in the fall of 1940. Immediately after Knudsen toured the nation's aircraft manufacturing plants, the Automobile Manufacturers Association (AMA) invited him to their meeting at the Waldorf-Astoria in New York on 15 October 1940 to express their appreciation for his work in the auto industry and in the defense program. Knudsen had already asked the automakers to voluntarily suspend future model changes to help conserve the stock of machines tools, and they had agreed to do so. He surprised his audience by asking the auto industry to produce half a billion dollars' worth of aircraft parts and subassemblies. Because the most pressing need was to increase the supply of heavy bombers, that would be the focus of their work. All of the auto companies represented at the meeting offered their factories to mass-produce standardized aircraft body parts and other components. On 25 October 1940, representatives from the auto companies, body and parts manufacturers, tool and die makers, and aircraft manufacturers met in Detroit and established the Automotive Committee for Air Defense (ACAD). A total of eighty-five men attended this organizational meeting, including U.S. Army Air Corps officers, a U.S. Navy representative, and several executives from the NDAC. Because the AMA boardroom could not accommodate this large group, they met in a former grocery store that occupied the ground floor of the New Center Building (now the Albert Kahn Building), where the AMA had its offices. A nearby funeral home provided the chairs.[29]

The ACAD's first task was to try to "get their arms around" hundreds of components entirely unfamiliar to them. The aircraft manufacturers and the Army Air Corps agreed to supply the ACAD with blueprints and the actual parts the automobile manufacturers were going to make. A committee of six men would visit the two plants where bombers were currently assembled. The ACAD would survey existing auto industry plants and equipment that might be suitable for aircraft parts production. The aircraft manufacturers were initially suspicious that the automakers might produce aircraft and become their competitors. Knudsen allayed their fears by promising that the car companies would serve as subcontractors to the aircraft makers, who would hold the primary contracts for the finished aircraft. The AMA

Automotive Committee on Air Defense display of Martin B-26 fuselage and wing, Detroit, December 1940 (*ACWP*).

appropriated $100,000 on 1 November 1940 to help finance the work of the ACAD, which named Clarence C. Carlton from the Motor Wheel Corporation in Lansing, Michigan, as its director. The work moved forward at a remarkably fast pace. By early November, the parts for the B-26, one of the bombers being manufactured, were shipped to Detroit and put on display in an 18,000-square-foot space the ACAD had leased at a vacant Graham-Paige Motors Corporation plant in Detroit. A complete B-25 bomber undergoing testing at Wright Field in Ohio was supposed to arrive in Detroit by mid-November.[30]

The ACAD required that technical experts from the aircraft companies be present at the exhibit of parts and blueprints to answer questions from the automakers. Bomber components from the Northrop, Consolidated, and Martin companies were on display, and over 2,000 automotive engineers and production managers representing 1,018 companies visited this display from November 1940 to the spring of 1941. In late December 1940, the government laid out the broad outline of its plan for bomber production. The government would build four large bomber assembly plants and place orders for delivery of a combined total of 1,200 bombers (B-24,

B-25, and B-26). One quarter of the work on the bombers would involve the fabrication of parts and another quarter the production of subassemblies, both to be carried out by the automobile industry. The old-line aircraft companies would make the airframes and complete the final assembly of the aircraft, with each operation involving roughly one-quarter of the total work (and dollar value) required. Educational orders would be used extensively for this initial production. Deliveries were to begin in January 1942. In early March 1941, the ACAD began to wind down its operations. By then, automobile manufacturers who had contracted to make aircraft parts or components included Ford, General Motors, Chrysler, Hudson, and Goodyear Tire & Rubber Company. After the ACAD ended its operations, Clarence Carlton noted that "out of these early meetings we distilled the pleasant discovery that we could plan together, work together, build together and exchange production secrets with each other." Brought together by William Knudsen, working voluntarily but motivated by patriotism, the Detroit automakers would make an early significant contribution to aircraft production.[31]

In late December 1940, Walter P. Reuther, the director of the General Motors Department of the UAW, offered a radical proposal to produce 500 metal fighter aircraft a day within six months. He argued that at least 20 percent of the production capacity of the auto industry was unused or underutilized, and he cited more than a dozen plants that were not using 50 percent of their space. Reuther proposed that this unused capacity be converted to the mass production of aircraft parts and components, which would be delivered to the aircraft companies for final assembly. Automobile production would continue at a rate of five million units per year, but the industry would leave the 1941 models unchanged, thus freeing up tooling and skilled workers. The most innovative and controversial part of Reuther's plan was the proposed method for managing aircraft *and* automobile production. The labor leader envisioned a nine-member board consisting of three representatives each from labor, the military, and the auto industry, which would manage space allocation, materials purchasing, production schedules, wages, and manpower. Reuther had first developed this proposal in May 1940, refined it over several months, and on 23 December 1940 Phillip Murray, the president of the Congress of Industrial Organizations (CIO), presented it to President Roosevelt.[32]

Although many of Roosevelt's New Dealers and the president himself found Reuther's plan attractive, it was dead on arrival in terms of the interests that mattered. It was anathema to the automakers, who had reluctantly recognized the UAW in 1937 and had ongoing struggles with the union. Ford did not recognize the UAW until May 1941, so it was automatically excluded. To some, this seemed like a blatant scheme to organize the nonunionized aircraft workers through the back door. None of the automakers was willing to share power with the union, and the military was even more adamant in rejecting this scheme. The military services preferred to negotiate procurement contracts directly with the manufacturers without outside interference. The Reuther plan had additional shortcomings. The military services and the American allies needed bombers, not fighter planes. In addition, Knudsen and the ACAD had already begun to mobilize the auto industry for aircraft production. At Roosevelt's request, Knudsen had a meeting with Reuther to discuss his plan. Knudsen quickly realized that Reuther had no understanding of the machine tools required to make aircraft components. He gave Reuther a set of blueprints for a Pratt & Whitney aircraft engine the government wanted to produce and challenged him to identify a plant that had the machine tools needed to make the engine. Reuther returned the blueprints a few days later, admitting that neither he nor his "tool designers" could understand the drawings.[33]

Right on the heels of Reuther's proposal, Franklin Roosevelt delivered his famous "fireside chat" in which he called on the United States to become the "arsenal of democracy" to provide weapons and materials to the United States' beleaguered European allies. Broadcast on 29 December 1940, the fireside chat addressed national security and the need to assist the European nations fighting against the Nazi onslaught.

> The people of Europe who are defending themselves do not ask us to do the fighting. They ask us for the implements of war, the planes, the tanks, the guns, the freighters which will enable them to fight for their liberty and for our security. What was needed was clear: We must be the great arsenal of democracy. For us this is an emergency as serious as war itself. We must apply ourselves to our task with the same resolution, the same sense of urgency, the spirit of patriotism and sacrifice as we would show were we at war.

A week later, on 7 January 1941, Roosevelt fundamentally restructured his efforts to rearm the nation when he replaced the NDAC with the Office of Production Management (OPM), with William Knudsen and Sidney Hillman as codirectors of an agency with much greater authority.[34]

The Demise of the NDAC

Although the NDAC had some success in starting industrial mobilization, it lacked clear legal authority to force mobilization and had to rely on persuasion instead. The lack of any clear-cut chain of command within the NDAC also weakened its efforts.

Franklin D. Roosevelt at microphone, radio talk on the
arsenal of democracy, 29 December 1940 *(FDRL)*.

The seven "commissioners" operated autonomously, sometimes promoted contradictory policies, and did not speak with a single voice. Within a month after he established the NDAC, Roosevelt named Donald M. Nelson, the executive vice president of Sears, Roebuck & Company, to the post of coordinator of national defense
purchases, in effect adding an eighth member to the NDAC. Roosevelt gave the
NDAC the authority to approve all defense contacts of $500,000 or more. Further
complications to procurement included Sidney Hillman's demand that all contracts
be reviewed in light of labor laws. The NDAC attempted to plan mobilization and to
organize the producers of war goods but was isolated from the buyers and users of
those goods, the army and navy. The military services strongly asserted their authority over war contracts, and their disputes with the NDAC delayed issuing critical
contracts for aircraft, trucks, and other war goods. Planning the production of war
goods to match the needs of the military services was extremely difficult given the
structure of the NDAC.[35]

Despite President Roosevelt's apparent support of organized labor and labor's support of Roosevelt, organized labor had little power over or influence on defense production policies before or during the war. Roosevelt had appointed Hillman, president of the Amalgamated Clothing Workers of America, as the labor representative on the seven-member NDAC on 30 May 1940 without consulting with the leaders of organized labor. The two most powerful American labor leaders, John L. Lewis, president of the CIO, and William Green, president of the American Federation of Labor (AFL), disliked and distrusted Hillman as much as they disliked each other. While serving on the NDAC and in later positions, Hillman faced a hostile labor movement, a suspicious Secretary of Labor Frances Perkins, and hostile or suspicious military and industrial leaders. In addition to heading the labor division of the NDAC, Hillman was the head of the labor division of the OPM, where he was the associate director with William Knudsen, and he served on the War Production Board (WPB) until April 1942. Hillman had little influence over labor policy in these positions despite Roosevelt's apparent support.[36]

When he first joined the NDAC, Hillman tried to implement a policy of punishing companies that violated labor laws by denying them war contracts. He was particularly incensed that war contracts went to companies such as Bethlehem Steel, the Ford Motor Company, and the International Shoe Company, among others, that openly violated the National Labor Relations Act. Many companies also broke labor laws protecting standards for wages, hours, and work rules. Within months after Hillman arrived at the NDAC, the military and industrial powers, including Knudsen, combined to effectively ignore Hillman's wishes. Roosevelt refused to intervene in the dispute, guaranteeing Hillman's defeat. Both the NDAC and the OPM ignored local and regional labor conditions, including shortages of workers and housing, in deciding where to build new war plants. The failure to follow a rational labor and social policy resulted in large pockets of unemployment in some parts of the country, such as rural Pennsylvania, and severe labor shortages in other parts, such as the West Coast.[37]

One of Hillman's duties was to head off or settle strikes at war production plants. They were rare in 1940 but increased sharply in 1941. The president created the National Defense Mediation Board (NDMB) on 19 March 1941 in an effort to tamp down the rising wave of strikes in the defense industry. The NDMB included representatives of labor, management, and the public, but organized labor argued that it undermined the normal collective bargaining process. Hillman was asked to intercede in a strike at the Allis-Chalmers Company (a defense contractor) in Milwaukee in March 1941. After Hillman botched the negotiations, Knudsen ordered the workers to return to work, and a threatened takeover of the plant by the army touched off a three-day riot that ended up being quashed by the state militia. The

NDMB took seventy-six days to settle the dispute. A wildcat strike of the UAW against the North American Aviation Company plant in Inglewood, California, in June 1941 was an even bigger disaster. Roosevelt sent in troops to break the strike and seize the plant, and the CIO blamed Hillman for this. Later that year, Hillman encouraged President Roosevelt to order the navy to seize the strike-bound Federal Shipbuilding and Drydock Company facility in Kearney, New Jersey.[38]

Perhaps because industrial leaders dominated the top positions, the NDAC showed little sense of urgency in pushing mobilization and took the position that it would bring minimal disruption to civilian production. The aircraft industry resisted the War Department's insistence that military aircraft receive top priority in expanding aircraft production and complained to the NADC about misplaced priorities. In November and December 1940, two of the largest aircraft manufacturers, Lockheed and Douglas, delivered twenty-nine commercial planes to customers but only six military aircraft to the War Department. Another aircraft company, more than year behind in deliveries to the War Department, was completing twelve large commercial planes a month. The NDAC created a committee to examine the issue and then approved the aircraft industry's proposal to double civilian aviation (and aircraft). This is not to suggest that the NDAC did little to advance mobilization. By October 1940, the government had 920 defense contracts in place with 531 manufacturers, with a total value of $2.85 billion. In June 1941, the auto industry alone had $2 billion in defense contracts, with 54 percent of the dollar value for aircraft and parts and another 25 percent for trucks and tanks.[39]

The OPM

By early December 1940, President Roosevelt concluded that the NDAC would not be able to manage full mobilization for a world war. Roosevelt informed Knudsen in mid-December that a new mobilization agency, the OPM, would replace the NDAC. The formal announcement came on 7 January 1941.

The OPM would be run by a four-man board, with Knudsen serving as director general and Hillman as associate director general. Secretary of War Henry L. Stimson and Secretary of the Navy Frank Knox were the other two members. The four would establish policies that Knudsen and Hillman would implement. The other NDAC commissioners would continue their work but would no longer have direct contact with the military and would instead report to the OPM. The new board immediately hired John Lord O'Brian to serve as the OPM's general counsel to handle all legal matters. The OPM's daunting task was to coordinate the production, purchasing, and priorities of all materials and products needed for rearmament.[40]

The demands the government placed on American industry to increase defense production escalated with the passage of the Lend-Lease Act on 11 March 1941. Despite widespread opposition to this act from prominent isolationist senators and groups like America First, Roosevelt carefully guided this bill through both houses of Congress, which approved it by wide margins. The Lend-Lease Act gave the president wide discretion to lend, lease, sell, or otherwise transfer military equipment and supplies to any nation whose defense the president determined was vital to the defense of the United States. It was initially intended to aid the British, who had exhausted their credits to buy war materials. The act made Roosevelt's call for America to become "the great arsenal of democracy" even more critical.[41]

The Lend-Lease program immediately put more strain on the American defense industry. In April 1941, before Lend-Lease requirements came into play, the contracts for war goods from the military services, from the Maritime Commission, and from British orders already amounted to $49 billion. The first appropriation for Lend-Lease, mainly to Britain, was an additional $7 billion. Following Hitler's attack on the Soviet Union in June 1941, Congress approved a Lend-Lease package for Russia costing $1.8 billion to start. Thirty-eight countries were certified as eligible to receive Lend-Lease assistance by late 1941, including nationalist China. Elberton Smith credits the Land-Lease requirements with touching off a second wave of defense plant construction, with the third wave starting after Pearl Harbor. Aid to Soviet Russia took greater precedence following Hitler's military successes against the Soviets. Total American aid delivered to the allies under Lend-Lease was roughly $51 billion, with $22 billion to Britain and $12 billion to the Soviet Union. The program also necessitated an enlarged U.S. Navy to protect those shipments. Lend-Lease aid consumed roughly one-third of American defense production over the span of the war.[42]

The efforts to mobilize the American economy for war remained limited throughout 1941 until the actual start of U.S. involvement in the hostilities. The OPM was responsible for organizing and jump-starting the production of military equipment and supplies, but the Roosevelt administration recognized that broader control over the entire economy would be needed for full mobilization. The supply of key materials to civilian industries would have to be controlled to ensure that the defense industry could expand its output. The government also needed to either convince or force private industry to curtail the manufacture of civilian goods and convert to military production. Put simply, "more guns meant less butter." The Roosevelt administration created additional government agencies (and bureaucracies) to tighten control over the civilian economy, but these agencies' responsibilities and powers were often overlapping or contradictory, producing confusion and conflict.

The first significant new mobilization agency after the creation of the OPM was the Office of Price Administration and Civilian Supply (OPACS), which began work on 11 April 1941. Headed by Leon Henderson, a veteran New Dealer, OPACS was created to help stabilize prices and control the allocation of supplies to the civilian sector of the economy. By then, key metals including aluminum, magnesium, and zinc were in short supply and crimping defense production, with steel supplies getting tight as well. OPACS had the authority to ration civilian goods as needed to further war production. OPACS was independent from the OPM and the two agencies often clashed, sometimes in unexpected ways. OPACS, which appeared to be responsible for protecting civilian supply, wanted to curtail civilian production at a faster pace than the OPM desired.[43]

The automobile industry was a case in point. From the start of OPACS, Henderson viewed automobile production as unessential and argued for production curtailments. In 1939 alone, automobiles consumed 90 percent of gasoline production, 80 percent of rubber output, 18 percent of national steel production, and 10 to 14 percent of the nation's copper, tin, and aluminum.

Automobile production increased in 1940, and in April and May 1941 it was 27 percent higher than it had been a year earlier. The automakers were not inclined to reduce output even though the industry was already causing steel shortages for the defense industry. In late May 1941, Knudsen announced an OPM agreement with the automakers for a 20 percent cutback in auto production between 1 August 1941 and 31 July 1942. Writing in *The Nation,* I. F. Stone blamed the auto industry and Knudsen for steel shortages and the general failure of the rearmament efforts: "Knudsen ought either to turn in his resignation and go back to Detroit or take a subordinate job where his real abilities as a production man could be utilized without requiring him to exercise the policy-making decision of which he has shown himself incapable."[44]

In summer 1941, the OPM and OPACS held simultaneous and conflicting negotiations with the auto industry. By July, Henderson demanded a 50 percent reduction in automobile output and threatened to reduce the supply of key raw materials to guarantee that outcome. The OPM, OPACS, and the auto industry finally agreed on 20 August 1941 to a retroactive 43.3 percent curtailment in 1942 model production starting from 1 August 1941. The curtailment in the first three months was only 6.5 percent, with most of the reductions scheduled to begin in 1942. OPACS was on the verge of announcing similar curtailment goals for household appliances and metal office furniture when Roosevelt replaced OPACS on 28 August 1941 with a new agency, the Supply, Priorities and Allocation Board (SPAB). Pearl Harbor rendered these curtailment agreements moot.[45]

Roosevelt created SPAB as a response to the supply crisis that had developed by mid-summer 1941 and to the widespread belief that the OPM catered to the needs of the military and private industry and was dragging its feet on mobilization. Chaired by Vice President Henry Wallace, SPAB included the leadership of both the OPM and OPACS (Knudsen, Hillman, the secretaries of war and navy, and Leon Henderson) but with two important additions: Harry Hopkins, representing the Lend-Lease program and the president, and Donald M. Nelson, who was the OPM's director of purchasing. Nelson also became the executive director of SPAB. Hopkins, Wallace, Hillman, and Henderson were all New Dealers and much less conservative than Knudsen and the military leaders. Under the new structure, Knudsen and the other leaders within the OPM reported to Nelson as the head of SPAB, even though within the OPM, Nelson reported to Knudsen. SPAB also replaced OPACS, which became the Office of Price Administration (OPA). The creation of SPAB did not end conflicting and overlapping authority over the rearmament program and did not immediately solve the supply crisis. Defense orders, which stood at $49 billion in April 1941, had ballooned to over $60 billion by September. Defense orders and actual production were two different matters. Actual defense production in the first half of 1941 was $1.46 billion, less than one-tenth of the orders on hand. American entrance into the war brought mandatory mobilization of the economy and the creation of a new and powerful coordinating body on 13 January 1942, the War Production Board (WPB).[46]

The OPM was the most influential federal agency in terms of initiating and coordinating rearmament and economic mobilization in 1941, but it was certainly not the only government agency with power and influence. Its ability to coerce the private sector into converting to defense production, much less control supply and prices, was limited until the declaration of war in December. The agency's structure and staffing also rendered it largely ineffective. Although OPM had a director general (Knudsen) and an associate director general (Hillman), neither man was a dynamic leader able to impose consistent policies for rearmament. The OPM consisted of three main operating divisions: the Priorities Division, headed by Edward R. Stettinius Jr.; the Production Division, directed by John D. Biggers; and the Purchasing Division, led by Donald Nelson. Hillman headed the Labor Division, which had little influence on mobilization. Because of the lack of centralized leadership, the production, purchasing, and priorities divisions operated autonomously and generally not very effectively. Performance improved once the OPM was placed under the control of SPAB but was still far from effective.[47]

The New Deal Democrats distrusted Knudsen because of his obvious links to big business. They complained to Roosevelt that Knudsen was appointing Republicans to most key jobs in the OPM. Roosevelt sent two memos to Knudsen in March 1941 noting that of the twenty-six "dollar-a-year men" Knudsen nominated, all but two were Republicans. Of these two, one had no affiliation, and one was a Willkie Democrat. Knudsen explained to FDR that he had hired the best-qualified people to work for him and admitted to not knowing their party affiliations. He agreed to provide Roosevelt with a list of possible Democratic appointees for FDR's approval. This was enough to quiet the Democratic Party critics. Once Knudsen informed them that these jobs paid one dollar a year, their interest quickly melted away.[48]

The OPM also suffered from internal and external infighting between the "all-outers," who wanted rapid conversion to military production and drastic curtailment of civilian output, and those who preferred a more gradual conversion. Economists, statisticians, planners, New Dealers, and labor generally supported all-out conversion, while industry favored a more gradual, conservative approach. The "all-outers" included men like Henderson, Nelson, Hillman, Wallace, and Hopkins. The military services generally sided with the business leaders, including Knudsen and Stettinius, in part because they shared similar political views and preferred to work cooperatively without the interference of the New Dealers. Both preferred a weak OPM. Pearl Harbor rendered this dispute moot.[49]

The Nye Committee's reports on the failures of the OPM helped force Roosevelt's hand. A Senate resolution of 1 March 1941 established the Senate Special Committee to Investigate the Defense Program with Senator Harry S. Truman (D-MO) as the chair. More commonly known as the Truman Committee, it held its first hearings on 15 April 1941. Some of its early investigations examined the supply of aluminum, the construction of military camps, and the use of small manufacturers in defense production, but the Truman Committee quickly zeroed in on the operation of the OPM. It noted that in July 1941, fifty-six companies held three-quarters of all army and navy supply contracts in terms of dollar value, with six accounting for nearly one-third of all contracts, while hundreds of small manufacturers were idle.[50]

The Truman Committee issued its first annual report to the Senate on 15 January 1942, but President Roosevelt received a copy of the report well before its official release. The report savagely criticized the OPM for its inability to coordinate and expedite war production. The lack of a single director with broad powers was cited as one source of the OPM's ineptitude. The Truman Committee also severely criticized the OPM's dependence on the "dollar-a-year men" and those who worked without compensation, the "w.o.c. men." This practice reflected questionable decision making at the highest levels of the OPM because these men acted with the best interests of the business sector in mind. They were prohibited from making decisions that directly affected the companies they worked for, but that was not the overriding issue. They typically made weak decisions or no decisions at all on vital matters. Even though they had a good deal of power, their actions were weak, vacillating, and inept. Roosevelt's decision to create the WPB under Nelson, announced on 13 January 1942, was facilitated by the Truman Committee's report.[51]

TWO

Planning Defense Production
after Pearl Harbor

Within five weeks after Pearl Harbor, the Roosevelt administration established a new government agency, the War Production Board (WPB), to control and coordinate defense production, as well as the Supply, Priorities and Allocation Board (SPAB). With the outbreak of war, the automobile industry fundamentally changed its attitude toward war production. The industry soon worked effectively with the WPB by creating a coordinating body to serve as a liaison between the industry and the government. The board of directors of the AMA reconstituted the organization as the Automotive Council for War Production (ACWP) on 30 December 1941. AMA president James Alvan Macauley (Packard Motor Car Company) called a meeting the following day of representatives of automotive parts suppliers, independent tool and die shops, and the makers of automobiles and trucks. By mid-January, the ACWP had established a Machine Tool and Equipment Listing Service to identify machine tools within the industry that might be available for defense production. More than eight hundred executives from the automotive industry, including suppliers, attended the first general meeting of the ACWP in Detroit on 24 January 1942. Ernest Kanzler, a former Ford Motor Company executive, attended as the director of the Automotive Branch of the WPB. The meeting established several ACWP divisions to share information about machine tools, tooling, and equipment, as well as information on the placement of contracts and subcontracts relating to war work. The ACWP also initially established five product divisions to coordinate the production of aircraft engines, airframes, ammunition, artillery, and tanks and armored cars.[1]

Ernest Kanzler quickly dismissed the rumor that Donald Nelson had sent him to Detroit to act as the "czar" of the auto industry. Kanzler was impressed by the early efforts of the auto companies to coordinate their defense work and concluded that compulsion, especially from Washington, would not speed up the conversion to war work. One of the government's goals was to get the auto industry to subcontract much of its work to suppliers and smaller manufacturers, and Kanzler believed the industry had the experience to subcontract efficiently. The challenge of mobilizing the automobile industry was monumental. At the time of Pearl Harbor, the industry had orders for $4.5 billion in military equipment in hand, and by June 1942 the auto industry had a backlog of orders amounting to $14 billion. At the end of March 1942, the ACWP issued its "Blueprint for Victory," a pamphlet outlining its accomplishments during its first three months of operation and its plans to better coordinate the auto industry's capabilities and the government's needs for war products.[2]

The ACWP kept comprehensive records of the auto industry's wartime production achievements. The industry's actual production of war materials increased impressively in the first part of 1942. If the industry's deliveries in January (nearly $172 million) were projected over the entire year, the total deliveries for 1942 would have been about $2 billion. Monthly deliveries accelerated so quickly that by July 1942 they were at the equivalent of $5 billion/year. By June 1943, monthly production would project to an annual output of $8.7 billion, which understates the actual physical output because the auto industry achieved price reductions ranging from 10 percent to 30 percent during this time. Deliveries in 1944 were a staggering $9.3 billion. By the end of the war, the auto industry, including suppliers, delivered $29 billion in war products to the government. The distribution of production is worth noting: aircraft engines, complete aircraft, and aircraft parts made up nearly 39 percent of the total value of the auto industry's war production, military vehicles other than tanks another 30 percent, and tanks an additional 13 percent, for a total of 82 percent of the value of all auto industry war production.[3]

Donald M. Nelson and the WPB

The Roosevelt administration had concluded well before Pearl Harbor that the OPM and the SPAB did not have the right organization or sufficient authority to manage war production. The First War Powers Act, passed by Congress on 18 December 1941, gave the president sweeping powers to reorganize the executive branch to

Automotive Council for War Production meeting in Detroit, 10 July 1942.
Left to right: Charles E. Wilson, president of General Motors; William S. Knudsen;
Donald Nelson; and K. T. Keller, president of Chrysler (*ACWP*).

better pursue the war effort. Roosevelt was legally empowered to create the WPB, which he officially announced on 16 January 1942. He named Donald Nelson, previously the executive secretary of SPAB, as chairman of the WPB. Nelson's experience as a Sears, Roebuck executive vice president would serve him well. William Knudsen had no role in the new agency and was no longer a key player in war production. The left wing of the Democratic Party had long despised Knudsen because of his association with General Motors and the perception that Knudsen had little interest in "all-out" mobilization and was more concerned with protecting automakers' profits. His contemptuous dismissal of Walter Reuther's plans for aircraft production did not help his standing with the left wing of the Democratic Party. There was also a widespread belief that Knudsen had neither the administrative talents nor the political skills to run a large government agency. Essentially, Knudsen was "kicked to the curb" with the creation of the WPB.[4]

President Roosevelt informed Nelson about the creation of the WPB and his appointment as its director in a meeting at the White House on 15 January 1942.

Knudsen received no official, much less personal, notification of the new agency or of his exclusion from any further leadership role. Nelson visited Knudsen and urged him to remain in the service of the government, but Knudsen was inclined to return to Detroit. Both Nelson and Harry Hopkins encouraged Roosevelt to find a position for Knudsen. The president appointed Knudsen director of production in the office of undersecretary of war, headed by Robert P. Patterson. Without consulting the War Department or Congress, Roosevelt also made Knudsen a lieutenant general in the U.S. Army. Knudsen then served until July 1944 as a troubleshooter and consultant for Patterson, who put an airplane at his disposal. Knudsen made hundreds of inspection trips to various defense plants around the United States, as well as long inspection trips to military bases in the Pacific. In two and a half years, he visited 1,200 factories and traveled about 250,000 miles by air.[5]

By mid-1943, the production of most weapons and supplies was moving ahead smoothly and roughly on schedule. The exception was the production of aircraft and aircraft engines, which remained problematic throughout the war. On 31 July 1944, the War Department named Knudsen to head the Army Air Force Materiel Command based at Wright-Patterson Field in Dayton, Ohio. When the War Department restructured the command as the Army Air Forces Air Technical Service Command on 1 September 1944, Knudsen became its director. He supervised the research, design and procurement, supply, and maintenance of the Army Air Force's aircraft. A grateful American government awarded Knudsen a Distinguished Service Medal on 24 May 1944, with the Oak Leaf cluster added on 29 May 1945. Knudsen resigned from the Army on 1 June 1945 and returned to Detroit, which honored him with a parade three weeks later recognizing his war work.[6]

In mid-January 1942, Patterson urged Nelson to strengthen the coordination of manpower for war production. When Nelson refused, President Roosevelt created a new super-agency in mid-April 1942 to take on this task: the War Manpower Commission (WMC). He passed over Sidney Hillman and named Paul V. McNutt as the director of this new agency. Most factions of organized labor detested Hillman because of his unwillingness to defend labor's interests. Hillman carried other "baggage" as well. In October 1941, Senator Harry S. Truman's Special Committee to Investigate the Defense Program had accused him of awarding defense contracts based on his preference for AFL unions over CIO-affiliated unions. Truman called for Hillman's resignation and for the dissolution of the OPM is favor of a stronger organization. When Roosevelt created the WMC, he asked for Hillman's resignation from the WPB but offered him an honorary advisory position, which Hillman declined.[7]

On the eve of the establishment of the WPB, President Roosevelt delivered a

Parade in Detroit honoring William S. Knudsen, 21 June 1945 (*GMCMA*).

message to Congress in which he set out specific production goals for 1942: 60,000 planes, 45,000 tanks, 20,000 anti-aircraft guns, 500,000 machine guns, and 8 million tons of merchant ships. The cost, estimated at $50–55 billion, was a fourfold increase from 1941 expenditures and would amount to roughly half of the projected GNP for 1942. Nelson and the economists advising the OPM argued that these goals were simply unattainable.[8]

The WPB staff disputed the practicality of Roosevelt's plans for aircraft production for 1942 and 1943. Roosevelt called for the production of 45,000 tactical aircraft and 15,000 training aircraft in 1942, a total of 60,000 airplanes. The WPB hired the consultant Mordecai Ezekiel to assess the aircraft industry's ability to achieve Roosevelt's goals. Ezekiel reported in late March 1942 that the actual production of tactical aircraft for 1942 would be approximately 33,000, or one-quarter fewer planes than the president wanted. When Robert Nathan, the chair of the WPB's Planning Committee, shared Ezekiel's report with Nelson, he reported that FDR's goal of producing 60,000 planes in 1942 was still possible. Roosevelt's goal for 1943 was an output of 100,000 tactical aircraft and 25,000 trainers, a total of 125,000 planes.

Ezekiel reported that the WPB had only 88,000 aircraft scheduled for production in 1943 and that a more realistic goal for 1943 would be 73,500 tactical planes and 31,500 trainers, a total of 105,000. Limited supplies of engines and propellers were the two main barriers to greater production. The aircraft parts manufacturers had to supply more spare parts than originally estimated, further limiting production.[9]

The WPB seemed destined to take control of the nation's military production. Granted broad powers by President Roosevelt and headed by a single chairman who reported directly to the president, the WPB seemed likely to become a "super-agency" and Nelson would become the "czar" of war production. The opposite happened in large part because Nelson was not a very aggressive, dynamic, or effective leader. In a move typical of his leadership style, Nelson arranged to have 1,100 employees of the WPB interviewed to help him identify and solve the organizational problems the WPB faced. These staffers were presumably loyal to Nelson, but the survey offered the following conclusion: "A majority [of the staff] believe that Mr. Nelson has more power than he is using. They wonder why he does not use it."[10]

Congress and the New Deal Democrats wanted a single agency to exercise civilian control of war production and the allocation of resources among the demands of the branches of the military and the civilian economy. The executive order establishing the WPB clearly granted Nelson broad authority over all procurement and supply decisions. However, Nelson left control over planning defense production in the hands of the armed services, which received first priority in the allocation of raw materials, factories, and manpower, leaving the civilian economy with the leftovers.

The armed services continued to control all procurement functions including purchasing through their contracts with the private sector, as they had done under the previous defense production agencies. Nelson argued that the military knew which products they required better than any civilian would and that they needed to be involved in inspecting and accepting any products delivered to them. He further argued that because most of the civilian executives in the WPB, the "dollar-a-year-men," had ties to industry, they would be severely criticized if they negotiated defense contracts. Nelson initially (and naively) believed that the military services could be convinced to work cooperatively with the WPB. When he later tried to impose civilian control over procurement, he faced a powerful alliance of most of the business executives within the WPB and the military leadership, which stymied his efforts. Nelson lost most of his authority when the White House placed the WPB under the control of a new agency created in May 1943, the Office of War Mobilization.[11]

Nelson and the WPB disputed the demands of the military services for enormous quantities of war goods on grounds of impracticality, touching off what has been called "the great feasibility debate" that raged from February to October 1942. Nelson created a Planning Committee on 19 February 1942 to examine the feasibility of producing the war goods the military demanded for 1942 and 1943. He chose economist Robert Nathan to head this committee, and Nathan promptly hired Simon Kuznets to serve as the committee's chief economist and statistician. Kuznets, the recipient of a Nobel Prize in Economics for his work in macroeconomic analysis, had developed national income accounting measures, including the concepts of GNP, GDP, and other national economic accounting tools.[12]

The armed services planned to purchase $58.2 billion in war materials in 1942, but in mid-March 1942, the WPB Planning Committee projected a maximum feasible output of $45 billion. For 1943, the WPB projected maximum feasible spending on war goods at $64 billion, roughly half of projected GNP. Roosevelt endorsed the WPB estimate, only to have the military services announce plans to spend $110 billion. Roosevelt ordered the War Department to reduce its spending plans to $75 billion, but by July 1942 the military's projected spending for 1943 had crept up to $88 billion, which the WPB claimed was an underestimate. Because part of the war production planned for 1942 would not be achieved that year, carryover into 1943 would push the spending program to at least $100 billion.[13]

Kuznets's feasibility report, released on 12 August 1942, dismissed the military's goals for war production for 1942 and 1943 as unattainable. The economy could not generate enough factory space, machine tools, raw materials, or labor to reach those goals. More realistic goals for the defense program would be $44 billion for 1942 and $75 billion for 1943. Attempting to achieve those higher goals would disrupt the entire economy. Lieutenant General Brehon Somervell, Commanding General of Services and Supply with the War Department, delivered a scathing attack on the Kuznets report to the Planning Committee of the WPB on 31 August 1942. Somervell rejected the statistical foundation of the report as unreliable and questioned Kuznets's abilities. His final comments summed up his disdain for Kuznets's work: "I am not impressed with either the character or the basis of the judgements expressed in the reports and recommend that they be carefully hidden from the eyes of thoughtful men." The day after a stormy WPB meeting on 6 October 1942 during which Kuznets's feasibility report was discussed, Undersecretary of War Robert Patterson, who reported directly to President Roosevelt and was Somervell's superior, ordered the general to accept maximum spending of $80 billion for 1943. Somervell had no choice but to accept the more modest figures. The WPB in fact had a better sense of economic feasibility than the military. Actual spending for 1942 totaled $30.2 billion; for 1943, it was only $57.2 billion.[14]

After first ceding control over procurement to the military services, Donald Nelson tried to reassert control during the last quarter of 1942 but with little success. In mid-September, he brought in two dynamic executives to run important parts of the WPB: Charles E. Wilson, president of General Motors, to head a newly launched Production Executive Committee, and Ferdinand Eberstadt to take charge of materials supply. Wilson and Eberstadt then became rivals, both hoping to succeed Nelson as the head of the WPB.[15]

In late November 1942, Nelson abruptly proposed that the military's control over production and procurement be transferred to the WPB. The military services, particularly Patterson, urged Roosevelt to replace Nelson at the WPB with either Bernard Baruch or Charles Wilson. In mid-February 1943, Nelson heard rumors that the president was ready to fire him and replace him with Baruch, who would name Eberstadt as his chief deputy. Nelson fired Eberstadt and named Wilson as his executive vice chairman as a preemptive strike, but Roosevelt did not replace Nelson at the WPB. In typical Rooseveltian fashion, the president instead created the Office of War Mobilization (OWM) on 27 May 1943, with former Supreme Court Justice James F. Byrnes in charge. The WPB reported to the OWM, ending Nelson's control over defense production.[16]

Nelson remained chairman of the WPB for another fifteen months, but the board was deeply divided during that time between the supporters of Nelson and those who favored Wilson. In October 1943, Wilson wanted to resign from his position at the WPB and return to General Motors. He argued that his work on increasing the production of aircraft, ships, radio, and radar was largely done. President Roosevelt convinced Wilson to stay with the WPB, and he remained on the job until late August 1944, shortly after Nelson resigned as chairman of the WPB.[17]

In early 1944, Nelson tried to regain control of the WPB by asserting control over reconversion policies and timing. First, Nelson rejected a reconversion plan that Wilson had proposed, further encouraging Wilson to resign. Nelson created controversy in March 1944 when he ordered the resumption of production of some consumer durable goods, and in June 1944 Nelson announced plans for the reconversion of the economy to civilian production. The military services, as well as many executives within the WPB, strongly opposed any early reconversion and won the day. Nelson had announced four new regulations to allow the start of reconversion, but the OWM suspended the new regulations. James Byrnes, the director of the OWM, generally sided with the military and industrial interests in opposing reconversion.[18]

Nelson resigned his post at the WPB in mid-August 1944 to participate in a high-level U.S. mission to China to help bolster that nation's struggling economy.

Roosevelt appointed Nelson to the cabinet-level position of Personal Representative of the President. FDR worried that the Chinese economy was on the verge of collapse and that China might leave the war against Japan and prolong the end of the war in the Pacific by as much as two years. Nelson established a Chinese War Production Board to increase war production. Roosevelt wanted the controversial Nelson out of Washington and out of sight. The fall election was not far away, and FDR's political advisors also wanted Nelson gone from Washington. Roosevelt named Julius A. Krug as his replacement as head of the WPB.[19]

Assessing Donald Nelson's thirty-one months at the WPB is a difficult task. In many respects, rearmament and war production were successful despite Nelson's efforts. He never accepted the military-industrial alliance that was emerging while he headed the WPB. Nelson associated most closely with New Deal reformers, making him suspect among the military and industrial leaders alike. Because he strongly disliked confrontation, he either ignored significant differences between himself and the military-industrial forces at work or looked for middle ground where it simply did not exist. As a result, he often appeared weak and indecisive, which only encouraged his enemies to ignore him. Nelson's ineffectiveness was not entirely his own doing. The military and industrial leaders became skilled at getting their way. Franklin Roosevelt, wanting to avoid open conflict that might damage war production, conceded control to the emerging military-industrial complex.[20]

Labor in the War

Maintaining a semblance of labor peace in the war plants proved challenging for the government as the war progressed. Ten days after Pearl Harbor, a conference of industry and labor leaders meeting in Washington signed a "no-strike, no-lockout" pledge for the duration of the war. The Roosevelt administration also established the War Labor Board (WLB) on 12 January 1942 to replace the largely ineffective National Defense Mediation Board (NDMB). The new board kept William H. Davis from the NDMB as its chairman. The NDMB could only offer recommendations for the settlement of disputes, but the decisions of the WLB were binding. The no-strike pledge did not bring an end to strikes during the war; in fact strikes were far more common in 1942 than they had been earlier. John L. Lewis, still president of the United Mine Workers (UMW) but no longer the head of the CIO, vehemently refused to uphold the no-strike pledge. Lewis and much of the CIO leadership interpreted the pledge to mean that labor agreed not to strike during the war in return for an implicit promise that government and industry would maintain traditional labor standards, including wages and hours, in the face of wartime pressures. A regional CIO convention held in Grand Rapids, Michigan, in June 1943 called for a repeal of the no-strike pledge. At the UAW National Convention in Grand Rapids in September 1944, more than one-third of the delegates voted to rescind the pledge. In March 1945, the UAW held a postcard referendum on the no-strike pledge and 45 percent of the voters rejected the no-strike pledge.[21]

In spite of the no-strike pledge, strikes occasionally crippled war production. There were fifty-one strikes that affected war production in a two-week stretch in June 1942. During the entire month of June, strikes cost war production about 132,000 man-days of work. The number of strikes increased in July and August 1942. The disruptions continued in 1943, when the government counted a total of 3,752 strikes at defense plants, with a loss of over 13 million man-days. Many of the walkouts were "wildcat" strikes carried out without union authorization and often after unions tried to stop them. Local unions and corporate managers often defied rulings handed down by the WLB after the board considered their disputes. Wages were typically the bone of contention. Although the government takeover of plants on strike was always a possibility, it rarely happened. In 1941–45, the government seized a total of sixty-four businesses, the most notable of which was the American railroad system (1.8 million employees) for three weeks starting in late December 1943. None of the takeovers involved the automobile industry or its suppliers, with the exception of the U.S. Rubber Company, which was subjected to a takeover starting in late July 1945 that lasted ten weeks.[22]

The overall labor supply was more than adequate for the growing defense industry before Pearl Harbor because of the lingering effects of the Great Depression. Unemployment, which stood at 9 million in June 1940, fell to 4 million by December 1941, when 51.6 million Americans had jobs or served in the armed forces. By December 1943, when a total of 61.3 million had civilian jobs or were in the military, unemployment stood at less than 800,000, the equivalent of zero unemployment. After unemployed men, the second largest addition to the labor force (those working or seeking work) were women, whose numbers jumped from 14.6 million in 1941 to 19.4 million in 1944. Women's share of the labor force increased during the course of the war from one-quarter to one-third of the total. The record of African American employment in the defense industries was less impressive but nevertheless showed substantial change. The percentage of African American workers holding civilian war jobs increased from 4.2 percent in 1942 to 8.6 percent in 1945.[23] The influx of women and African Americans into the defense industry will be considered in greater detail in a later chapter.

The War Production Contracting System

The system employed by the military to purchase equipment and supplies changed drastically before the onset of war. Through 1938, the military services purchased weapons and materials though a competitive bidding system, although price was not the sole determinant in awarding contracts. Congress permitted the army and navy to enter into cost-plus-a-fixed-fee (CPFF) contracts without advertising and, starting in 1939, to negotiate the contracts with three or four reputable, experienced contractors. The Split Award Act (March 1940) allowed the services to divide contracts for aircraft among the three lowest bidders. For the year ending June 1940, 87 percent of War Department purchases still were the result of competitive bidding, but the share fell to 27 percent over the next nine months. For navy contracts awarded from July through December 1941, only 16 percent were the result of competitive bidding. Under the First War Powers Act, passed on 18 December 1941, Congress gave the military services discretionary power to enter into negotiated contracts. This power was vested in the WPB after its creation. Finally, WPB Directive No. 2, issued on 3 March 1942, ordered the military services to use negotiated contracts exclusively.[24]

The CPFF contract became the most common type of defense contract, particularly early in the war, with fees generally limited by law to 6–7 percent of the estimated costs. Price was less of a consideration in awarding contracts than the speed at which contractors could convert to war production and the speed at which contractors could deliver the goods. The CPFF contract was a logical way to award contracts, given the fact that most recipients of these contracts had no previous experience making the product they contracted for and therefore had no idea what the costs would be. The old way, a fixed-price contract, would not work. The president of the Edward G. Budd Company of Philadelphia, a major subcontractor for the B-29, was asked about possible contractual arrangements with the Army Air Force, and he replied, "it will be cost plus or nothing."[25]

The military services also awarded fixed-price contracts with escalator clauses to allow manufacturers to adjust prices to take into account increases in labor and materials costs. CPFF contracts were most commonly used for construction projects and large contracts for "big-ticket" items such as aircraft, ships, and ordnance. War supply contracts valued at $10 million or more awarded by all the military services from June 1940 through December 1944 totaled $110.5 billion, with CPFF contracts comprising 45.3 percent of the dollar total. The share peaked at 51.8 percent in January–June 1942 and then gradually declined to 39.8 percent in July–December 1944. Congress criticized the CPFF contract because of the potential for profiteering but nevertheless recognized the need to rely on this device.[26]

Congress took several approaches to avoid repeating the abuses that had occurred in World War I that had enabled many defense contractors to earn massive profits. Congress suspended the Vinson-Trammell Act, intended to control the profits of military contractors, in October 1940, but replaced it with the more generic Excess Profits Tax Act of 1940, which applied to all businesses. In April 1942, Congress passed the Renegotiation Act, which required the military services to include in all contracts for more than $100,000 a clause allowing renegotiation of the contract price to eliminate excess profits. The act did not, however, define "excess profits." Congress enacted a new statute in February 1944 that raised the minimum contract size from $100,000 to $500,000 and created a War Contracts Price Adjustment Board to administer the act. The renegotiation process typically resulted in war contractors reducing contract prices on future contracts and returning funds to the government to pay back perceived overcharges.[27]

Renegotiation, along with excess profits taxes, resulted in lower profits for war contractors. Because smaller contracts were exempt and renegotiation of contract prices did not begin until April 1942, some war production was not covered. Contracts subject to renegotiation for 1942 through 1946 amounted to $223 billion. In 1940 and 1941, the government issued an additional $10.7 billion in contracts for munitions and $5.7 billion for government-built factories and military bases. A closer examination of the profits earned by war contractors reveals how well the system of renegotiation worked. Profits as a percentage of sales before renegotiation ranged from a high of 16.2 percent for 1942 to a low of 9.4 percent for 1946, with an overall average for the war of 12.7 percent. Once adjusted by the renegotiated prices, profits ranged from a high of 9.0 percent in 1942 to a low of 7.5 percent in 1946. These are healthy rates of profit after adjustment but can hardly be called excessive, and excess profits taxes reduced them further. The war profiteering of World War I was not repeated.[28]

Modest wartime profits were certainly the rule in the automobile industry. General Motors' net profits on sales (after taxes) ranged between 4.0 percent in 1943 and 1944 to a peak of 7.3 percent in 1942, with an average for 1942–45 of 4.9 percent. Similarly, the Chrysler Corporation's net profits on sales ranged from 2.3 percent in 1944 to 3.8 percent in 1945, with an average of 2.8 percent for the four wartime years. Ford's profits were even lower, ranging from a loss of 4.2 percent in 1945 to a profit of 6.1 percent in 1943. The four smaller independent automakers had similar or worse results for 1942–45: the Studebaker Corporation averaged 3.5 percent net profits on sales; the Packard Motor Car Company earned profits averaging 2.8 percent; Nash Motors earned an anemic 1.9 percent; and the Hudson Motor Car Company earned just 1.5 percent.[29]

The Role of the Defense Plant Corporation (DPC)

War production depended on the availability of appropriate factory space of the proper size, design, and location. The Reconstruction Finance Corporation (RFC) established the DPC on 22 August 1940 to provide financing to build the needed facilities. The aircraft industry was the defense industry slated to expand more rapidly than any other and the one needing the most specialized factories in terms of size and design. The DPC's first major projects involved funding the construction of aircraft engines: an agreement in September 1940 to fund a factory operated by Packard to build Rolls-Royce aircraft engines and a contract a month later to finance an enormous plant for the Wright Aeronautical Corporation in Lockland, Ohio. The DPC partially or entirely funded the construction of fourteen of the fifteen largest aircraft engine plants built during the war. The largest of these was the Dodge-Chicago plant, which will be discussed in a later chapter, costing $170 million. The DPC also signed agreements in fall 1940 for major new aircraft assembly plants to be operated by the Curtiss-Wright Aircraft Corporation, Consolidated Aircraft Corporation, and Ford Motor Company. By 31 December 1945, the DPC had invested $1.357 billion in aircraft engine factories, $592 million in aircraft assembly plants, and $665 million in factories producing aircraft parts, for a total of $2.614 billion. Investment in aircraft production amounted to 37 percent of the DPC's total wartime investments of $6.982 billion.[30]

DPC investments in other types of military hardware included the production of transport ($301 million), ordnance ($285 million), and ships ($132 million). DPC spending to increase production of basic materials, including iron and steel ($951 million), synthetic rubber ($740 million), aluminum ($684 million), and magnesium ($428 million), amounted to $2.8 billion or 40 percent of the total invested. The investments were made to support the expansion of a few large corporations. More than half (55 percent) of the DPC's spending built facilities for twenty-five large corporations. Six of these made complete aircraft or aircraft engines or both (Curtiss-Wright, Ford Motor Company, General Motors Corporation, United Aircraft, Bendix Aviation, and Continental Motors, which made aircraft engines). Another six were former manufacturers of automobiles or auto parts (Chrysler, Goodyear Tire and Rubber, Studebaker, Packard, B. F. Goodrich, and Nash-Kelvinator) that were engaged in aircraft parts production during the war. Most of the remaining companies in the top twenty-five made steel, chemicals, other metals, or petroleum products.[31]

The automobile-industry-turned-defense-industry and a considerable number of other defense producers would not have been able to increase production as rapidly as they did before and during the war without new factories. The speed at which the DPC was able to build many of the largest plants was breathtaking. The time between the signing of a contact for a new plant and the installation of machinery to start production often ran from four to six months. A single architectural firm was the dominant force in building factories: Albert Kahn and Associates, Inc. Architects and Engineers, based in Detroit. As early as 1905, Kahn revolutionized architectural practice in the United States. He created an interdisciplinary, full-service practice that offered clients integrated architectural, engineering, and construction management services. Kahn subdivided the work into discrete tasks and created, in effect, an architectural assembly line that mass-produced plans. He could offer clients rapid completion of design and construction. Between 1915 and 1925 Kahn completed more commissions, in terms of value, than any other American architect. His firm expanded throughout the 1920s, then faced difficult times in the early Depression before rebounding in the late 1930s. Albert Kahn Associates produced nearly one-fifth of all architect-designed factories in the United States in 1938, when the firm had a staff of four hundred. From December 1939 through December 1942, Kahn won more than $200 million in contracts for defense plants from the U.S. government. In 1941 alone, Kahn's office completed plans for more than 20 million square feet of space for defense plants, employing a staff of more than 650 by Pearl Harbor. His firm had adopted the practice of using standard architectural features, such as doors and windows, in multiple buildings, saving design time and cost. During the war, he designed buildings based on materials known to be immediately available for purchase, such as steel girders of a particular size. He bought his materials "off the shelf," so construction was not delayed by shortages.[32]

Before working on defense plants in the United States, Kahn also helped the Soviet Union, America's future ally against the Nazis, to establish a strong industrial base by designing factories in Russia. In April 1929, his firm agreed to a contract with the Soviet government to design and build a $40 million tractor plant near Stalingrad. The two parties signed additional agreements that totaled 521 plants worth $2 billion. These included an enormous diesel tractor factory at Cheliabinsk (1932) and a steel-making complex at Magnitogorsk. The tractor factories quickly converted to tank production with the coming of the war. Kahn established a Moscow office, which at its peak employed 1,500 draftsmen and women. When Kahn's contracts lapsed in March 1932, his firm had helped train nearly 4,000 Russian architects, engineers, and draftsmen and women. The work done for the Soviet Union helped Kahn's practice remain afloat in a difficult period but also strengthened the Soviets' ability to fight Nazi Germany.[33]

Kahn's architectural firm also specialized in large aircraft factories, and a good

Albert Kahn, November 1941 (CKH).

share of its prewar and wartime commissions involved the aircraft industry. Kahn designed enormous manufacturing plants (1929, 1937, 1939) at Middle River, Maryland, for the Glenn L. Martin Company. In 1940–42 alone, Kahn designed ten large factories for the Curtiss-Wright Corporation and its subsidiaries, plus an additional dozen aircraft and aircraft engine plants. The two most notable, the Ford Motor Company Willow Run Bomber plant (1941) and the Dodge-Chicago plant (1942), which produced engines for the B-29, will be discussed in detail in chapter 4. Other significant commissions included the Chrysler Tank Arsenal (1941) near Detroit; the American Steel Foundries Cast Armor plant (1941) in East Chicago, Indiana; and the Amertorp Torpedo plant (1942) in Chicago. Kahn's defense work was concentrated in 1939–42, although his firm designed additional plants for the duration of the war. Kahn also designed several types of military installations. In 1939–41, his firm completed plans for more than a dozen Naval Air Stations, as well as ten hangers for navy bases, docks, and submarine bases at Midway and at Kodiak, Alaska. Albert Kahn died on 8 December 1942, a year and a day after Pearl Harbor, long before his defense plants help bring Hitler's defeat.[34]

Financing and building defense plants was only part of the DPC's work. It also supplied most of the machinery and equipment needed to operate the plants it built. Between 25 June 1939 and 31 December 1945, the RFC authorized $9.783 billion for defense and war facilities. This is a larger figure than the one cited earlier because authorized spending was considerably more than the funds actually spent. Only 35 percent of the authorized spending was intended for facilities construction, while 63 percent was to be spent on equipment. The remaining 2 percent was for real estate purchases and loans to construction contractors. Supplying equipment and machinery, especially machine tools, was a greater challenge for the WPC than erecting factories.[35]

Supplying defense industries with vital machine tools for defense production is the greatest "untold story" of World War II. In 1940, the American machine tool industry consisted of 200 plants that made machine tools exclusively and another 200 that manufactured other products in addition to machine tools. These were small firms that employed highly skilled labor but had limited capital resources. In 1940, they employed roughly 57,000 workers and produced about 200,000 tools per year with a combined value of $440 million, more than double the output for 1939. Two hundred of these firms accounted for 95 percent of the total dollar value of machine tool production, with 30 companies accounting for 62 percent. The abrupt ending of World War I and the equally abrupt cancelation of war contracts had left many suppliers of machine tools with excess capacity that still remained twenty years later. They were unwilling to bear the risks of accepting contracts with private contractors, such as aircraft manufacturers. At the same time, private contractors who operated war production plants did not want to own the machine tools they needed for production.[36]

In a curious attempt to influence war production, Walter Reuther submitted a proposal for increasing machine tool production for the war effort to Donald Nelson at the WPB in January 1942. Reuther called for auto industry-wide pooling of tool-making facilities and equipment. He claimed that a recent survey of 104 tool-making shops in the Detroit area with a total of 4,624 machine tools showed that only 53.7 percent of the available machine time was actually used. Reuther assumed that these machine tools could be operated twenty four hours per day and seven days a week. He proposed that tools needed for defense work be produced at that pace, with expanded training to produce enough skilled machinists to run these machines. Reuther would leave all decisions concerning machine production to the machinery makers and to the arms manufacturers. He believed that this improved use of existing machines would allow the United States to surpass the Axis in tank production within six months. This appears to have been another Reuther "pie-in-the-sky" proposal, as running machinery on a "24-7" schedule is completely unrealistic. He also seemed unaware of the efforts already under way by the DPC to expand and coordinate machine tool production nationally or the efforts by the auto industry to coordinate machinery with defense production requirements. There is no evidence that Nelson took any action in response to Reuther's proposal.[37]

The Roosevelt administration recognized the critical importance of machine tools to defense production from the start. The National Defense Advisory Commission (NDAC) launched its Tools Branch, soon renamed the Tools Division, in July 1940. When the NDAC gave way to the OPM and the OPM in turn was replaced by the WPB, the Tools Division came under the control of each successor agency. The DPC also became the buyer of machine tools to equip defense plants at no cost to the defense contractor. At the request of the NDAC, the DPC established a "machine tool pool" in December 1940 and by May 1941 had agreed to purchase $235 million in machine tools to be used in the defense industry.

"Pool" orders originated with the Tools Division and had to be approved by the Machine Tool Committee of the Army-Navy Munitions Board (ANMB) before the DPC placed the orders. The DPC would purchase machine tools from the manufacturers for the "pool" and then decide which defense contractor would get them. They could order machine tools for a particular war product and take delivery before knowing which manufacturer would have a contract for that product, saving as much as six months in delivering machine tools where they were needed. The DPC also provided machine tool makers with a 30 percent cash advance on the value of the contract, providing them with much-needed working capital to start production.[38]

DPC pool orders jumped from $284 million in 1941 to a peak of $1.361 billion in 1942 and then fell to $229 million in 1943. DPC tool orders for 1944 and 1945 combined were only $77 million, reflecting the declining number of new defense plants. Actual shipments of DPC pool-ordered tools amounted to $1.6 billion in 1941–43, when the total production of the machine tool industry was $3.3 billion. The overall accomplishment was impressive: machine tools in use in American industry increased from 941,898 in 1940 to 1,771,137 in 1945. The machine tools in place in factories making aircraft and aircraft engines jumped from only 8,780 machines in 1940 to 276,466 in 1945. The DPC served two additional roles with regard to machine tools. The agency identified unused machine tools and reallocated them to where they were needed. In 1941 and 1942, when machine tools were in short supply, the DPC served as a central clearing house. It also rationed machine tools in accordance with the priorities established by the military services.[39]

The DPC had two principal leasing arrangements with contractors who used DPC-owned plants. The first was the "dollar per year lease," used when a plant was producing exclusively for the government. A factory making tanks, such as the Chrysler Tank Arsenal, would typically have one of these leases. The contractor could not charge the government any facilities costs, including depreciation, so this was a simple arrangement. The DPC used "dollar per year leases" for only 199 plants, but these were the largest plants, representing nearly half of the DPC's investments. A second type of lease was intended to include the depreciation costs of the plant during its use. The contractor was expected to include the depreciation costs in the price of the goods supplied to the government. Rents were typically based on a fixed percentage of the original cost of the facilities (930 leases) or on a percentage of sales (529 leases). Over the period ending 30 June 1945, the DPC collected a total of $540 million in rents from its facilities. Leases based on original construction costs and/or sales accounted for 86 percent of the total rent collected. The rest came from leases of DPC-owned machinery and flying schools.[40]

Overall Success

Despite continued bickering within and between different parts of the government's war production planning apparatus, the conversion of industry to defense production, false steps and glitches aside, was reasonably successful by 1943. President Roosevelt was willing and able to replace dysfunctional agencies and their leaders with better ones. The military services, other government agencies, and private industry managed to muddle through the conversion process. The contract system, for all of its warts, allowed the production of military equipment and supplies to take place without undue delays or profiteering. The DPC provided the resources required to build the expanded industrial capacity the military services needed.

The best way to understand the size and structure of the war effort is to examine expenditures. Between 1 July 1940 and 31 August 1945, the United States spent $315.8 billion on its war program. Munitions accounted for $185.4 billion of this (58 percent of the total). Another $16.1 billion (5 percent of the total) was spent on industrial buildings, machinery, and equipment, while construction of military bases, housing, and other nonindustrial facilities cost an additional $15.3 billion. The remaining $99.9 billion went mainly toward military pay ($60.5 billion), pay for civilians employed by federal war agencies ($10.6 billion), and transportation services ($12.1 billion). Military spending before Pearl Harbor was modest, amounting to $3.6 billion in 1940 and $17.8 billion in 1941. Expenditures more than tripled in 1942 ($57.4 billion), increased substantially to $86.2 billion in 1943, and then peaked at $93.4 billion in 1944. With the war winding down, defense spending in 1945 fell off to $57.4 billion.

The distribution of spending on munitions, totaling $185.4 billion, illustrates the relative importance of the major war goods and the industries that produced them. Expenditures on aircraft, some $44.8 billion (24 percent of the total), were followed closely by spending on ships, totaling $41.2 billion (22 percent). The latter figure includes all U.S. Navy ships built during the war and thousands of civilian cargo ships. Spending on "combat and motor vehicles," which included tanks and trucks, came to $20.3 billion (11 percent of spending on munitions). Ammunition ($18.1 billion) and guns ($9.9 billion) together made up 15 percent of spending on munitions. Communications and electronic equipment, mainly radio and radar hardware, cost $10.7 billion. The remaining equipment and supplies not categorized above cost $39.5 billion (21 percent of the total). The automobile industry was substantially involved in making all of the above-mentioned products other than ships.[41]

The chapters that follow are a series of case studies of critical areas of war production in which the automobile industry played a major, if not dominant, role. There will be discussions of the manufacture of aircraft engines, aircraft components, and complete aircraft; tanks; trucks and jeeps; and other war goods.

THREE

Aircraft Engines and Propellers

This chapter will highlight the work of a half-dozen automakers in producing two significant aircraft components: engines and propellers. The history of the production of these key components is largely unknown, although vital to the aircraft industry. Because they are not very sexy, aircraft engines and propellers have not generated the interest that fighter and bomber aircraft have. Because no single company manufactured these components, their production is barely mentioned in aircraft histories. American industry produced approximately 300,000 military aircraft and 802,161 aircraft engines in 1940–45. The U.S. Army Air Force purchased 81 percent of the aircraft engines produced during the war and the U.S. Navy bought most of the rest. The automobile industry produced 56 percent of all the aircraft engines built for the military. In August 1944, when production reached its highest level, automobile companies produced more than two-thirds of all the aircraft engines and three-quarters of the engines for use in combat aircraft. There was no simple transition from making automobile engines to manufacturing aircraft engines. The latter were much larger and more complex than any engine the automakers had previously manufactured. They were typically air-cooled engines using a radial design and upward of eighteen cylinders. The largest produced 2,200 horsepower, dwarfing any automotive or truck engine. North American industry also produced 708,268 propellers over the course of the war, and automobile manufacturers accounted for 36 percent of the total.[1]

There were only three significant manufacturers of aircraft engines before the war: the Wright Aeronautical Corporation, operating an engine plant in Patterson, New Jersey; the Pratt & Whitney Aircraft Division of United Aircraft Corporation in East Hartford, Connecticut; and the Allison Division of General Motors Corporation, with a plant near Indianapolis. The government decided to concentrate production on the existing (and proven) air-cooled radial engines already developed by Wright and Pratt & Whitney. Allison had developed a liquid-cooled engine that was in full production in 1940, and the Packard Motor Car Company produced liquid-cooled Rolls-Royce Merlin engines a year later. The British had great success with the Merlin engines, but the U.S. Army Air Corps preferred air-cooled radial designs. They believed the radial engines were less vulnerable in battle, were more durable, and were easier to service and repair.[2]

Wright preferred to manage the final assembly of its engines and built huge branch plants near Cincinnati and at Wood-Ridge, New Jersey, to supplement production at its main factory in Patterson. In November 1940, at the insistence of the Army Air Force, Wright licensed the Studebaker Corporation to manufacture one of its engines in South Bend, Indiana. Wright granted its only other license to the Dodge Division of the Chrysler Corporation to build engines for the B-29 at its Dodge-Chicago plant. Licensees accounted for only 37 percent of the 223,036 Wright engines made between July 1940 and August 1945. Studebaker, with total production of 63,789 engines for the B-17 Flying Fortress, and Dodge-Chicago, with 18,349 engines for the B-29 Superfortress, accounted for virtually all of the Wright engines manufactured under license. As a result of Wright's insistence on managing most of its production, the company's management was spread thin and it struggled to satisfy all its contracts.[3]

Pratt & Whitney in contrast licensed production of its engines to a wide range of manufacturers while expanding its East Hartford plant and operating a branch plant in Kansas City. Licensees included Ford, Buick, Chevrolet, Nash, Continental Motors, and the Jacobs Aircraft Engine Company. Over the course of the war, Pratt & Whitney produced 355,985 engines, with licensees accounting for 60 percent of the total. The most important licensees were Buick, which produced 74,198 engines in Melrose Park, Illinois; Chevrolet, which turned out 60,766 engines at its Tonawanda, New York, factory; and Ford, which manufactured 57,178 engines at its River Rouge complex in Dearborn, Michigan. The Allison Division of General Motors also produced 69,305 liquid-cooled engines during the war, and Packard completed 54,714 Rolls-Royce Merlin liquid-cooled engines. Eight additional manufacturers produced another 100,390 smaller engines producing less than 500 horsepower each.[4]

Each automobile company that manufactured aircraft engines faced a unique set of circumstances and challenges, and it is instructive to consider the experiences and the records of the eight automakers-turned-aircraft-manufacturers. The chapter will begin with the four earliest examples of aircraft engine production: the Allison Division of General Motors and the Packard Motor Car Company, both making liquid-cooled aircraft engines; the Ford Motor Company, which manufactured Pratt & Whitney Engines under license; and the Studebaker Corporation, which built Wright engines under license. Three automakers that began production in 1942 and manufactured Pratt & Whitney engines—the Buick and Chevrolet divisions of General Motors and the Nash-Kelvinator Corporation—will be considered together. Finally, the Dodge-Chicago plant of the Chrysler Corporation, which produced its first Wright engines for the B-29 bomber in January 1944, will be examined in some detail.

The Early Engine Makers

The Allison Division of General Motors began as Allison Engineering, established in 1915 by James A. Allison, one of the founders of the Indianapolis Speedway. The firm initially manufactured precision components such as gears and bearings for automotive and marine use. The chief engineer at Allison, Norman Gilman, took the reins of the company following the death of James Allison in 1928. After General Motors acquired Allison Engineering the following year, Gilman decided to develop a liquid-cooled engine for aircraft to replace the outmoded Curtiss V-12. The new engine, dubbed the V-1710 after its displacement, was a 12-cylinder engine and the first specifically designed to use ethylene-glycol coolant. The engine developed 650 horsepower when first run in August 1931, but Allison quickly increased the output to 750 horsepower. The Army Air Force, however, wanted an engine that had 1,000 horsepower. Allison developed a modified engine, the V-1710-C, and in April 1937 tested it at full power for 150 hours and passed all the air force requirements for acceptance. This was the first 1,000-horsepower engine to do so. Allison also had the distinction of manufacturing the only American-designed liquid-cooled engine used in military aircraft during the war.[5]

Although Allison had no firm contracts in hand, it nevertheless broke ground in May 1939 for a 360,000-square-foot addition known as Plant 3. The air force placed an initial order for 969 engines in June 1939, the French government ordered 700 engines in February 1940, and the British followed with an order for 3,500 more in May 1940. The U.S. Army Air Force followed up with an order for 3,691 engines in December 1940. To fulfill these orders, Allison eventually enlarged its factory at Speedway, Indiana (near Indianapolis), by 650,000 square feet in three phases, with the U.S. government, through the DPC, contributing $62.5 million for the factory and the needed machinery. Allison turned out only 48 engines in 1939, but completed 1,153 in 1940 and 6,433 the following year. By March 1942, its plant in Speedway encompassed over 1.2 million square feet of space and was producing 1,100 engines per month. In 1942, Allison built a two-million-square-foot plant (Plant 5) in nearby Maywood, Indiana.[6]

The experience at Allison in manufacturing aircraft engines illustrates the differences between making automobile engines and aircraft engines. In addition to their larger size and complexity, aircraft engines typically developed between 500 and 2,200 horsepower and involved more than 8,000 parts, which required greater precision than automotive engine parts. More than 70,000 inspections were performed before an Allison engine was delivered to the Army Air Force. Because weight matters much more with engines destined to power aircraft, designers paid particular attention to reducing weight. Passenger car engines in the late 1930s typically weighed between five and seven pounds for each horsepower produced. For large aircraft engines, the ideal weight-to-power ratio was one to two pounds per horsepower.

Because aircraft engine parts required more accuracy in manufacturing than automobile engine parts, the factory environment was different. The Allison plant was designed to be fully air-conditioned to eliminate large fluctuations in temperature and humidity. Large temperature shifts affected the metals being turned, bored, or otherwise finished and altered the dimensions of the machine tools, negatively affecting the accuracy of the work. Relative humidity was kept at a constant 50 percent, greatly reducing rusting on various metal surfaces. The enlarged engine plant of 1941 was one of the earliest American "black-out" plants; it had no windows and was illuminated by a florescent lighting system, new at the time. This architectural style was adopted to better insulate the building to make air-conditioning feasible, not to protect it from nighttime bombing raids.[7]

Allison had the luxury of having GM's other divisions, especially Cadillac, available to supply many of the precision parts needed for aircraft engines. Long-recognized for its competence in precision manufacturing, Cadillac became a major supplier starting in 1939, providing Allison with connecting rods, piston pins, crankshafts, camshafts, and various other parts. Once Allison was in full-scale production, Cadillac established a separate Aircraft Division, which had 6,000 workers and more than 1,500 machine tools engaged exclusively in making engine parts. The work fully occupied a four-story building at Cadillac's main plant in Detroit. One of Cadillac's notable achievements was the complete redesign of the manufacturing system to produce the engine's supercharger rotator vanes. Cadillac's production engineers moved this manufacturing operation from the Speedway plant, where the vanes were hand-built, and designed a new machine to accurately cut the vanes. Cadillac reduced the production time needed for the vane from 125 to 10 hours. Allison machined only 20 percent of its engine parts and relied on Cadillac, Chevrolet, Delco-Remy, and outside vendors for the rest.[8]

As a result of modifications in its design, the Allison V-1710 produced 1,150 horsepower in late December 1940 and 1,425 horsepower by December 1942. By October 1943, it had a combat rating of 1,750 horsepower. This engine powered the Lockheed P-38 Lightning (29,862 engines), the Bell P-39 Airacobra (13,149 engines), the Curtis P-40 Warhawk (14,087 engines), and the Bell P-63 Kingcobra (5,024 engines), among others. By the spring of 1944, production reached more than 2,000 engines per month and Allison had delivered 50,000 engines to the government. Allison, which had fewer than 800 employees in 1939, reached a peak employment of 23,000 in October 1943. By the end of the war, this GM division had completed 69,305 engines, including the V-3420, a 24-cylinder, liquid-cooled engine, which was basically a four-bank version of the V-1710. The V-3420 saw limited use in two experimental aircraft, the XB-19 and the XB-39. Allison also manufactured 313 turbojet engines in the last months of the war.[9]

Detroit's Packard Motor Car Company is the other automaker-turned-aircraft-engine-manufacturer that produced liquid-cooled aircraft engines. In May 1940, Secretary of the Treasury Henry Morgenthau Jr. asked the Chrysler Corporation to produce the liquid-cooled V-12 Rolls-Royce Merlin aircraft engine. Chrysler's engineers disassembled and measured two of these engines and declined the opportunity to make them. They argued that the engine would have to be entirely reengineered to American specifications. A month later, Edsel Ford, the president of Ford Motor Company, agreed to manufacture 9,000 of the Rolls-Royce engines, with 6,000 going to the British and the remaining 3,000 to the U.S. Army Air Force. Henry Ford vetoed the agreement and even a face-to-face appeal from Knudsen would not change the elder Ford's mind. Later in June, Knudsen asked Alvin Macauley, the chairman of Packard, if his firm would make these engines. Max Gilman, Packard's president, and Jessie G. Vincent, Packard's vice president for engineering, met with Knudsen on 24 June at his home on Grosse Ile, south of Detroit. They agreed that Packard would take on this project. Vincent sent several Packard employees to inventory the Merlin engine drawings that Ford held and then transferred them to Packard on 10 July 1940. The first engine contract was signed on 3 September 1940. The DPC issued its first lease to a private firm when it agreed on 8 September 1940 to purchase $8 million in needed machinery for Packard.[10]

Because of its experience in making marine engines and aircraft engines, Packard was a logical choice to build the Merlin engine. Under the direction of Vincent, Packard developed its first aircraft engine in 1915, a V-12 design with 300 horsepower. Other similar designs followed, and Packard typically tested them in race cars. With the U.S. entrance into World War I, Packard assisted the U.S. Army in developing a V-12 aircraft engine that developed 400 horsepower. Packard became one of the principal manufacturers of this engine, dubbed the Liberty 12. Between late 1917 and the end of the war, four American automakers—Packard, Lincoln, Ford, and Buick—turned out 19,585 Liberty engines or 94 percent of the total made in the United States. Packard made 6,857 of these (one-third of the total). Packard developed additional aircraft engines, which it sold in small quantities to military and civilian customers until 1934, when the company abandoned the business. Packard also made marine engines in the 1920s and in 1939 won a navy contract to make 1,200-horsepower engines for PT boats. Over the course of World War II, Packard made 12,115 PT boat engines while simultaneously producing the Merlin aircraft engine.[11]

Packard's entrance into military aircraft engine production was clouded by a complicated contract and the enormous problems Packard encountered in using Rolls-Royce's blueprints for mass-producing the engine. The contract signed on 3 September 1940 and approved ten days later involved three parties: Packard, the U.S. War Department, and the British government, through the British Purchasing Commission. There were actually two contracts, one for 6,000 British Merlin engines—models 28, 29, and 31—and a second one for 3,000 American V-1650-1 engines. The four models were virtually identical. They were V-12 liquid-cooled engines that developed 1,800 horsepower and had a displacement of 1,650 cubic inches. Packard officials estimated that the cost of all the buildings, machinery, and tooling required for this contract would be about $35 million. The value of the 9,000 engines produced would be more than $165 million, or more than $18,000 per engine. The same basic contracts remained in effect for the duration of the war but with 199 supplemental agreements, which made the final contract a foot thick. This was also the first large CPFF contract executed by the War Department. Allocating costs between the two contracts was a bookkeeping and accounting nightmare. To make matters worse, Packard began work on the engines in a building still devoted to automobile production.[12]

Packard encountered multiple problems when it took the Rolls-Royce drawings and prepared to mass-produce the Merlin engine. Packard assigned two hundred engineers and draftsmen to create a complete set of production drawings by late November 1940. They discovered that Rolls-Royce did not prepare detailed drawings of subassemblies or generate parts lists because their engines were "handmade." The drawings Packard received from Rolls-Royce often did not match the dimensions of the sample engines Rolls-Royce had sent Packard, and the British did not always specify manufacturing tolerances for the engine parts. It was British production practice to make "shop modifications" to the design without bothering to change the blueprints. Rolls-Royce had changed the dimensions of many castings without making changes to the blueprints. The blueprints Rolls-Royce sent to Ford specified a one-piece cylinder block, but the British manufacturer changed this to a two-piece design without informing Packard. The Packard engineering staff had to redo all of the existing drawings and create thousands more.

An additional headache developed because Rolls-Royce used four different threads and then modified so many of them that Packard ended up using a total of 140 different external threads. Packard had problems getting machines to duplicate these threads from their customary suppliers, who were not familiar with these British thread standards. Packard also struggled to get the 3,575 machine tools needed for this contract, along with roughly 60,000 fixtures and jigs, gauges, and tools. As a result, the first hand-made engine was not completed until 20 March 1941, and the first production engine came off the line in late October, both three months behind the original schedule. Jessie Vincent directly managed the Merlin engine project at Packard from start to finish.[13]

The DPC financed the construction of three new buildings at the Packard factory site in Detroit: a motor assembly building, including a four-story office wing; a building housing a heat-treating department and machine shop; and a building containing twenty-six dynamometer test cells and tear-down and reassembly facilities. Ironically, the motor assembly building stood on the site of Packard's Liberty Engine assembly building, which had to be demolished before construction could begin. Packard later converted its iron foundry into an aluminum foundry in 1943, at government expense. A summary of aircraft engine production by company in December 1944 showed Packard employing 36,100 men and women in engine production and using 2.8 million square feet of factory space for this purpose. By the end of the war, the DPC had invested $38.3 million in Packard facilities to produce the Merlin engine.[14]

By late April 1941, when Packard issued its *Annual Report* for 1940, the company had 1,600 employees preparing the machinery and tooling, purchasing the needed materials, and planning production. The automaker projected it would need 14,000 workers once production reached peak levels. Output grew slowly at first, reflecting the learning curve that Packard faced. Production in December 1941 was only 25 engines, but increased to 100 in January, then jumped to 500 in April, and reached 800 in July 1942. Peak monthly production of 2,752 engines occurred in August

Packard Rolls-Royce engine plant, Detroit (*WPRL*).

1944. After their initial order for 6,000 engines, the British ordered an additional 14,000 engines on 31 June 1942, followed by an order for 8,400 a year later. In February and March 1944, the British placed multiple orders for 31,200 engines. After its first order for 3,000 engines in September 1941, the U.S. Army Air Force made only more substantial order when it contracted for 13,352 engines in June 1943. The British government accounted for 82 percent of all the Merlin orders placed, a total of 76,341 engines, although only about 55,000 were actually delivered.[15]

The Rolls-Royce/Packard Merlin engines underwent thousands of design modifications over time, initiated by either Rolls-Royce or Packard. The most important design change was the introduction of a two-stage, two-speed supercharger to improve power and performance at high altitudes. After reviewing Packard's proposed design, the Army Air Force awarded the company a contract on 7 February 1942 to produce two supercharger units by early July. Packard completed the first unit in late May and installed it on an engine for testing. The supercharger automatically changed engine operating speeds with changes in altitudes, freeing the pilot from making those adjustments. The first Packard-built two-stage American Merlin, dubbed the V-1650-3, went into production on 17 April 1943. It was rated at 1,600 horsepower, significantly more than the power of the first generation of Packard Merlins, all rated at 1,260 horsepower. The first two-stage British Merlin, the Merlin 68 (1,710 horsepower), was completed on 9 December 1943. By strengthening the engine and changing gear ratios in the supercharger, yet another version of the American Merlin (the V-1650-7) developed 1,720 horsepower at 6,200 feet. Packard later introduced water-alcohol injection in an engine that went into production in April 1945. The new engine, designated the V-1650-9, had a rating of 2,280 horsepower at 3,700 feet. The Rolls-Royce/Packard Merlin engines were more powerful and much improved by the end of the war.[16]

Merlin engine production, along with the manufacture of marine engines and industrial engines, made up virtually all of Packard's war work. Packard's gross sales for 1942–45 amounted to $1,236,774,000; Merlin engine production accounted for 74 percent of the total ($909,830,000). As was the case with the other automakers, defense contracts were not particularly lucrative. Packard's profits on gross sales varied during the war years between a peak of 2.1 percent in 1942 to a low of 0.5 percent in 1945. Although Packard did not manufacture defense products with great visibility such as aircraft, tanks, trucks, or jeeps, the company made a substantial contribution to the war effort by supplying engines to the British and American air forces. Packard-built Merlin engines powered British Lancaster bombers, British Spitfire fighters, Curtiss P-40 Warhawk fighters, and North American P-51 Mustang fighters, among others.[17]

After Packard, Ford Motor Company was the next automaker to start production of aircraft engines. Although William Knudsen was clearly miffed by Henry Ford's reversal of Edsel Ford's commitment to build Rolls-Royce Merlin engines for the United States and Britain in late June 1940, he nevertheless approached Ford Motor Company in mid-August 1940 about producing aircraft engines designed by Pratt & Whitney. The engine in question, designated as the R-2800 ("R" indicated a radial configuration of the cylinders and 2800 referred to the displacement in cubic inches) Double-Wasp, was an 18-cylinder, air-cooled radial engine, with two banks of nine cylinders arranged back-to-back. Edsel Ford, Charles Sorensen, and a group of Ford engineers visited the Pratt & Whitney plant in East Hartford on 20–21 August to view the manufacturing process. Two days later, Ford informed the War Department of its willingness to manufacture 4,000 engines, and on 23 August the government sent Ford a letter of intent covering 1,092 engines. Ford sent a dozen engineers to the Pratt & Whitney plant on 1 September to study production and plant layout. Pratt & Whitney was building engines using the "station assembly" technique long abandoned by the automakers. There, engines were built one at a time at a fixed location with skilled craftsmen adding one part at a time until the engine was complete. A second letter of intent came on 10 September committing the government to take delivery of 2,949 engines. None of these letters mentioned any dollar amounts.

On 17 September 1940, the War Department issued a letter of intent to spend $14.3 million to construct and equip a plant to make 4,401 engines. The same day, Ford broke ground for its stand-alone aircraft engine plant located in an area that had been used for parking lots. After several additions, the two-story plant eventually measured 360 by 1,408 feet, with an attached wing containing engine test cells measuring 270 by 952 feet. When finished, the new buildings enclosed 1,286,344 square feet of floor space and cost $39 million, not counting machinery and equipment. By the end of the war, the DPC spent a total of $59.5 million at the Rouge, primarily for the aircraft engine plant and related facilities. Ford finally received a contract from the War Department on 31 October 1940 calling for the production of 4,236 engines. The automaker would pay Pratt & Whitney a nominal fee of $1 for each of its engines Ford made under license.[18]

Work on the new plant proceeded at breakneck speed. A little more than three months after the groundbreaking, the structural steel framework was completed and encased in a fiberboard "winter cocoon," which allowed the work to continue throughout the Michigan winter. The first machine (a drill press) was set in place in early February, and the installation of machinery was largely completed by the end of April 1941, when limited production of airplane engine parts started. At the end of July, the first completed engine test house ran a series of tests on an engine provided by Pratt & Whitney. Ford assembled the first complete Pratt & Whitney engine on 23 August 1941, slightly more than ten months after Ford broke ground for the new plant, but the government did not accept the first engine until 5 October.

The first engines built by an automobile manufacturer to actually power a military airplane were Ford-built Pratt & Whitney engines installed in a Martin B-26 medium bomber and flown by Glenn L. Martin Company test pilots at their plant near Baltimore on 14 February 1942. Among the dignitaries present at this demonstration were Donald Nelson, head of the WPB; Merrill C. Meigs, head of the Aviation Division of the WPB; and Charles Sorensen and Benson Ford, representing Ford Motor Company. The War Department issued a contract to Ford for an additional 6,281 engines on 26 September 1941, bringing the total ordered to 10,517. By the end of the war, the government had ordered a total of 60,869 engines, but Ford built only 57,178, with production ending on 31 August 1945. Although the Pratt & Whitney Double-Wasp engine was a new product (to Ford), the automaker quickly accelerated production. Ford completed only twenty engines in September 1941 but 182 in December 1941 and 805 the following December.[19]

In manufacturing aircraft engines, Ford was confronted with a broad spectrum of challenges it never faced in making automobiles, and the company responded with many innovative practices. Much like the Allison Division of General Motors, Ford had to install air-conditioning in its aircraft engine plant to better control heat, humidity, and dust. This was the first building at the Rouge to be fully air-conditioned, with temperatures maintained at a steady 75 degrees. Because the aircraft engines required a lot of aluminum and magnesium castings, Ford built a new aluminum foundry, a magnesium smelter, and a magnesium foundry. The aluminum foundry went into production in December 1942 and cast 553,968 cylinder heads over the course of the war. The government authorized the construction of a magnesium smelter on 16 January 1942, and it started production four months later. In time, the smelter included 96 furnaces enclosed in a building measuring 280 by 800 feet. Ford's new magnesium foundry was in operation in October 1941, using magnesium from outside sources. The foundry served double duty, making 26 different castings for the Pratt & Whitney engines and 23 castings for the B-24 Liberator bomber. As was the case with virtually all defense products, Ford had to contend with design changes to the engine. When substantial engineering changes were made, the engines that included the changes were given a new model designation, such as R-2800-5, R-2800-27, and so forth. The first 951 engines produced were rated at 1,850 horsepower, but the remainder of the engines developed 2,000 horsepower. By the end of the war, Ford had produced eleven variations on the original design.[20]

Because Ford workers had no experience in aircraft engine parts manufacturing, assembly, inspection, and repairs, the company established an aircraft engine school at the Rouge complex. The first classes began on 1 June 1941, with 1,100 employees enrolled by the end of the month. Pratt & Whitney had shipped a complete aircraft engine to Ford in March to help Ford's engineers, draftsmen, and toolmakers prepare for production. Ford put the engine on the floor of the aircraft engine plant, where it was disassembled and reassembled multiple times. The first group enrolled in the aircraft engine school were trained in parts manufacturing; the second group learned the fine points of assembly; the third group were trained as inspectors and engine test operators; and the final group were trained as engine mechanics. Once engine production was well under way starting in February 1942, the school was used to train enlisted men in the U.S. Army Air Force Service Command as airplane engine mechanics. By the time the school closed in 1945, it had trained 5,270 Army Air Force personnel to service and repair the R-2800 engine.[21]

Ford and the other automakers-turned-aircraft-engine-manufacturers had to carry out far more thorough inspections and testing than were required for automobile production. At the end of June 1944, when aircraft engine production reached its peak, Ford employed roughly 15,500 workers at its engine plant. The Inspection Department alone employed 2,958 inspectors and clerks and 181 foremen. Finished engines were subject to extensive testing in special "cells" in the Test House. They underwent dynamometer testing to measure their horsepower production, but they were also closely monitored for temperature, fuel consumption, oil usage, and other elements of performance. Ford put fifteen test cells into service in mid-June 1942 and another thirteen in August 1943. Ford eventually built a total of eighty test cells. In typical Ford fashion, the company connected the engines undergoing testing to electrical generators that provided 95 percent of the electric power used in the aircraft engine plant. The first engine to come off the production line underwent grueling 150-hour dynamometer testing, but once the plant was in production, the standard test ran four hours. Standard procedure at aircraft engine plants, including Ford's, was to completely disassemble the engine after testing to find any defective or worn parts. This was carried out by a team of Army Air Force and Ford inspectors. If nothing was amiss, the engine was reassembled and underwent a second four-hour test before being cleaned and packed for shipment. When worn or broken parts were found, they were replaced and the engine subjected to a two-hour penalty test and then disassembled again. If the replacement part held up, the engine was reassembled and subjected to an additional four-hour test before receiving final acceptance.[22]

Ford modified the methods used to fabricate many key components, resulting in savings in both materials and costs. The company produced cylinders and cylinder heads through a centrifugal casting process, replacing forging, which was the practice used by Pratt & Whitney and the rest of the aircraft engine industry. This technique reduced the cost per cylinder from $13.38 to $10.50, mainly because Ford's technique saved thirty-five pounds of steel per cylinder. The Army Air Force reluctantly accepted this innovation, but Pratt & Whitney never abandoned forging. Ford production engineers and toolmakers modified existing machine tools or designed entirely new ones to produce interchangeable parts for the engine. Ford designed 8,128 new machine tools and used only 844 of their existing tools in aircraft engine production. In time, Pratt & Whitney and two of its licensees, Chevrolet and Buick, adopted Ford's machine tools.[23]

Ford also achieved great cost savings merely by adopting automotive moving assembly line methods in building these engines, which consisted of 220 subassemblies and a total of 11,723 parts. The final assembly area was 1,400 feet long and 60 feet wide, and employed 1,424 workers (1,177 men and 251 women). Two assembly lines ran the length of the building and were fed by mechanized subassembly lines on both sides. All materials moved by way of overhead monorails, Hy-cycle rails, electric cranes, and hoists. Each worker had only one or two tasks to perform. Ford had essentially replicated the moving assembly line the company had developed at its Highland Park plant in 1913–15. The aircraft assembly line was continuously fine-tuned throughout the war. Between 1943 and the end of production, the number of workers required to assembly sixty engines per shift fell from 650 to 231. Ford became the most efficient manufacturer of Pratt & Whitney aircraft engines in terms of manpower required. The War Department generated monthly reports on aircraft engine production by manufacturer, comparing the combined horsepower of engines shipped with the number of employees. This was the only way to develop comparative information, since each plant produced engines of varying capacities. For December 1944, Ford shipped engines developing an average of 132 horsepower per employee, followed by Chevrolet (91), Nash-Kelvinator (87), Buick (83), and the main Pratt & Whitney plant in East Hartford (66). Ford's mass-production expertise, combined with the enormous toolmaking resources of the Rouge plant, made it the most efficient producer.[24]

As was the case with most defense contractors, Ford had to contend with demands by the Army Air Force for increased production. In March 1943, Ford was completing 1,075 engines a month as it continued to expand production to reach the government's goal of 1,800 engines a month. Without warning, the air force announced a new goal of 3,400 engines a month. There were substantial obstacles to reaching the goals of the "3,400 Program," as Ford called the new schedule. One was space. The Aircraft Engine Building was fully utilized, and there was no vacant space available at the Ford Rouge plant. The second was manpower: there was simply very little labor available in the Detroit labor market. Ford's solution was to decentralize engine parts production, moving a significant share of production to several of its other plants, which had available space and a better likelihood of finding labor. The Aircraft Engine Building became primarily an assembly operation.

The Ford Highland Park plant, which had 312,000 square feet of available space, took on the work of finishing the propeller shafts and making all the gears in the engine. Ford moved 1,241 machines from the Aircraft Engine Building to Highland Park. Parts production and the necessary machines were shifted to Ford's branch assembly plants in Memphis (413 machines), St. Paul (290), and Kansas City (156). Miscellaneous parts production was moved to "the farm building" in Dearborn, along with 267 machines. As a result of these moves, Ford increased its capacity to 3,400 engines a month by September 1944, but the air force never ordered that many engines. Ford's peak production was 2,431 engines in August 1944. Ford's program to shift parts production to its branch assembly plants helped ease the labor shortage in Detroit. In mid-March 1944, Ford employed 32,202 workers in aircraft engine production, but fewer than half (15,596) worked in the Aircraft Engine Building. The Ford Motor Company had great success in making the Pratt & Whitney Double-Wasp engine. Operating on a very similar timetable, the Studebaker Corporation based in South Bend, Indiana, prepared to manufacture, under license from the Wright Aeronautical Corporation, a 9-cylinder, air-cooled aircraft engine.[25]

The Studebaker Corporation was the fourth automobile company to manufacture aircraft engines and was one of only two to be licensed by Wright Aeronautical Corporation. By mid-1940, Wright had fallen behind its scheduled deliveries of its R-2600 Cyclone 14 engine, which developed 1,600 horsepower, to the British government and to the U.S. Army Air Force, so it was willing to make an exception to its preference for "in-house" production. The Army Air Force issued a contract to Studebaker in December 1940 to build 6,500 of these engines, to be used mainly in the North American B-25. This was a CPFF contract. Studebaker would build three new plants—at South Bend, Indiana; at Fort Wayne, Indiana; and in Chicago—to produce these engines. The new facilities would incorporate 1,500,000 square feet of floor space and would be financed with $50 million from the DPC. In December 1944, Studebaker was using 2,861,000 square feet of floor space for aircraft engine production alone.[26]

Studebaker broke ground for its new aircraft assembly plant on Chippewa Street in South Bend in January 1941 and the plant was completed eighteen months later. The company deliberately built additional factories in Fort Wayne and in Chicago to draw on labor supplies away from South Bend. Studebaker had already purchased a good deal of tooling for the R-2600 Cyclone 14 engine when the air force abruptly decided in mid-1941 to have Studebaker make the more urgently needed R-1820 Cyclone 9, a 9-cylinder, 1,200-horsepower engine used to power the Boeing B-17 Flying Fortress. Because many of the tools purchased for the production of the R-2600 engine could no longer be used, Studebaker delivered more than $1.75 million in excess tools to the Army Air Force, which ultimately sold most of them for scrap.[27]

Studebaker encountered the same challenges faced by the other automakers who turned to aircraft engine production. The R-1820 Cyclone engine had 8,000 parts that required more than 80,000 machining operations to create the precision finishes needed. The production operations were subject to 50,000 distinct inspections along the way. The initial running test of the completed engine, called the "green" test by all engine manufacturers, ran for four hours, the normal time at factories making Pratt & Whitney engines. At South Bend as elsewhere, the engines were completely disassembled after the initial test to identify excessive wear or defective parts and then thoroughly tested a second time. The Army Air Force terminated Studebaker's contract in May 1945 and the last engine came off the line in June. By then, Studebaker had delivered 63,789 engines to the air force, and for the last twenty months of the war, Studebaker was the exclusive supplier of engines for the B-17 Flying Fortress. As one of only two licensees of Wright Aeronautical, Studebaker turned out more than three times (63,789 versus 18,349) as many engines as the Dodge Division of the Chrysler Corporation, which started production of a much larger 18-cylinder engine three years after Studebaker had finished its first engine.[28]

Other Pratt & Whitney Licensees

Buick's involvement in manufacturing aircraft engines followed a path similar to that of Ford. In August 1940, William Knudsen approached Harlo H. Curtice, the head of the Buick Motor Division of General Motors, about Buick manufacturing Pratt & Whitney aircraft engines. Engineers and production specialists from Flint visited the Pratt & Whitney plant in East Hartford on 9–11 October to observe aircraft engine assembly. Curtice placed orders for $10 million in machine tools before any formal contract was issued. Buick and GM officials conferred with Army Air Force and WPB representatives in Washington in late December 1940 to finalize contract details. The air force issued a formal contract in January 1941 calling for the production of 500 Pratt & Whitney 14-cylinder, Twin Wasp R-1830 engines per month. Until there was a signed contract, Buick's production engineers could not look at Pratt & Whitney's engine blueprints and specifications, which were stored in a locked cabinet. Once the engine contract was in place, Pratt & Whitney shipped a complete engine to Flint to allow Buick's engineers to examine it more closely.[29]

Buick's production experts made many visits to East Hartford and discovered, much as had been the case for engineers from other automakers visiting aircraft manufacturers, that Pratt & Whitney hand-built and hand-fitted its engines. Buick initially planned to build an engine plant in Grand Blanc, Michigan, a small town southeast of Flint. When the Army Air Force doubled the monthly production quota to 1,000 engines, Buick and GM officials recognized that there would be a severe shortage of labor in the Flint area once the automobile and parts plants there converted to war work. They quietly bought a 120-acre parcel in the Chicago suburb of Melrose Park, on the western outskirts of the city. Groundbreaking for the Melrose Park plant took place on 17 March 1941. The DPC paid for the land, buildings, and the machinery installed there, and ultimately spent a total of $110 million on the project, the fourth most expensive DPC facility built during the war.[30]

Buick Melrose Park (IL) engine plant test cells (*SA/KU*).

Once the Melrose Park plant construction was finished on 17 September 1941, the installation of machinery continued at a frantic pace. The first complete engine built at Melrose Park came off the line on 7 January 1942 and passed its tests. The initial contract called for the delivery of 110 engines by the end of March 1942 and Buick easily met that goal. The air force increased the size of the contract to 3,000 engines in July 1942, to 4,400 engines in December 1942, and to progressively higher numbers over the next year. Buick consistently beat its production schedules for the engines. The first 7,000 engines were scheduled to be delivered to the Army Air Force by September 1943, but Buick completed that part of its contract by November 1942, some ten months early. Buick carried out roughly half of the manufacturing work for these engines in various plants in Flint, with the remaining half carried out in Melrose Park, along with engine assembly and testing.[31]

The process for inspecting the engine parts and then testing the completed engine was virtually the same at all plants making Pratt & Whitney engines, as specified by the Army Air Force. At Melrose Park, a Buick employee and a U.S. Army Air Force representative independently inspected each of the 6,266 engine parts. The testing protocol was exactly the same as the protocol followed at Ford.[32]

At the request of the War Department, Buick built and operated a large aluminum foundry in Flint to cast cylinder heads for the aircraft engines built at Melrose Park.

Construction began in February 1942, and by the end of the year three-quarters of the plant was completed and operating. The foundry, built by the DPC at government expense, cost $10 million. Although it had little experience casting aluminum, Buick took on the challenge. By the end of the war, Buick turned out more than 3.2 million cylinder heads, enough to provide 225,000 engines with fourteen cylinder heads each. Buick provided all of the cylinder heads needed at Melrose Park and the rest were sold to other aircraft engine manufacturers.[33]

Much like the other automakers-turned-aircraft-engine-manufacturers, Buick became much more efficient over time. Under the initial contract with the government, Buick would deliver the engines at a price of $16,000 each. By June 1943, the price fell to $8,000 and by the end of the year to only $6,400. Buick's success in meeting and exceeding its production quotas and drastically lowering costs brought additional work. In late April 1944, the Army Air Force signed new contracts with Buick to build additional Pratt & Whitney R-1830 14-cylinder Twin Wasp engines and the R-2800 18-cylinder Double Wasp engine to be used in the C-54 cargo plane. The additional supply contracts provided that upward of $60 million would be spent on the two engines. There is little available documentation on Buick's experience with the R-2800 Double Wasp engine. Because the R-1830 and the R-2800 had very few common parts, this was in effect a brand-new production job. Buick assembled the engine in Flint using parts manufactured in Buick plants in Flint and from other suppliers.[34]

Buick hosted a dinner at the Drake Hotel in Chicago on 22 October 1943 to celebrate the delivery of the 25,000th Buick-built engine to the air force. Less than nine months later, on 13 July 1944, Buick hosted a dinner at the same hotel to mark the delivery of the 50,000th Buick-built aircraft engine to the government. An advertisement in the middle of the dinner program was titled "Battle Song of the Liberators" and stated that all 50,000 Buick-built engines up to that point went into B-24 Liberator bombers.[35]

In late April 1941 the Army Air Force approached the Chevrolet Division of General Motors Corporation asking for a proposal specifying the contract price and a production schedule to produce 1,000 Pratt & Whitney R-1830 aircraft engines per month and an additional supply of spare parts equal to 10 percent of the contract. This was the same engine Buick was building. A letter of intent followed on 28 June 1941 calling for production to begin in October 1942 with twenty-five engines. Chevrolet engineering and production executives visited the Pratt & Whitney plant in East Hartford between 2 and 10 July. The two parties signed a supply contract on 7 October 1941 calling for 1,000 engines per month, but this was amended twice in six months. An amendment on 11 December 1941 called for 2,000 engines a month,

Chevrolet production of Pratt & Whitney engines,
Tonawanda, New York, January 1943 *(ACWP)*.

plus 17 percent spare parts, but this was altered again in March 1942 to provide for 3,000 engines per month and 29 percent for spare parts, retroactive to all previous contracts. The March 1942 contract called for the monthly production of 1,000 R-1830-43 engines, built for B-24 bombers, and 2,000 R-1830-92 engines, installed mainly in C-47 cargo planes. The two aircraft engine models were not identical; 316 parts were unique to one or the other engine. The March 1942 contract called for the production of 40,550 engines at a total cost of $617,662,568, with peak production to be achieved by June 1943. Chevrolet quoted a price of $16,000 per engine on the first 2,000 it delivered, $13,500 on the next 5,000, and $11,500 on the balance.[36]

At the onset of its work on aircraft engines, Chevrolet operated two plants in western New York: an assembly plant in Buffalo and the Tonawanda Motor and Axle plant in nearby Tonawanda. Chevrolet sold the Buffalo Assembly plant to the DPC for its book value and gave the government the use of its Tonawanda plant at no charge, but Chevrolet retained ownership. The Buffalo plant provided 546,390 square feet of space and the Tonawanda plant an additional 873,860 square feet. Once the government awarded the engine contract, the DPC built a new factory (Aviation Engine Plant No. 1) next to the existing Tonawanda plant, providing an additional 286,266 square feet. In the early stages of engine production, Chevrolet used 1.7 million square feet of floor space in western New York. The DPC also invested slightly more than $86 million for the machinery and tooling needed to equip the plant to make 3,000 engines a month, including machinery already owned by Chevrolet. The total DPC investment in buildings and equipment amounted to $120 million, making this the third most expensive DPC project completed during the war.[37]

The original supply contract called for Chevrolet to complete the first twenty-five engines by October 1942, but the automaker assembled its first engine in March 1942 and monthly output had already reached 866 engines in August. By the end of July 1942, Chevrolet employed 12,850 workers at its aircraft engine plants. When Chevrolet achieved peak engine production in August 1943, it employed 37,431 workers on engine work, nearly half of the 79,424 workers it employed throughout its operations. As was the case with the Ford Motor Company, Chevrolet mass-produced aluminum forgings at a plant it operated in Saginaw, Michigan, making Chevrolet the second-largest producer of aluminum forgings in the world. The plant turned out propeller blades, propeller hubs, engine crankcases, and engine pistons. Chevrolet also converted a large gray iron foundry in Saginaw to produce magnesium castings for the Pratt & Whitney engines. In the final year of the war, Chevrolet produced the Pratt & Whitney 18-cylinder R-2800 engine on the same Tonawanda engine assembly line that produced the two versions of the 9-cylinder R-1830 engine. These engines did not share any common parts. Chevrolet met this manufacturing challenge by carefully scheduling production and coordinating the delivery of components.[38]

In early 1941 Pratt & Whitney asked Nash-Kelvinator to make components for one of its aircraft engines, but not the complete engine. In July, the automaker sent some of its engineers to East Hartford to observe production and by July had leased the REO Motor Car Company truck plant on Mt. Hope Avenue in Lansing, Michigan, to use for producing engine parts. Nash-Kelvinator began production in Lansing later in 1941, but the government inked a new agreement with Nash-Kelvinator on 12 February 1942 making the automaker a prime contractor for Pratt & Whitney R-2800 Double Wasp engines. The company would complete the final assembly and testing of the engines. The first contract called for production of 350 engines a month using an enlarged plant in Lansing. However, the government soon called on Nash-Kelvinator to increase engine production to 700 a month, creating a huge shortage of factory space in Lansing. The solution was to shift the manufacturing of aircraft engines to Kenosha, Wisconsin, the site of Nash-Kelvinator's main plant. By early March 1942, the company had moved machinery from Lansing to Kenosha and began buying additional equipment.[39]

On 9 April 1942, the DPC agreed to build a new engine factory in Kenosha on a ten-acre parcel that had previously served as the Nash athletic fields. The factory building of 204,800 square feet included twenty-four test cells. Work began on the new plant on 1 April 1942 and production started on 1 July. The engine plant cost the government $5.2 million for the building and $26.2 million for the machinery and equipment, including engine test equipment, for a total of $31.4 million. The navy reached an agreement with Nash-Kelvinator on 25 May 1942 for the production of 1,500 engines and spare parts, with 870 engines going to the navy and 630 to the British government. Nash-Kelvinator shipped its first five aircraft engines on 29 December 1942, only nine months after work began on the factory.[40]

In March 1943, the government asked Nash to increase engine production from 700 to 900 per month. Construction of ten additional engine test cells, one flight test cell, and one dynamometer cell began in September 1943. The buildings were ready in January 1944 and additional equipment in place by 1 March 1944, at a total cost of $2.6 million. Nash-Kelvinator achieved its peak production of aircraft engines in June 1944, turning out 901 engines. Peak employment on aircraft engines reached 11,500 at that time, including workers in Kenosha and Milwaukee. Before the war, the Kenosha plant employed only fifteen women, but during the war average total employment was 9,215, including 2,353 women, more than one-quarter of the total.[41]

One of the most demanding parts of aircraft engine production was the inspection process. Nash-Kelvinator inspected practically every individual part, or roughly fifteen million parts every month. In addition, the inspection department gave 600,000 parts per month a magnetic inspection to check for surface defects, casting defects, or forging cracks. This alone involved 110 full-time employees. The inspectors also checked for the presence, location, and size of hundreds of oil holes on each engine, necessary for proper lubrication. They inspected each engine 100 percent before the four-hour "green test run" that each engine endured. Inspectors then disassembled the engine, gave it another 100 percent inspection, and ran another four-hour test.

The exhaustive inspection process required the use of 70,000 gauges to check the dimensions on all aspects of the machines making the parts. The company maintained a staff that in turn checked the dimensions of the close-limit gauges twice a week and the other gauges every two weeks. When production reached 800 engines per month, the inspection department had 1,050 employees: 475 male inspectors, 425 female inspectors, 60 foremen and supervisors, and 90 clerks.[42]

Nash-Kelvinator manufactured the B Series version of the Pratt & Whitney R-2800 engine. In early 1944, the government planned to move production of the more advanced C Series engines from Pratt & Whitney's East Hartford plant to Kenosha to free up Pratt & Whitney to produce an even more advanced E Series engine. The government issued letters of intent to Nash-Kelvinator on 2 May and 30 June 1944 for 2,550 of these C-type engines but then canceled the plans in mid-October. By the end of the war, Nash-Kelvinator was producing three versions of the B Series engines: the R-2800-8, used in the Vought-Sikorsky Corsair; the R-2800-10, installed in the Grumman Hellcat; and the R-2800-65, used in the twin-engine Northrop P-61 Black Widow night fighter.

As Nash-Kelvinator perfected its use of mass-production techniques in making the engines, costs fell substantially. The estimated cost per engine in the first contract (May 1942) was $26,600, but by the spring of 1945 the actual cost to the government was only $13,483 per engine. Nash-Kelvinator manufactured 17,012 aircraft engines during the war at a cost to the government of $303,919,125, including the company's fixed fee (profit) of 6 percent.[43]

Pratt & Whitney and the Automakers

The evolving relationship between Pratt & Whitney (P & W) and the automobile companies that manufactured its engines throws light on the success of the automakers as aircraft engine manufacturers. The interactions between these partners is delineated in some detail in a reminiscence/report by Edmund L. Eveleth, who was in charge of customer relations at P & W during the war and had the task of hosting a flood of visitors from the automobile industry to East Hartford. This seventeen-page document, titled "The Greatest Wedding of American Industry," describes the relationship between P & W and its licensees. Eveleth kept records of the number of men from each automaker who visited the P & W plant in East Hartford and the number of visits they made. His compilation includes the four automakers discussed earlier in this chapter (Ford, Buick, Chevrolet, and Nash-Kelvinator) and two firms not included: the Jacobs Aircraft Engine Company and the Continental Aviation and Engine Company. Between August 1940 and December 1943, a total of 1,303 men made 2,143 visits to P & W. Ford had the fewest number of men visit (138), while Chevrolet had the most (305). The automakers developed a "friendly" competition over who would produce their first Pratt & Whitney engine in the shortest time. This was in fact an "apples and oranges" competition. Buick and Chevrolet produced the same engine, the R-1830 Twin Wasp, and needed fifteen months and nine months, respectively, between their initial visit to P & W and their first production engine. This engine had been in production for months before Buick and Chevrolet took on its manufacture. In contrast, Ford needed thirteen months to turn out its first production R-2800 Double Wasp engine, but this was a brand-new, untried engine that P & W had not yet manufactured.[44]

Edmund Eveleth recalled the initial visit of Ford Motor Company executives on 20–21 August 1940. During this visit, the Ford and P & W executives toured the factory and then returned to P & W's executive offices. The aircraft engine company's chief production engineer addressed the two sets of executives and told them that they were among the best musicians in the world. He then noted to the Ford executives, "You play the piano, while we play the violin. In fact you play the piano better than anyone else in the world. Therefore, if you are willing to play the violin you will build a satisfactory aircraft engine, but if you try to play the violin the way you play the piano, you will never build a Pratt & Whitney Aircraft engine." The Ford executives returned to the factory floor to reexamine P & W's production methods and realized the challenges they would face. Ford's top production experts returned to East Hartford in September, were initially discouraged by what they saw, but then took off their jackets, rolled up their sleeves, and went to work to master P & W's methods.[45]

The automakers did not imitate P & W's methods; they improved them and forced P & W to alter many of its practices to meet the needs of mass production. Eveleth admitted that P & W knew that once the auto companies made their aircraft engines exactly as designed, then P & W would benefit from the production expertise of the automakers. He claimed that at some point, "we all realized that we were the outstanding engineering firm and they were the outstanding production firms to do the job." Eveleth conceded that P & W's blueprints and specifications were often incomplete and inadequate for use in mass production in part because they did not incorporate the "know-how" of the skilled machinists who did the work. P & W adapted its blueprints to meet the demand of the automakers, while the automobile companies had to learn how to replicate the high finish required on aircraft engine parts. The two parties cooperated and learned a great deal from each other, which made the aircraft engine production miracle possible.[46]

The Dodge-Chicago Plant and the Production of B-29 Engines

The final case study of aircraft engine manufacturing by the automobile industry involves the Wright Cyclone engine (R-3350) made for the B-29 Superfortress by the Dodge-Chicago Division of the Chrysler Corporation in a sprawling government-built factory complex in Chicago. This was an air-cooled 3,350 CID engine that developed 2,200 horsepower and had eighteen cylinders (two sets of nine) arranged in a radial configuration. As was typical with large war contracts involving complex products, the initial planning process was fraught with various delays, contradictory signals from the government, and conflicts among the contractors. Following prelim-inary discussions about Chrysler's possible interest in making aircraft engines, the Wright Aeronautical Corporation and the Aircraft Production Branch of the WPB approached Chrysler at the end of December 1941 about a contract.[47]

At first, the Army Air Force proposed that Chrysler take over existing factory space near Milwaukee or Chicago, but by 20 January 1942 the WPB decided that they would need a new plant and Chicago ended up being the only location under consideration. After some wrangling over possible sites, the government agreed to Chrysler's choice, a site at 75th Street and Cicero, near Chicago's southwest border. DPC was to build the plant, but its chief engineer, W. L. Draeger, argued against hiring Detroit's Albert Kahn as the architect, claiming that Kahn's office had too much work already and was not providing good service. Chrysler staunchly defended Kahn's track record and won the day.[48]

The initial supply contract of 27 February 1942 called for Chrysler to produce 10,000 engines, with deliveries starting in March 1943 and continuing through August 1944. Production would reach 1,000 engines per month in January 1944. This was a CPFF contract, with an estimated cost of $253,146,200 for the engines, plus $43,034,854 for spare parts ($296,818,054 total). Chrysler would be paid a fixed fee of 6 percent on the contract, or a little less than $18,000,000. In late March, the DPC approved spending of $103,751,231 for the project, including $68,000,000 for machinery and tools. The balance covered the land (375 acres) and the buildings, which would provide 3,370,523 square feet of floor space.

The air force changed the initial contract in early April, increasing the peak pro-duction from 1,000 to 1,500 engines a month; they wanted Chrysler to produce both a 2,220-horsepower *and* a 2,300-horsepower version of the R-3350. The total cost of the original supply contract increased by $57,130,426 to reflect the larger production figure. The DPC would acquire an additional 120 acres of land and increase total floor space to 5,551,744 square feet. In time, the Dodge-Chicago plant incorporated 6,430,000 square feet of floor space, as much space as the entire aircraft engine industry used in January 1941. Projected employment also jumped from 27,000 to 45,000 workers. Given the enormity of this project, Chrysler's presi-dent, K. T. Keller, created an independent Dodge-Chicago Plant Division of the Chrysler Corporation, mainly for administrative purposes, and named L. L. Colbert as its general manager.[49]

Construction of the Dodge-Chicago plant began at the same time Chrysler's pro-duction engineers and planners wrestled with designing the needed machine tools and the production line. The WPB announced the selection of the George A. Fuller Company of Chicago as the general contractor in early May 1942 but then faced protests from local and state politicians who tried to have the decision reversed. They objected to Fuller only because the firm was not a contributor to their political campaigns. The WPB did not back down, but Fuller's problems were not over. In June, the DPC delayed construction by disputing Fuller's requests for equipment. The Army Air Force called a meeting of all the parties on 27 June 1942 and Colonel Charles Russell asserted that the plant "was the number one job in the country" and ordered the DPC to cooperate with Fuller. Colonel Russell was authorized to jump-start this project by Brigadier General K. B. Wolfe, head of the U.S. Air Force Production Division.[50]

The general contractor broke ground for the tool shop on 4 June 1942, and by mid-August a dozen buildings were under construction and Fuller had 7,000 men working two shifts. A month later, the labor force had grown to 12,000, and by November more than 16,000 construction workers were on the job, working around the clock. This was a monumental plant by any standard. The major structure, the machining and assembly building, measured 2,340 feet by 1,520 feet, enclosing 3,556,800 square feet (nearly 82 acres) under one roof. The complex also included two forges and a heat-treat and die shop; a set of fifty large test cells for engine testing and a propeller test building; an enormous aluminum foundry and an equally large magnesium foundry; two boiler houses; a tool shop; a personnel building and main office building; and various other buildings. Despite monumental problems as a result of materials shortages, equipment shortages, and bad weather, the George Fuller Company finished the sixteen major buildings of the complex by April 1943. However, at that date, Chrysler was still nine months away from starting production of the Cyclone engine.[51]

The major buildings incorporated innovative design features. After Chrysler presented Kahn's building plans to the Army Air Force on 9 May 1942, the WPB rejected the design because it used too much steel. According to L. L. Colbert, the government decided that this would be a "temporary" plant, designed to last only seven to ten years. Chrysler's building engineers and Kahn's organization jointly designed a novel structural system that used reinforced concrete in place of steel. The roof consisted of reinforced concrete arched roof slabs supported by reinforced concrete columns and beams. The machining and assembly building alone required 6,200 separate ribs and 3,363 columns. The aluminum and magnesium foundries, the tool shop, and other buildings in the complex also used the arched roof design. The contractor poured the concrete roof slabs in traveling forms mounted on wheels and tracks. Once the concrete had set, the panel would be lowered into place and the form moved to the next position. Fuller used fifty of these traveling forms, called "Trojan horses," during plant construction.

Kahn's innovative design used only 2.56 pounds of steel per square foot of space versus the 5.5 pounds of the original conventional plan, saving over 18,000 tons of structural steel. According to one calculation, this was enough steel to build fourteen destroyers or more than 300 medium tanks. Kahn also replaced the normal steel window sash with "wood victory sash" and designed a wooden security fence four miles long, which saved another 125 tons of steel. Chrysler installed its own Airtemp air-conditioning equipment in the final assembly area, some twenty acres of floor space. Because magnesium, aluminum, and steel have different coefficients of expansion, controlling temperatures was necessary to ensure that assembled parts would fit properly. Chrysler installed eighty-one air-conditioning units, which circulated 1,500,000 cubic feet of air per minute, in penthouses on the roof.[52]

Building the massive Dodge-Chicago plant turned out to be the most simple, straightforward part of the effort to produce aircraft engines. Chrysler had to contend with two daunting problems: an unfinished engine design and long delays in getting the machine tools needed to start production. In early March 1942, Chrysler's management complained that Wright Aeronautical Corporation was not providing them with the blueprints, specifications, parts lists, tool lists, and other information. At the end of the month, Chrysler had received only 700 of the 960 blueprints, and the missing drawings covered the largest and most complex components. Wright forwarded a list of 4,999 machine tools Chrysler would need for production but then admitted that the list was far from complete and would need major revisions.

Chrysler soon discovered that Wright had not even finished the design for the engine, much less produced any of them. Colbert accused Wright of misleading Chrysler and, worse, of failing to cooperate in moving the work forward. A group of Chrysler engineers had gone to the Wright test facility to witness a "tear-down" test of the engine, but the Wright officials would not allow them to see the actual tear-down. Instead, Wright only allowed them to look at the parts afterward. Carl Breer, one of Chrysler's chief engineers, reported that Chrysler disassembled several Wright engines and discovered that the parts were not interchangeable. Further, the engines they examined did not follow the drawings with respect to tolerances. These were in effect handmade engines, unsuitable for mass production.

Even the drawings were problematic. When Chrysler's engineers carefully studied them to ensure proper "fit" of the components, they discovered over two hundred "interferences" that required changes in design tolerances. With decades of experience in mass-producing automobiles, Chrysler's production engineers were ready to mass-produce the Wright engine, while the Wright engineers were not prepared for the task. In time, the Wright and Chrysler engineering staffs worked together to improve the engine design before it went into production.[53]

Long delays in getting machine tools moved the start of production back from March 1943, as the original contract specified, to July 1943 and then to January 1944. Chrysler had initially intended to have its production "pilot line" operating by December 1942, but by late March 1943 only half the pilot line machinery had arrived. Chrysler simultaneously ordered the equipment needed for full-scale production, more than 7,000 machines tools in total, and these came even more slowly. In early April 1943, the Dodge-Chicago plant had only one-third of the machines on order and five months later still had less than three-quarters of the needed machines. Colbert blamed the machinery shortages on the lack of foresight by both the air force and the WPB, but he also believed that certain air force officers at Wright Field were deliberately sabotaging Chrysler by diverting the needed machinery elsewhere. Given the severe shortages of machine tools needed for the defense industry in 1942 and 1943, plus the fact that the design of the engine and of the B-29 itself were still undergoing revision through 1942, the WPB simply diverted machinery to other war plants.[54]

As Chrysler finally began to receive the machine tools needed to start mass production, the Army Air Force informed Chrysler in mid-October 1943 that it would not produce the second version of the engine (RB-3350-BB) after all, even though Chrysler had bought machine tools for that purpose. The pilot line began operating on 1 December 1943 and the main assembly operations started up in January 1944, when the plant produced fifteen engines. Once Dodge-Chicago began to produce engines in quantity (507 in July 1944), the Army Air Force raised its production targets considerably. The plant was initially set up to make 750 engines per month, but by February 1944 the air force already planned for production to reach 1,600 engines per month by May 1945 and 2,200 a month later in the year. Dodge-Chicago production was 1,327 engines in January 1945 and then reached a peak of 1,697 engines in July 1945, the all-time record for the war period.[55]

Once the machine tools arrived and the plant came into full production, Dodge-Chicago consistently exceeded the air force's production goals, which they constantly revised upward. Employment climbed quickly from 10,104 in late August 1943 to 19,245 in December 1943. A year later, 31,828 worked at the complex; employment peaked at Dodge-Chicago at 33,245 in February 1945. Although the plant could draw from the Chicago labor market, maintaining a workforce was difficult despite extensive use of female and African American workers. In late July 1944, when 27,251 worked at the plant, women made up over one-quarter of the total (7,575). During the eight months ending 30 June 1944, Dodge-Chicago hired 23,404 new employees, but 10,483 left for military service or for other jobs.[56]

The air force wanted to replace carbureted fuel systems in all of its aircraft engines with fuel-injection systems, which would improve fuel distribution, provide better acceleration, and reduce fire risks. In early June 1944, the WPB granted Chrysler an educational contract to build ten fuel-injected engines, with the intent that production of the new design would begin in October. Initially, Dodge-Chicago was to build 4,160 fuel-injection engines using a system built by the Bendix Aviation Corporation. By mid-December 1944, Chrysler had contracted to build a total of 5,880 fuel-injection engines, but Bendix was still in the midst of modifying its design and had not delivered the promised quantities. The Army Air Force did another "change order" allowing Chrysler to buy parts for carburetors for the 5,880 engines so that production did not come to a complete halt.[57]

Planning and then managing production of the Wright Cyclone engine at the Dodge-Chicago plant was the most frustrating experience Chrysler faced during the war. The organization had to incorporate 6,274 design changes to the engine, usually involving dozens of parts, resulting in 48,500 change notices from engineering to the planning and production divisions of the plant. Chrysler was originally supposed to manufacture 110 of the engine's parts, but because of problems finding reliable suppliers, the automaker ended up making 160 parts. In August 1944, Chrysler asked the DPC for an additional payment of $5,500,000 to cover extra expenses they had incurred since the start of the engine contract.[58]

In February 1945, the WPB informed Chrysler that the government wanted to change the engine contract to a "fixed-cost" basis. Chrysler vehemently objected to this plan, pointing out that under the existing contract, the average cost of the engines had dropped from $25,314 to $14,500. Given the long history of delays in machinery deliveries and thousands of engineering changes to the engine, Chrysler was not willing to risk a fixed-price contract. The automaker also argued that it would have to shut down the plant for fifteen days to complete a thorough inventory, with the resulting loss of 800 engines. The WPB reconsidered and then dropped its plan.

With the last engine assembled on 7 September 1945, Chrysler's Dodge-Chicago plant had achieved an impressive production record. This single plant manufactured 18,413 R-3350 engines, or 60 percent of the total made during the war. Production include 16,427 carburetor engines; 1,577 fuel-injected engines using the Bendix system; and 409 fuel-injected engines that used a Chrysler-designed fuel system. The engine contract amounted to $872,129,295, nearly three times the original estimate, including Chrysler's fixed fee of $37,724,176. The U.S. government declared the Dodge-Chicago plant surplus after the war, but Chrysler had no interest in buying it. Instead, Preston Tucker leased part of it in 1947 to produce his ill-fated automobile.[59]

Propellers

Automatic controllable variable pitch propellers were another key component of military aircraft. The structure of their production during the war closely paralleled that of aircraft engines. Two established manufacturers and one newcomer dominated propeller production on the eve of the war: Curtiss Electric, a subsidiary of Curtiss-Wright, which made a propeller system controlled electrically; Hamilton Standard, a subsidiary of United Aircraft, which used hydraulic controls on its propellers; and the Aeroproducts Division of General Motors, established in 1940 to produce hydraulically controlled propellers. Much like its parent company, Curtiss Electric preferred to directly produce its propellers, while Hamilton Standard licensed other manufacturers. At war's end, propeller production was 708,268 units. Hamilton Standard accounted for 33 percent of the total, followed by Nash-Kelvinator, its licensee, with 22 percent. Curtiss Electric accounted for another 20 percent, while the other independent manufacturer, the Aeroproducts Division of General Motors, produced only 3 percent of the total. The remaining 22 percent came from other licensees of Hamilton Standard, primarily Frigidaire (11 percent), Remington Rand (9 percent), and Canadian Propellers Ltd. (2 percent).[60]

In March 1941, the OPM asked Nash-Kelvinator to build 1,500 Hamilton Standard hydromatic variable pitch propellers per month. The automaker would build these under license from the Hamilton Standard Propeller Division of United Aircraft Corporation using government-supplied equipment. Nash-Kelvinator representatives visited the Hamilton Standard factory in Hartford, Connecticut, in April to see production firsthand.[61]

The variable pitch propeller that the pilot could adjust in flight was a major refinement in aircraft design because it allowed the pilot to change the pitch (angle) of the propeller blades, providing maximum power (RPM) for takeoffs and climbing but lower RPMs at cruising speed. Ground-adjustable propellers date from 1908 (Geoffrey de Havilland), and in the late 1920s several inventors in Europe and the United States developed mechanisms that allowed the pilot to adjust pitch in flight. One of them was Thomas Dicks at the Standard Steel Propeller Company. The United Aircraft Corporation merged Standard Steel Propeller with the Hamilton Aero Manufacturing Company in 1929 to form the Hamilton Standard Propeller Company. In 1938 the company introduced its hydromatic propeller that used double-acting hydraulic controls that changed blade pitch faster and over a wider range than other systems. This allowed the engines to operate at a constant speed. Hamilton Standard and its licensees supplied 75 percent of all the propellers used by the United States' European allies.[62]

The OPM announced on 19 May 1941 that Nash-Kelvinator would build the propeller assembles at the former REO Motor Car Company plant on Cedar Street in Lansing, which had been recently purchased by the DPC. The automaker expected to employ 2,000 to 3,000 workers at the plant. The Army Air Force issued a contract on 28 June 1941 for 5,000 Hamilton Standard hydromatic propellers, which Nash-Kelvinator was to deliver to the British government starting in January 1942. The Army Air Force issued a second contract on 11 October 1941 for 7,000 propellers for its own use, followed by a third contract (26 May 1942), which they frequently amended through the end of the war.[63]

Work on the rehabilitation of the Cedar Street plant was under way in August 1941, with $8.5 million committed by the DPC to convert 450,000 square feet of the REO plant for propeller production. Work continued for the rest of the year, with the needed machinery installed over several months. Meanwhile, groups of supervisory staff and skilled workers went to the Hamilton Standard plant for instruction in August and September 1941. Nash put the first pilot line into operation in January 1942, and the plant built the first acceptable propeller in February. Production then jumped quickly to 135 units in March and 700 in May. The Lansing plant achieved a major milestone in June 1942: it sent two of its propellers, each with more than 1,000 parts, to the Hamilton Standard plant in Hartford to be disassembled; their parts were then intermixed with those from two Hartford-produced propellers. Workers randomly reassembled parts to make four propellers and all the parts fit perfectly.[64]

A second Nash-Kelvinator plant in Lansing, the former REO Motor Car Company truck plant on Mt. Hope Avenue, initially assembled Pratt & Whitney aircraft engines, but the increased demands on Nash-Kelvinator for propeller assemblies and aircraft engines brought a realignment of production facilities. Aircraft engine production moved to Kenosha, Wisconsin, in March 1942 and Nash used the Mt. Hope plant to make blades and for final assembly, while building the hubs at the Cedar Street plant. In December 1942, Nash-Kelvinator increased blade production by using part of its Grand Rapids, Michigan, factory space. In September 1943, the Lansing propeller plants received the Army-Navy "E" production award. Peak monthly production was reached in October 1943 when Nash-Kelvinator assembled 7,015 complete propellers, making the firm the largest propeller manufacturer in the world for that month, exceeding Hamilton Standard. All of the propellers Nash-Kelvinator built in the early years of the war had three blades. Production problems increased when the company agreed in March 1944 to make 8,564 four-blade propellers for the Corsair Navy fighter and the A-26 Invader Fighter-bomber. The firm delivered the first four-blade propellers in September 1944 and completed 4,972 by war's end.[65]

Nash-Kelvinator propeller plant, Lansing, MI (*CKH*).

Nash-Kelvinator's propeller manufacturing operations were impressive by any measure. The firm used more than 1,032,000 square feet of factory space in Lansing and another 393,000 square feet in Grand Rapids. Peak employment in all the facilities combined was 10,582. By the end of the war, Nash had completed 158,134 propeller assemblies, along with 85,656 spare blades. The automaker was second in terms of total output only to Hamilton Standard (233,021 propellers) and was slightly ahead of Curtiss Electric (144,863). Three additional licensees produced another 172,250 propellers, for a grand total of 708,268 North American–made variable pitch propellers. This was a more than adequate supply for the 802,161 aircraft engines built during the war because these propellers were not installed on all aircraft, especially small, single-engine trainers. More than twenty-five American and British aircraft used them, including the B-17, B-24, and B-29 bombers. As was usually the case in war contracts, the cost to the government decreased over time as the firm achieved economies of large-scale production. The unit cost of propellers under the first Nash-Kelvinator contract was $2,650, but this declined steadily to only $1,205 under the final contract.[66]

The contributions made to defense production by the automakers who built aircraft engines and propellers cannot be exaggerated. Aircraft engines were the key component that aircraft companies were simply not able to build on their own. The automobile companies not only produced 56 percent of the more than 800,000 aircraft engines built during the war, they also enabled the established aircraft engine manufacturers to expand their in-house production well beyond their own expectations. Wright Aeronautical and Pratt & Whitney in particular adopted the precision mass-production techniques of the automakers to greatly expand their output of engines. Early in the war, all parts for any given Pratt & Whitney engine were perfectly interchangeable, whether manufactured by Pratt & Whitney, Ford, Chevrolet, Buick, or Nash-Kelvinator. More important, there is no evidence that the delivery of aircraft was significantly delayed by a shortage of engines or propellers.

Airplanes cannot fly without engines and engines require propellers to work, but neither has any value unless placed in an airframe. The next chapter will examine the role played by the automobile industry in the aircraft "production miracle" achieved during the war. The automobile industry and the independent auto body companies also produced a wide range of key aircraft components other than engines and propellers, including fuselage sections, nose sections, tail sections, cabins, wings, wing flaps, landing gear, and engine cowlings. In many cases, the existing aircraft manufacturers became mere assemblers of components made by the automobile companies and others.

FOUR

Aircraft and Aircraft Components

The production of military aircraft was the archetypical example of the "production miracle" achieved by American industry during World War II. American aircraft production, a paltry 5,856 units in 1939, peaked at 96,318 aircraft in 1944 before falling off to 49,761 aircraft in the final year of the war.

This chapter will examine the operation of the procurement system as it applied to aircraft. The aircraft production system and its accomplishments will also be considered in some depth. The chapter will focus on the auto industry's production of aircraft components and complete aircraft. There will be no attempt to summarize the work of the fifty-three companies directly involved in aircraft manufacturing, much less the hundreds of automotive and non-automotive subcontractors supplying parts and components. The chapter will include four detailed case studies of the production of complete aircraft: the Ford Motor Company's production of B-24 Liberator bombers at its Willow Run plant in Michigan; the Grumman Aircraft Corporation–General Motors joint venture to produce carrier-based naval aircraft; Ford's manufacture of wooden gliders at its Iron Mountain, Michigan, plant; and Nash-Kelvinator's production of Sikorsky helicopters. The only other "automaker" to build complete aircraft was the Goodyear Aircraft Corporation, a division of the Goodyear Tire & Rubber Company, which assembled 3,940 Vought Corsair fighters for the navy in a large factory in Akron, Ohio. Three companies built the Corsair: the Chance-Vought Corporation, Goodyear, and the Brewster Aeronautical Corporation.[1]

The Evolving Production System

The broad production system for military aircraft was first established in the fall of 1940 through an informal alliance of the military services, the airframe manufacturers, and automobile industry (see chapter 1). The Automotive Committee for Air Defense (ACAD) served as a coordinating body and clearinghouse to link automobile manufacturers (as suppliers of components) with aircraft companies, who would complete the final assembly of the aircraft. This method of organizing production was naturally reflected in the procurement system. The basic production system for aircraft established by the ACAD continued throughout the war, with few exceptions. The primary contracts for aircraft went to aircraft companies who would then subcontract most of the work on components, including engines, to other manufacturers, who for the most part were automakers. This was a radical change from the prewar production system, in which airframe manufacturers subcontracted less than 10 percent of the content of their planes. A typical example of the new arrangement was the Glenn L. Martin Company, which assembled B-26 bombers at a new plant in Omaha, Nebraska. Martin bought engines from Pratt & Whitney or one of its licensees and the rest of the components from Chrysler, Hudson, and Goodyear Aircraft Corporation.[2]

The enormity of the task at hand forced a revolution in the way the aircraft manufacturers and their component suppliers operated. Over the course of the war, the aircraft industry produced 150 different types of military aircraft but a total of 417 distinct models or versions of those aircraft. Each of these models typically underwent thousands of design changes in the course of production. The sheer volume of aircraft produced during the war, slightly more than 300,000 in total, added to the enormous challenges faced by industry. The U.S. Army Air Force purchased 54 percent of the total, followed by the U.S. Navy (25 percent), Great Britain (13 percent), and the Soviet Union (5 percent). In 1938, the aircraft industry operated a total of fifteen plants producing airframes, engines, and propellers. By the end of 1943, there were eighty-six plants in operation, with most of these gigantic compared to prewar factories.[3]

Before the war, the aircraft industry was highly competitive, with each producer carefully guarding its designs and manufacturing techniques. The companies did a complete about-face during the war, however, in part because of the structure of production mandated by the military services and partly out of patriotism. Seven West Coast manufacturers formed the Aircraft War Production Council to share technical information, production methods, and components. Shortly thereafter, the major East Coast manufacturers followed suit, and in April 1943 the two groups merged to form the National Aircraft War Production Council. The military services typically issued contracts to at least two companies and sometimes as many as seven to make the identical product, whether an airplane, engine, or propeller. The practice helped "spread the work" but also provided insurance against a catastrophic event at a single factory. For example, Boeing, Douglas, and Lockheed shared the production of the B-17 Flying Fortress; Consolidated-Vultee, Douglas, North American, and Ford assembled the B-24 Liberator; and Boeing, Bell, and Martin all produced the B-29 Superfortress.[4]

Between 1 July 1940 and 31 August 1945, the U.S. government spent $44.8 billion on aircraft, some 24 percent of all spending on munitions. Aircraft production was in many respects a much larger part of the defense industry that the raw statistics suggest. Because few existing factories were suitable for aircraft or aircraft engine production on the scale required for the war, the DPC spent a disproportionate share of its investment on new plants for aircraft production. Out of the twenty-six most costly facilities built by the DPC, involving a total investment of $1.539 billion, nineteen involved aircraft or aircraft engine production and used three-quarters of the funds spent. Eight of the nineteen were plants operated by automobile companies, and these accounted for $728 million of DPC spending.[5]

With few exceptions, the existing aircraft manufacturers became almost exclusively assemblers of airplanes using components supplied by others. The DPC greatly expanded their production capacity by building additional plants, typically far removed from their "home" plants. There was a conscious effort to build new plants in the Great Lakes region and in the Midwest, partly for security reasons but also to tap underutilized labor markets. One exception was the Lockheed Aircraft Corporation, which operated two enormous plants in Burbank, California. The Bell Aircraft Corporation based in Buffalo, New York, added an assembly plant in Atlanta; the Boeing Aircraft Company, with its original plant in Seattle, added new factories in Renton, Washington, and in nearby Vancouver, British Columbia, as well as in Wichita, Kansas; Consolidated-Vultee's original factory was in San Diego, but the company added new plants in Downey, California, Nashville, and Fort Worth, Texas; the Curtiss-Wright Corporation, with its original facilities in Buffalo, New York, added new factories in Louisville, St. Louis, and Columbus, Ohio; the Douglas Aircraft Company had major factories in Long Beach and Santa Monica, California, but built new assembly plants in Tulsa, Oklahoma City, and Chicago; North American Aviation, based in Inglewood, California, operated new factories in Dallas and in Kansas City, Kansas; and finally, the Glenn L. Martin Company, with its base in Baltimore, built a new assembly plant in Omaha, Nebraska.[6]

A closer look at defense production by the "Big Three" automakers reveals the extent to which the automakers specialized in aircraft and aircraft components. The Ford Motor Company fulfilled defense contracts totaling $3.962 billion, with aircraft and engine production accounting for 61 percent of the company's war work. At General Motors, aircraft work accounted for 40 percent of its $13.2 billion in defense contracts. Chrysler's war contracts totaled $3.518 billion, with its B-29 engine contracts ($872 million) alone accounting for one-quarter of the total. Chrysler also completed work on other aircraft components, including nose sections and wing edges for the B-29; nose sections, center wing sections, and flaps for the Martin B-26 Marauder bomber; cockpit enclosures for the Boeing B-17 Flying Fortress; and 5,660 sets of center wing sections for the Curtiss-Wright Helldiver dive bomber built for the U.S. Navy. The value of these contracts is not clearly stated in Chrysler's war records, but they would likely increase the share of Chrysler's war work devoted to aircraft components to close to 40 percent of its war contracts. For the automobile industry as a whole, aircraft and aircraft components contracts amounted to $11.2 billion, or 38.7 percent of the value of the industry's war work.[7]

The Contract System

The contract system developed by the Army Air Force to purchase aircraft and aircraft components resulted from the need to quickly expand production with a minimum of slowdowns because of excessive rules and bureaucratic controls. The contract system used to buy aircraft will be considered here, but essentially the same systems were developed by the U.S. Army Ordnance Department and the Quartermaster Corps, as well as by the U.S. Navy. The system of competitive bidding on military contracts that had been used since World War I was jettisoned in favor of contracts negotiated directly between the military services and the suppliers. Aircraft manufacturers were reluctant to enter into contracts with the government, fearing losses from producing newly designed aircraft. The CPFF contract, with escalator clauses, was the only way to get the aircraft companies onboard. The government would issue a letter of intent promising to negotiate a contract, while agreeing to reimburse the manufacturer for all costs incurred before the formal signing of the contract. Engineering, tooling, and even production could get under way before the contract would be finalized, sometimes months into the future. Contract lawyers needed to compose the agreements and various officials needed to approve the contracts. For contracts of under $100,000, only the approval of the contracting officer was required, but at the other end of the scale, contracts worth more than $5 million had to be approved by the undersecretary of war.[8]

Procurement and contracts for aircraft were under the control of the Supply

Division of the Office of the Chief of Air Corps based in Washington, but the work was carried out by the Materiel Command, which had been based at Wright Field in Dayton, Ohio, since 1926. The Army Air Corps also created an Industrial Planning Section (IPS) based at Wright Field to engage in long-term planning for procurement. Wright Field became the center for air force procurement, which was a daunting challenge because the variety and numbers of aircraft multiplied with the onset of war. By the end of 1942, the air force was dealing with 7,000 prime contractors and more than 60,000 subcontractors. The Materiel Command at Wright Field was negotiating an average of 392 formal contacts per month in 1942, along with 2,500 informal contracts or purchase orders per month. The staff of the Materiel Command, which stood at 1,900 in 1939, ballooned to 43,821 (34,304 civilian employees and 9,517 military) in 1944. Having authority to make decisions divided between Wright Field and Washington further complicated the operations of the Materiel Command. Starting in 1939, the chief of the Materiel Command was based in Washington, which made decision making at both locations difficult. Despite efforts to speed the contract process, roughly thirty days were required to negotiate the terms of a contract, and an additional seventy-eight days were needed to have a signed, legally binding contract in hand.[9]

Negotiating contracts was a messy business at best. The Army Air Force had a bevy of estimators who worked with the contractors to determine costs. In estimating direct labor costs, they employed a "learning curve," which assumed that whenever production of a new product doubled, the amount of direct labor required per unit fell by roughly 20 percent. The first B-17 produced by Douglas at Long Beach, California, required more than 100,000 hours of labor, but the 1,000th B-17 required only 16,000 hours. "Fixed fees" (profits) were the cause of friction, but generally these were held at 6 or 7 percent of the production costs. Auditing thousands of contracts to verify expenses submitted for reimbursement was a costly and time-consuming but necessary part of the contract system. The General Accounting Office (GAO) carried out this function from Washington.[10]

The Army Air Force tried to convince contractors to eventually convert their CPFF contracts into fixed-cost contracts but had little success. The air force announced in 1944 that only sixty-seven manufacturers held CPFF contracts, but they held contracts with a face value of $22.5 billion: 70 percent of the value of airframe contracts and 50 percent of the value of engine contracts. Virtually all the CPFF contracts included escalator clauses to protect the manufacturer against inflation of wages or materials costs. The Army Air Force also aggressively renegotiated prices paid under existing contracts because most manufacturers reduced costs over time as they moved up the "learning curve." The Boeing B-17, which cost the air force

$301,000 each in 1939–41, cost only $204,300 in 1944. Consolidated's B-24s cost dropped even more dramatically over the same period, from $379,000 per airplane to only $215,500 by 1944. Given the enormity of the task of issuing tens of thousands of contracts over the course of the war, the Army Air Force was remarkably efficient.[11]

The Manufacturing Challenges

Manufacturing large numbers of newly designed large military aircraft using a network of several prime contractors and dozens of subcontractors created tremendous problems in designing the aircraft, organizing production, and coordinating the work all of the parties involved in this enormous endeavor.

Early in the war, many conflicts, disputes, and misunderstandings developed among the three primary actors in the aircraft procurement campaign: the military services, the prime contractors (the airframe manufacturers), and the subcontractors, mostly automobile manufacturers. In time, compromise and innovation overcame these problems. The military services learned how to better work with private industry, both the airframe companies and the component manufacturers. The demands of war production forced the airframe manufacturers to develop new methods for cooperating with other airframe companies and in developing more effective working relationships with their component suppliers, who were mostly automobile manufacturers. The airframe companies learned from the automobile companies how to apply mass-production methods to aircraft manufacturing. At the same time, the automakers learned that the process of building airplanes was not the same as that involved in assembling automobiles.

Aircraft are much more complex machines than automobiles. A midsized automobile might have 5,000 individual parts, excluding screws and other fasteners, while the nose of a B-29 contained 8,000 parts (excluding 50,000 rivets) supplied by more than 1,500 subcontractors. The B-25 had 165,000 separate parts excluding the engines, instruments, other equipment, and 150,000 rivets. The B-24 bomber had 152,000 parts, with 30,000 of them entirely different. When Consolidated Aircraft Corporation licensed the Ford Motor Company to build the B-24 bomber, Consolidated provided Ford with more than 30,000 drawings to enable the automaker to start a production line.[12]

Complete aircraft, aircraft components, aircraft engines, and propellers were very different from automobiles in terms of their design and the way in which they were manufactured. Wartime engineering literature discussed those differences and the need for the aircraft manufacturers and the automakers to cooperate and learn from each other, which they did. Automobile companies taking on an aircraft contract typically asked the aircraft company for blueprints for the component they were going to make, but this was only the start of the relationship. The auto companies then sent their top engineers and production managers to study the production methods used at the "home" factory. Most of the auto companies modified their mass-production methods, including tooling, to get into production quickly. The Ford Motor Company, discussed later in this chapter, was the most rigid automaker in that it often refused to modify its normal production methods. The Eastern Aircraft Division of General Motors, also examined in detail later in this chapter, was perhaps the most flexible in terms of adopting aircraft manufacturing methods.[13]

The approach taken by the Murray Corporation of Detroit, a large independent supplier of bodies to the auto industry, reveals an ability to adjust its "normal" methods to meet the particular requirements of aircraft component manufacturing. In early 1941, Murray agreed to make outer wings, wing tips, and nacelles for the B-17 Flying Fortress. Nacelles are the enclosures that held the engines and other power equipment used in the aircraft. In late 1942, as Murray was ending the B-17 contract, the body company began producing wings for the Republic P-47 Thunderbolt fighter. From the start of production, Murray adopted existing aircraft industry methods for stamping the aluminum sections that made up the aircraft components. They did, however, develop specialized fixtures to rigidly hold the components in place to ensure accuracy. For final assembly, Murray used a combination of straight-line and "merry-go-round" moving assembly lines. Aircraft manufacturers visiting the Murray plant would view (mostly) familiar production and assembly methods.[14]

For their part, aircraft manufacturers adopted many of the mass-production methods of the automakers in order to satisfy the enormous demands of the military services for aircraft. They used "straight-line" moving assembly lines that mimicked auto industry practice. They also made enormous strides toward achieving interchangeability for their major components. Each of the major airframe companies operated multiple assembly plants that received components from hundreds of suppliers; interchangeability was essential if they were to achieve quantity production.[15]

To achieve mass production of automobiles, the Detroit automakers set up the necessary tooling and dies at the start of the model year, and these remained unchanged throughout the model run. In essence, the design of the car was frozen; the basic design of the Model T from 1908 through 1927 is an extreme example of this. Virtually all of the aircraft and other weapons used during World War II were new and untested designs. The airmen, soldiers, and sailors who used them in battle were in effect conducting field tests. Throughout the war, there was conflict between the need to produce the maximum volume of aircraft versus the need to improve aircraft designs. Every major weapon system underwent continuous improvements, which meant design changes. Engineers and draftsmen produced blueprints showing the changes, and the machinery used to fabricate and assemble the changed part had to be altered as well. Often the redesign of one component required the redesign of scores of components. Flight testing of the B-29 generated 900 engineering changes to the plane before the first production plane came off the assembly line. Before agreeing to assemble B-24s, Henry Ford wanted the design frozen as a condition of his involvement, but the Army Air Force refused. In the course of building the first 2,268 bombers at the Willow Run plant between September 1942 and mid-March 1944, Ford carried out 697 master changes to the airplane's design, with each master change involving scores of engineering changes.[16]

Design changes wreaked havoc not only on the factory floor but also among the engineering staffs at the aircraft companies and the automobile companies alike. North American Aviation kept detailed records on the hours expended by its engineering staff in modifying its B-25. North American spent 329,415 direct engineering hours on the B-25 in 1940; this expenditure peaked at 695,488 hours in 1942 before falling off to 200,321 hours in 1945. Rather than compromising production even further by ordering that every design change be done at the factory, the Army Air Force shifted some of these changes to "modification centers" away from the factories. The repair and maintenance shops of the major airlines were the logical place to locate these centers because they already had hangars, runways, and skilled mechanics in place. By May 1942, ten of these modification centers were in operation, and the Army Air Force built another twenty during the war.[17]

The demands placed on airframe manufacturers and their subcontractors mandated the development of innovative methods to achieve coordination of all the work. Early in the war, prime airframe contractors making the same plane developed means of coordinating their efforts. Working relations between the prime contractors and their subcontractors, mainly automobile companies, also improved in the course of the war. Before Pearl Harbor, Boeing, Douglas, and Vega (later a subsidiary of Lockheed) agreed to make the B-17 Flying Fortress, a Boeing design. After a group of Douglas engineers met with their counterparts at Boeing in May 1941, they established what became the BDV (Boeing-Douglas-Vega) Committee. This committee coordinated the production activities of the three prime contractors and their related subcontractors. The committee consisted of representatives of the three airframe companies and a representative of the Chief of the Production Division of the Materiel Command at Wright Field. When there were disputes that could not be resolved, a rare event, the Army Air Force representative made the final decision.

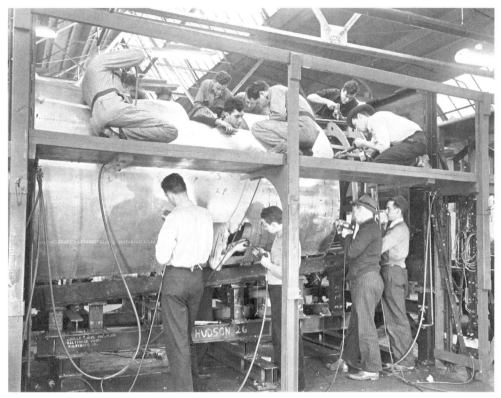

Martin B-26 Marauder fuselage assembly at the Hudson plant, Detroit *(CKH)*.

The BDV Committee had an engineering subcommittee that coordinated all design changes and a tooling committee that controlled the supply of machine tools to the various plants. Over the course of the war similar coordinating committees oversaw the production of the B-24, B-26, B-29, and other planes. None of these worked as smoothly as the BDV Committee, but they did well enough to produce the needed aircraft.[18]

Automotive subcontractors were commonly frustrated by the failure of the prime airframe contractor to deliver complete, accurate engineering drawings in a timely fashion. For example, the Hudson Motor Car Company, under contract to supply Wright Aeronautical Corporation with pistons and rocker arms for radial aircraft engines, was hopelessly behind its delivery schedule by mid-September 1942 because Wright had failed to deliver the plans and specifications when promised.[19] The Glenn L. Martin Company, the design prime contractor for the B-26 Marauder, also failed to provide its subcontractors with updated drawings. It opened a second assembly plant in Omaha, Nebraska, and the main subcontractors supplying this plant were the Chrysler Corporation (wings) and the Hudson Motor Car Company (fuselage tail sections). There was a coordinating committee established for the B-26, but it did not work as well as the BDV Committee, whose members were experienced aircraft manufacturers who could operate on an equal footing. Chrysler and Hudson were subcontractors with no experience in aircraft design who depended on Martin to accept their work before they were paid. Their committee seldom met, and Martin did little to help solve production problems. An Army Air Force report issued in late December 1942 that examined the delays in B-26 production praised Chrysler and Hudson for their efforts and blamed Martin for its failure to provide the subcontractors with engineering changes in a timely fashion and for its failure to provide leadership in coordinating production. Drawings for modifications that were to take place in the factories in October 1942 were not delivered to Chrysler and Hudson until December. By the end of the war, Chrysler produced 1,586 nose sections, 1,586 center fuselage sections, and 1,895 sets of wing flaps for the B-26, despite the initial problems with Glenn Martin.[20]

The history of producing the Boeing B-29 Superfortress also included false starts, conflicts, and coordination challenges. The sheer size of the B-29 (twice the weight of a B-17) and the complexity of its mechanical and electrical systems made it the most difficult World War II airplane to build. The B-29 was still undergoing flight testing in December 1942 and production did not get under way until July 1943. The initial production plans developed in early 1942 called for Boeing to build 300 B-29s at a new plant in Renton, Washington, and another 765 from a second new plant in Wichita, Kansas; Bell Aircraft of Buffalo would build 400 B-29s in Marietta, Georgia, near Atlanta; North American Aviation would assemble 200 B-29s at its plant in Kansas City, Kansas; and the Fisher Body Division of General Motors would build 200 B-29s at a new plant in Cleveland. Executives from the four companies established the B-29 Liaison Committee in February 1942. The committee included representatives from the major subcontractors—Chrysler, Hudson, Goodyear, McDonnell (St. Louis), and Republic Aviation (Long Island). The Army Air Force did not establish tight control over the committee and gave the aircraft companies, especially Boeing, free rein.[21]

By June 1942 the liaison committee had become dysfunctional, and there were widespread complaints about Boeing's slow response to requests for blueprints and specifications. Boeing's leaders did not trust General Motors, which owned a controlling interest in North American, and worried that it would lose control over the bomber that it had designed. Army Air Force planners decided to drop North American Aviation from the B-29 program and have the company assemble B-25s in Kansas City instead. By the end of the war, North American assembled all 9,816 of the Army Air Force's B-25 bombers, a two-engine aircraft. Among multiple aircraft com-

B-29 cockpit assembly, Chrysler plant, Detroit (*ACWP*).

ponents it built, the Fisher Body Division of General Motors manufactured wings, fuselage sections, and complete tail sections for 5,214 B-25s. Boeing dropped Fisher Body as an assembler of B-29s, but the GM division instead built the B-29 nacelles at its Cleveland plant. The four nacelles for each bomber housed the engines, superchargers, heating and cooling systems, and the aircraft's major controls. The nacelles were the second most important component of the B-29 after the center wing. By the end of the war, Fisher had completed 13,772 nacelles, enough to equip 3,443 B-29s, as well as outer wings sections and complete tail sections for the B-29, all in Cleveland. Glenn Martin, which was building B-26 Marauders in its Omaha plant, agreed in July 1943 to convert that plant to B-29 production. Martin converted its main subcontractors—Chrysler, Hudson, and Goodyear—from B-26 work to B-29 contracts. Chrysler produced 586 nose sections and 559 leading wing edges, while Hudson made 802 fuselage tail sections. Briggs Manufacturing Company, one of three large Detroit auto body manufacturers, supplied dorsal fins and stabilizers to all of the B-29 assembly plants. With this restructuring completed, Boeing shared the final assembly work with only two companies—Bell Aircraft and Glenn Martin—both old-time airframe manufacturers.[22]

Production was slowed by hundreds of design changes to correct design defects discovered in flight. The process of training crews to fly the new plane was also delayed while the problems were fixed. Hundreds of newly minted B-29s went to modification centers at Marietta and Omaha, which fixed defects and made design changes. The mere presence of these airplanes near the factories demoralized workers and management alike, so air force planners moved the modification centers elsewhere. Continental Airlines ran a B-29 modification center at the Denver airport and Bechtel-McCone-Parsons built one at Birmingham, Alabama, where they employed 5,200 workers. Production of the Superfortress in 1943 was disappointing: the Army Air Force accepted delivery of only 92 B-29s, 87 of which came from the Wichita plant. In an effort to break the various production bottlenecks, in February 1944 the Commanding General of the Army Air Forces, Henry H. "Hap" Arnold, put General William Knudsen in charge of coordinating B-29 production. In 1944 1,161 B-29s were produced from the four assembly plants, and in 1945, an additional 2,642 aircraft were completed. While at full production during the final year of the war, both the Wichita and Renton (Washington) plants averaged more than 100 B-29s a month, hitting their stride as the war ended. The eventual output of 3,895 B-29s was accomplished in a little more than two years of production.[23]

Both Hudson and Chrysler manufactured additional key aircraft components. In a sense, they teamed up to help with the production of the Curtiss-Wright Helldiver dive bomber. Hudson turned out 4,280 sets of outer wings and Chrysler manufactured 5,669 center wing sections. Chrysler also manufactured 4,100 cockpit enclosures for the Douglas B-17 Flying Fortress and 688 flight stations for the Lockheed PV-2 Ventura bomber. Finally, Chrysler produced 10,202 sets of landing gear and arresters ("tail hooks") for the Chance-Vought Corsair, a carrier-based fighter aircraft.[24]

Greater insight into the ongoing interaction between automakers, airframe manufacturers, and the military services can be gained through detailed case studies. The rest of this chapter will consist of four case studies. The first is the well-known Ford Motor Company Willow Run plant, where Ford built B-24 Liberator bombers under license from the Consolidated-Vultee Aircraft Corporation. The second is the lesser-known production of Navy Wildcat fighters and Navy Avenger torpedo bombers by the Eastern Aircraft Division of General Motors, in cooperation with the Grumman Aircraft Engineering Corporation. The remaining two are the little-known production of wooden gliders by the Ford Motor Company and helicopters by Nash-Kelvinator.

The Ford Motor Company Willow Run Bomber Plant

The gigantic bomber plant operated by the Ford Motor Company in Willow Run to assemble B-24 Liberator bombers is easily the most famous World War II factory. It was widely publicized well before it produced a single bomber owing to the work of Henry Ford's relentless publicity machine. The plant is an instructive example of the difficulties faced by an automaker trying to manufacture aircraft using the same mass-production methods that worked so well with automobiles. In time, Ford overcame its production problems and became the sole example of a non-airframe company producing enormous quantities of bombers. Because the Willow Run plant was situated in a rural area far from a ready source of labor, adequately staffing the plant was also a monumental challenge.

Henry Ford had some experience in airplane manufacture. He had purchased the Stout Metal Airplane Company from William B. Stout in February 1925 and began manufacturing a trimotor airplane to be used initially to deliver mail, freight, and passengers from Ford's airport in Dearborn. The Ford Trimotor had a wingspan of 70 feet and could carry eight passengers. Sales peaked in 1929 at 86 planes, then fell to 36 in 1930 and to only three in 1932. Ford permanently shut down aircraft manufacturing in July 1932.

Henry Ford constantly interfered in the design of the plane, ousted William Stout from the operation, and consistently lost money on his aircraft venture. This episode did not give Ford much valuable experience he could use in manufacturing the B-24 Liberator bomber. The Ford Trimotor was a small, simple airplane compared to the B-24 Liberator. Ford made only a small number of Trimotors as opposed to the mass-produced B-24.[25]

Ford Motor Company's involvement in making the B-24 Liberator began with modest expectations. After Henry Ford had vetoed a plan for Ford Motor Company to build Rolls-Royce aircraft engines for the British, he agreed in November 1940 that Ford would make 4,000 aircraft engines under license from Pratt & Whitney. With the elder Ford's approval, his son, Edsel, and Charles E. Sorensen, Ford's production boss, visited the Consolidated Aircraft Company plant in San Diego in January 1941 to observe the production of Consolidated's B-24. Edsel's sons, Henry II and Benson, accompanied them, along with several members of Sorensen's production staff. Consolidated planned to build one B-24 a day or 350 a year, nowhere near the number of planes the Army Air Force needed. Even so, Consolidated was ill equipped to reach even that modest goal. Consolidated would need much larger facilities to mass-produce the B-24, but the air force opposed plant expansions on the West Coast, where they would be vulnerable to Japanese attacks.[26]

Sorensen and his staff closely observed Consolidated's manufacturing operations and were appalled by what they saw. The planes were not mass-produced with interchangeable parts but were custom-built, one plane at a time. William Pioch, Ford's head of tooling, noted that no two fuselages were alike and no two wings were alike. To make even matters worse, the final assembly of the B-24 took place outside, under the California sun, which distorted the structural steel fixture used in final assembly. When Consolidated mated the center wing with the fuselage, they used shims to fill in the gaps in the joints. Consolidated proposed that Ford Motor Company build wing sections for the B-24, but Sorensen knew that they could not built standardized wing sections with any hope of fitting given the assembly methods used. Sorensen bluntly informed the air force representatives and Major Reuben H. Fleet, Consolidated's president, that the entire production system would need to be radically changed to achieve quantity production. They challenged Sorensen to show them what he would do.[27]

The Ford production boss spent much of the night at the Coronado Hotel in San Diego designing a factory and assembly line to mass-produce B-24 Liberators. He discussed his plan with Edsel Ford over breakfast on 9 January 1941, and the younger Ford approved the concept. Sorensen and Edsel Ford then met with Reuben Fleet and the air force officials and presented them with a plan for a mile-long assembly line that would build a B-24 every hour, or 540 planes a month. The rest of the factory would produce seventy major components that would be fabricated and then moved by conveyors to the main assembly line to produce the complete airplane. The factory, which Ford would operate, would cost $200 million. Consolidated and the air force wanted to limit Ford to the production of components, but the key decision makers at Ford—Charles Sorensen, Edsel Ford, and Henry Ford—wanted to make complete aircraft in a new factory the Ford Motor Company would manage. The Army Air Force proposed two alternative arrangements, which were rejected: one had Ford buying Consolidated; the other had Ford, Consolidated, and Douglas establishing a new company to make Liberator bombers.[28]

Ford initially offered to build complete bombers, but the OPM rejected Ford's proposal. In early February 1941, General Oliver P. Echols, the Army Air Corps Chief Procurement Officer, agreed in principle to grant Ford an educational order to make a complete B-24 and a contract to make aircraft components. On 21 February, Ford received a letter of intent to produce fuselage assemblies for 1,200 bombers to be built by Consolidated in Fort Worth and by the Douglas Aircraft Company in Tulsa for a total of $200 million. On 13 March, the Army Air Force awarded Ford an educational contract for $3,418,000 to build a single B-24. On 1 May, Ford received verbal assurance that it could build complete B-24s. The Army Air Corps issued Ford a letter of intent on 5 June 1941 to build 800 complete aircraft, and a contract for 795 bombers followed on 26 September 1941. The $429 million contract included $52 million for the factory and the adjacent airport, with $368 million for complete bombers. Five months later, on 25 February 1942, the Army Air Force granted Ford a contract increasing the production of "ships" (aircraft) to 4,495. Groundbreaking for the giant factory at Willow Run had already taken place on 18 April 1941. Ford's intention from the start to build complete aircraft can be seen in the plans for the plant. The main manufacturing building covered sixty-seven acres of floor space and the complex included runways and fifteen additional buildings. This scale suggests that Ford planned to turn out much more than a few hundred sets of components per month.[29]

Getting the Willow Run plant into production was hampered by the frequent lack of cooperation and coordination between Ford and Consolidated. After Ford stumbled for a year, the Army Air Force brought Ford and Consolidated officials together at Wright Field on 24 March 1942 and forced them to establish a B-24 Liaison Committee. Despite the well-known success of the BDV Committee launched in May 1941 to coordinate B-17 production, Consolidated opposed establishing a committee for the B-24. They were suspicious of Ford, and the army and had a "full plate" of their own problems at their San Diego plant. The new committee met regularly for the first year, then once a month until early 1944, and then on an "on call" basis thereafter. Much like the BDV Committee, the B-24 group delegated most of the work to an engineering subcommittee, which handled design issues, and a tooling subcommittee, which took care of acquiring machine tools.[30]

Ford encountered enormous problems in trying to prepare the tooling to mass-produce the B-24. Ford dispatched a team of two hundred engineers, designers, toolmakers, and draftsmen to the Consolidated plant in San Diego in March 1941 to copy all of the drawings and blueprints of the B-24 and the machinery and tools used to fabricate and assemble the entire plane. These men spent two months in San Diego and photographed more than 30,000 drawings, which they shipped back to Dearborn in two railroad freight cars. Ford's engineers and draftsmen worked on the blueprints in an old airplane factory building on the site of Ford Airport in Dearborn. They broke down the B-24 into sixty-nine major components and produced an average of eleven blueprints for each component. Each of those drawings was then broken down into hundreds of drawings to cover each subassembly and individual part. The B-24 had 152,000 parts, 30,000 of which were unique. These were held together by more than 313,000 rivets of 520 types and sizes.

Once they carefully studied the drawings, Ford's engineers were shocked to discover that the drawings did not incorporate design changes that had been made over the previous six months. As was the case throughout the aircraft industry, the Consolidated B-24 was "shop-engineered" and was designed to be assembled by skilled workers who would modify the components during final assembly. These workers followed the general practices of "file to fit" or "bump to suit" to bring the parts together. Ford engineers found hundreds of discrepancies in drawings for the same part or component. The two companies also used different methods of measurement in their drawings, further complicating the transfer of information to Ford. Consolidated used fractional dimensions in its blueprints, whereas Ford had long used the more precise decimal dimensions. The aircraft company also employed idiosyncratic signs and symbols on its drawings without any explanation of their meaning. Ford had to redo all 30,000 drawings simply to begin planning for production, and because there were thousands of design changes that were not yet incorporated into the original drawings, they had to redo most of the drawings a second time.[31]

Aircraft manufacturers adopted a process known as "lofting," first used by shipbuilders, to create full-size drawings of the aircraft frame and all exterior surfaces to ensure that once parts were fabricated they would come together correctly to form the finished product. The drawings could then be used to make templates or dies to be used in production. Consolidated and Ford both referred to their B-24s as "ships" and not aircraft. The design of a finished ship would typically begin with a three-dimensional model that showed the ship's "lines" in broad form. Detailed blueprints drawn to scale would follow, and the full-size drawings, known as "loft boards," would be produced from the blueprints. Consolidated used lofting in preparing for production of the B-24, and Ford followed the same practice with some refinements. Ford covered its lofting tables, the largest measuring 16 by 64 feet, with 16-gauge steel plate painted with two coats of white paint. The painted surfaces were large enough to allow for full-size renderings of the center wing section, which was 55 feet long, and the fore or aft fuselage sections, which were smaller. Draftsmen drew directly on the painted surface, which then became a permanent master template. Most companies following this practice allowed the loft board drawings to deviate up to 1/32nd of an inch from the blueprints, but because of the use of the steel plates, Ford allowed deviations of only 1/100th of an inch. Ford copied all of Consolidated's loft boards for the B-24 but found hundreds of discrepancies between the loft boards and the detailed drawings they were supposedly derived from.[32]

While wrestling with these issues, in March 1941 Ford began to prepare the plant site for construction by clearing more than five square miles of land of its trees. The site chosen for the plant was property Henry Ford had purchased in the late 1920s as part of his Ford Farms program. Located four miles east of Ypsilanti, the property straddled Wayne and Washtenaw counties and named Willow Run after a small creek that traversed the property. It was the home of Camp Willow Run, a cooperative farm that provided summer employment for schoolboys, who grew vegetables there. This was an entirely illogical and inappropriate place to build a gigantic factory because it was located twenty-four miles west of Detroit, the source of much of the labor the plant would need. Henry Ford insisted that the plant be built on his property and he got his way. The government took additional land by eminent domain, resulting in a parcel of 1,878 acres. Plant construction was delayed because Henry Ford insisted that the entire plant be redesigned to fit entirely within Republican-controlled Washtenaw County rather than extend into Democratic-controlled Wayne County. Plant construction proceeded quickly following groundbreaking on 18 April 1941. The first concrete was poured two days later and the steel frame erection began on 5 May. Limited parts production started in September 1941, but the plant was not completed until September 1942. Ford finished assembling the educational order B-24 on 15 May 1942, but the first production plane was not completed until 10 September.[33]

Detroit architect Albert Kahn, who had designed Ford's Highland Park and River Rouge plants, also planned the Willow Run plant. Kahn initially designed a 1,176,900-square-foot factory to manufacture knock-down B-24 components to be shipped elsewhere. Once Ford had approval to build complete airplanes, the factory expanded to 4,734,617 square feet, at the time the largest factory in the world under one roof. The plant initially made knock-down B-24s, which were trucked to the Douglas Aircraft Company assembly plant in Tulsa, 950 miles away, and later to the Consolidated plant in Fort Worth. Shipments to Tulsa began in July 1942 and continued through August 1944. Shipments of knock-down units to Fort Worth began in January 1943 and ended in June 1944. Four special trailers, each sixty-three feet long, were needed to ship a complete B-24. Ford used a total of eighty-six trailers and the trip took four days. The Willow Run plant produced a total of 1,894 knock-down planes, with 955 sent to Tulsa and 939 to Fort Worth. Ford completed its first "fly-away plane" on 10 September 1942, and the army accepted it for delivery on 30 September.[34]

The Willow Run plant was much like an automobile assembly plant except on a much larger scale. It was an L-shaped building, with the base of the "L" some 1,280 feet wide. The base housed the machine shop, die room, tool room, punch presses, and several manufacturing operations. The main assembly line extended easterly more than 3,000 feet along the narrower part of the building, which ended just short of Wayne County. Along the longer section of the building, Ford had conveyors delivering various subassemblies to two parallel assembly lines. A gigantic drive built into the floor moved the B-24s along the length of the building. Once the plant reached

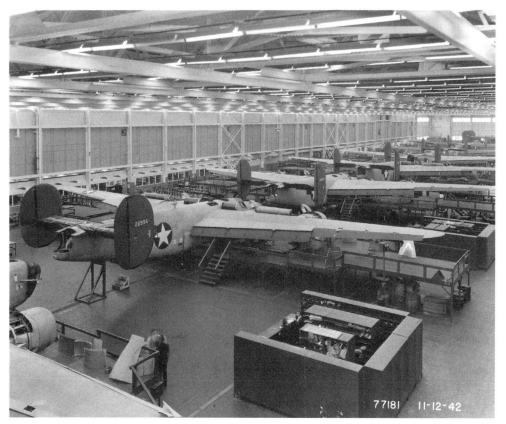

B-24 assembly line, Willow Run bomber plant (*NAHC*).

full production, about ninety ships were at some stage of construction within the plant. At the east end of the building, the two assembly lines made a 90-degree right turn heading south, using turntables to rotate the aircraft. The line extended only a short distance farther and then the B-24s exited the building. Counting the assembly lines for the components and subassemblies, the lines extended for 5,460 feet, giving Sorensen his mile-long assembly line.[35]

While the Willow Run plant was impressive, the way in which Ford manufactured and assembled the B-24 bombers was often revolutionary. Although Ford substantially changed many of the production methods used by Consolidated, in some cases it had to modify even its own plans because airplane assembly was quite different from automobile assembly. For example, Ford changed the types of dies used to create the numerous aluminum stampings that made up the skin of the B-24 fuselage, wings, tail, and nose section. Consolidated used soft kirksite dies, consisting of 92 percent zinc and 7 percent aluminum and copper. A rubber pad under the part being formed spread the pressure on the aluminum more evenly. The Consolidated engineers argued that because aluminum stretched much more than sheet steel in the stamping process, steel dies would stress the aluminum and weaken it.[36]

The Ford production engineers objected to soft dies because they quickly lost their precision dimensions in high-volume production, resulting in parts that would not be interchangeable. In addition, Ford conducted tests showing that aluminum parts stamped with hard metal dies did not lose any strength. Ford's production engineers did, however, discover that hard steel dies often scratched the aluminum stamped sheets, resulting in irregular surfaces. Using highly polished dies eliminated the problem. Using a single stamping operation sometimes produced distortion in the stamped piece because aluminum had a greater tendency to "spring back" than steel, so Ford was forced to change stamping operations that would normally be completed in a single pass into one requiring several passes. At Willow Run, the dies used for stampings simultaneously punched holes for rivets. One die alone punched 781 holes at once, saving Ford substantial labor costs compared to the process used by Consolidated, where workers bored the holes by hand. Through April 1945, Ford purchased or built 30,739 dies, but only 15,659 were in use, with nearly half of these at locations other than Willow Run. The remaining dies had been scrapped or were in storage. Because the thin aluminum panels that made up the outer skin of an airplane were more flexible than steel metal panels, assembly required elaborate holding devices (fixtures) to keep the panels properly positioned before they were riveted together.[37]

Consolidated built a complete fuselage and then installed wiring and hydraulic lines by pushing them though openings and then dragging them the full length of the fuselage. This was an awkward and time-consuming method because the workers installing the wiring had to work in small spaces. Sorensen described Consolidated's method as resembling "a bird building his own nest while sitting in it." Ford instead built the fuselage in two sections (fore and aft of the section holding the wing), installed the wiring and hydraulic lines into those open sections, and then connected the two halves. The Ford method allowed more laborers to work on installing these lines and, more important, facilitated constant inspection of the work.[38]

The Willow Run plant combined the use of precision machinery, which turned out interchangeable parts, with fixtures and jigs, which precisely held the parts and allowed easy assembly. The mechanization of production reduced the required man-hours to build the plane and allowed Ford to use an unskilled workforce. Ford employed more than 1,600 machine tools and 11,000 fixtures and jigs to hold work in place, although the company built a total of 21,000 fixtures and jigs. The total cost of all the tooling at Willow Run was between $75 million and $100 million, while the factory and land cost only $86.6 million.[39]

The most impressive operation at Willow Run was the machining and assembly of the 55-foot-wide center wing, which was completely fabricated and assembled before being mated with the fuselage of the aircraft. Each center wing had 6,439 parts, not including the 1,000 bolts and 78,606 rivets. Ford used a set of five fixtures in assembling the center wing, each used sequentially to put the wing together. At its peak operation, the Willow Run plant ran seven banks of wing fixtures, each holding five separate wings, so there were thirty-five center wings being assembled simultaneously. Each of the center wing vertical fixtures was 60 feet long, 18 feet high, 13 feet wide, and weighed 27½ tons. They were so large and complex that only Ford's Tool and Die Department at their River Rouge plant was capable of building them, and they needed three months to build the first unit.

Perhaps more impressive was the gigantic machining apparatus Ford used to simultaneously complete forty-two machining operations on the assembled center wing section before it was inserted into the fuselage. The Ingersoll Milling Machine Company built this enormous piece of equipment for Ford at a cost of $168,000. The labor required for these machining operations alone fell from 500 to 3½ man-hours and, in time, to a mere 35 man-minutes. More important, the work was much more accurate than was possible with hand methods. The mounting pads that held the four engines were milled and drilled simultaneously and resulted in perfect alignment of the four engines. Once Ford's production managers and workers climbed the steep learning curve with the mechanized center wing assembly operations, the labor savings were enormous. Center wing #59, assembled on 3 October 1942, required 3,813 man-hours of labor, but center wing #178, completed on 17 December 1942, needed only 933 man-hours. By October 1944, the labor requirement had been further reduced to only 433 man-hours.[40]

Ford's engineers also designed a set of large fixtures that enabled the accurate mating of the center wing section with the bomber's fuselage sections. They constructed a set of four "leveling towers" that sat on blocks of reinforced concrete eighteen feet deep and resting on bedrock. Two additional towers that served as hydraulic jacks held the center wing and maneuvered it onto the leveling towers, which then adjusted the wing to the correct fit in the fuselage section directly above the wing. The much larger fore and aft fuselage sections were then moved on "mating cars" to be connected to the wing section fuselage. The fore section was mated first, followed by the aft section. The tail section, engines, outer wing tips, and wing flaps were sequentially added later in the assembly process.[41]

Although Willow Run was primarily an assembly plant, there was substantial manufacturing there as well. According to one estimate, roughly 50 percent of the workforce assembled the bomber, but 20 percent manufactured parts and another

20 percent assembled components. The remaining 10 percent carried out other functions such as security, testing, and so forth. Severe shortages of labor at Willow Run, which will be treated later in this chapter, caused Ford to ship as much manufacturing as possible to other plants. Starting in March 1943, Meade Bricker, the general manager of Willow Run, began moving work to other Ford facilities, including the branch plant at Hamilton, Ohio, the Lincoln plant in Detroit, and the Highland Park plant. He moved the fabrication of the B-24 horizontal stabilizer, a major component of the tail, to the unused tire plant at the Rouge complex, freeing up 1,100 employees at Willow Run to work on other jobs. In mid-1943, 22,000 workers were employed outside of Willow Run to manufacture bomber parts. By early January 1944, Ford had shifted 3,477 assembly jobs and a total of 6,182 dies to plants at River Rouge, Highland Park, and Hamilton; the Lincoln plant; and the factories of twenty-seven subcontractors. The vast majority of the jobs and dies were moved to Ford's other plants. Subcontractors had 19 percent of the assembly jobs, but only 9 percent of the dies. Providing all of the raw materials and components needed at Willow Run was a monumental task as well. Over time, 965 suppliers from thirty-eight states were needed to serve the Willow Run plant.[42]

Production began slowly at Willow Run, as there were substantial quality problems and other setbacks that lingered for nearly a year after assembly work began. Critics and skeptics derisively referred to the giant bomber plant as "Will It Run?" There were many reasons for Willow Run's shaky start-up. The problems Ford faced in deciphering Consolidated's blueprints contributed to the delays. Ford also faced shortages of the machine tools it needed and eventually built many of the machines in-house. The single most important barrier Ford faced, however, was a shortage of labor, especially skilled or experienced workers, and high rates of labor turnover. In this case, these labor shortages were largely due to the isolated location of the plant.

Charles A. Lindbergh served as an advisor to the Ford Motor Company, focusing on the Willow Run plant, from March 1942 until March 1944 and his *Wartime Journals* reveal the start-up problems. He visited Willow Run on 7 April 1942 and was impressed by the extensive tooling in place and the more than 9,000 workers already employed there. Lindbergh visited the Douglas plant in Tulsa in mid-May 1942 after a shipment of components from Willow Run had arrived there. The Douglas inspectors pointed out hundreds of manufacturing defects, including rivets that were missing, misplaced, badly finished, of the wrong size, or split.

Lindbergh observed, "It was the worst piece of metal aircraft construction I have ever seen; yet it was passed by both the Ford Company and the Army inspectors at Willow Run." He recommended that Ford truck all of the parts back to Willow Run and work on resolving the quality problems. Lindbergh noted that a team of eleven riveters who produced faulty work included only one worker and the foreman who had attended Ford's riveting school. On 26 October 1942 Lindbergh attended a meeting of the top Ford Motor Company officials responsible for getting Willow Run into full production. Edsel Ford argued that the current labor force of 30,000 should be quickly enlarged, but Meade Bricker, Sorensen's top lieutenant, countered that Ford should focus on training its existing workforce to improve their job performance rather than bringing in hordes of additional unskilled and inexperienced workers.[43]

Ford had already begun to devote resources to train its inexperienced workforce, who for the most part had no experience in factory work, much less in building aircraft. In mid-January 1942, the automaker started construction of the Ford Airplane School located next to the factory and it opened six months later. This two-story building had eighteen classrooms, thirteen labs, a library, an auditorium, a study hall, and a bookstore. Ford spent $500,000 to build and equip the school. By April 1943, the school had 3,800 students and a staff of 165 teachers. This was an apprentice school that gave workers the needed skills to fabricate and assemble aircraft, but it also produced draftsmen and inspectors.[44]

In the early discussions about the bomber plant, at least one estimate put the labor force needed at 110,000 workers. Sorensen argued that 90,000 would be required, but 30,000 of these would be employed off-site in other Ford facilities or by subcontractors; thus the Willow Run plant would need 60,000 workers. The first "mancount" for the plant, dated 19 December 1941, showed a total of only 661 workers, with the vast majority of them working on construction, maintenance, stores and supplies, and plant protection. Only 117 were employed in small parts production and exactly seven worked on the center wing. A detailed estimate of manpower requirements to produce 13 ships, presumably in a single shift, dated 5 December 1941, projected a need for 54,156 workers after 6,459 jobs were moved off-site. The estimate included 14,699 employed in manufacturing (27 percent of the total), 27,798 engaged in assembly (51 percent), and 11,659 in "non-production" work (22 percent).[45]

Peak employment at Willow Run reached 42,331 in June 1943, which included 10,000 women. About 10,000 workers transferred to Willow Run from other Ford facilities, and Ford received permission from the United States Employment Service to recruit workers from Tennessee, Kentucky, Iowa, Illinois, and Texas. Ford offered to pay workers' transportation expenses to get to Willow Run. The plant's employment department compiled a list of the states of origin for workers hired at Willow Run between 1 March 1943 and 31 May 1945. Local Michigan residents, presumably from southeastern Michigan, accounted for fewer than half (18,628 of 39,249) of the workers included in this compilation. The numbers also included workers transferred to Willow Run from other Ford plants. Out of 20,613 workers hired to work at Willow Run from outside southeastern Michigan, 4,945 came from other parts of Michigan; thus 15,668 were from other states.[46]

Ford managed to hire a large number of new workers but faced a devastating turnover rate among those who worked at Willow Run. By the time bomber production stopped at the end of June 1945, Ford had hired 114,000 people to maintain an average labor force of 27,400. Of these, 12,197 quit within the first ten days; 34,533 stayed for less than three months; and only 30,021 stayed on the job for more than a year. A substantial amount of turnover was due to men and women (a total of 10,320) leaving for military service. The draft was indiscriminate, often depleting key departments of all of their skilled workers. In time, Ford and the (Detroit) draft board came to an arrangement whereby Ford would supply the board with lists of men eligible for the draft drawn from all departments in the plant. Sorensen reported that in July 1943, Ford hired 3,078 workers, but 3,614 quit during the same month. In addition to the high turnover rate of workers, typical absenteeism was 15 percent of the workforce. Ford was not alone in facing an extremely unstable labor force. Airplane manufacturers like Lockheed and North American faced similar turnover rates.[47]

Rancorous labor relations also disrupted production at Willow Run. Most of the auto industry recognized the UAW as the collective bargaining agent for their workers in 1937, but Henry Ford refused to recognize the UAW until May 1941. Ford's right-hand man, Harry Bennett, had kept the union at bay for nearly a decade. Bennett was put in charge of hiring at Willow Run and brought in as many southerners as possible, hoping to minimize the UAW's influence at the plant. At first, most Willow Run workers belonged to UAW Local 600, which represented Ford workers at the River Rouge plant, but the UAW established a separate "Bomber Local" (Local 50) for the Willow Run workers in late June 1943. The UAW established an Educational Department at the plant early in 1942 to familiarize the new workers with the union and its procedures. Still, Bennett's tactics led to several short-lived wildcat (unauthorized) strikes, which further hindered operations at the plant. An Army Air Force evaluation of the Willow Run plant in 1946 concluded that strikes were relatively rare and brief. The study claimed that only six strikes had taken place in 1942, but the number rose to thirty-three in 1943 and to twenty-three in just the first quarter of the following year.[48]

Serious housing shortages near the plant also reduced the workforce and increased labor turnover. In April 1942, when the bomber plant employed nearly 8,000 workers, no rooms were available to rent within a fifteen-mile radius of the plant. The two closest communities were Ypsilanti (population of 15,000) and Ann Arbor (30,000), neither of which was capable of accommodating the influx of workers and their families. Hundreds of workers had already parked trailers or built shacks in willy-nilly fashion on any available land near the factory. On 26 April 1942, the Federal Housing Administration (FHA) announced plans to build a large residential development to house the anticipated workforce of 110,000 and their families. Known as Bomber City, the housing development, to be located north of Ypsilanti in Superior Township, would consist of five independent communities. The cost of the proposed housing quickly ballooned from $35 million to $108 million. The major local interest groups, including the real estate boards of Ypsilanti and Ann Arbor, the Ann Arbor Builders Association, the Washtenaw County Board of Supervisors, and the Ford Motor Company, jointly signed a letter to the Truman Commission, dated 22 July 1942, opposing the construction of any public housing in the area. They argued that the housing would lower property values throughout the county, and they feared that when the war ended the housing would be vacated. Henry Ford opposed this housing because he believed it would bring thousands of Democratic voters to Republican-controlled Washtenaw County. This grandiose plan for federally built housing quickly died, in large part because of severe shortages of materials and housing's low priority in the war effort.[49]

As a result, few bomber workers lived near the factory. When employment at the plant stood at 30,660 in October 1942, there were only 302 dwellings in close proximity to the plant and half of these were trailers. When employment peaked at 42,331 in June 1943, the area adjacent to the plant had 630 dwellings and 54 percent of these were trailers. The FHA finally built dormitory-style housing for single employees and the first units opened in mid-February 1943. The dormitories, named Willow Lodge, eventually became a fifteen-building complex that housed 3,000 single workers. In December 1943, the FHA opened 1,728 units of temporary housing dubbed Willow Village. In June 1943, government housing accommodated only 2.4 percent of those living near the bomber plant, but as more housing was finished, this share jumped to nearly 9 percent in December 1943. Many wives of men who worked at the plant were willing to work there but could not because of the almost total lack of child-care facilities at Willow Run.[50]

One solution to the shortage of labor and housing at the bomber plant was the construction of a limited-access, divided-highway system connecting the plant with the western edges of Detroit. The first expressway section looped around the plant, and the southern segment extended 9.1 miles east to Hannan Road in Romulus. Construction began in November 1941. The federal government paid the construction costs ($5.95 million) and the State of Michigan paid $1.03 million to buy the right-of-way. The highway was officially opened on 12 September 1942 and fifteen thousand bomber plant workers attended the dedication ceremonies. An extension of this expressway further east was already under construction and opened in December 1942. Dubbed the "Detroit Industrial Defense Expressway," it extended 11.5 miles further east to Southfield Road in Dearborn, literally at the gates of the Ford Rouge plant. The new highway system greatly facilitated the movement of components from the Rouge plant to Willow Run but did not entirely solve the problems workers had getting to Ypsilanti. Even with the expressways, workers might spend forty-five minutes getting to the plant when there were many other defense jobs much more conveniently located. Tire rationing, which started in 1942, was another problem workers faced. Sorensen considered using Ford's tire plant at the Rouge complex to retread workers' tires, but the shortage of rubber made this offer moot. Workers carpooled or took buses operated by the Detroit Street Railway Company, but many struggled to get to work and simply quit.[51]

The Willow Run operation also suffered from the Ford Motor Company's dysfunctional management team, with two factions struggling for control of the company. The company's founder, Henry Ford (1863–1947), was seventy-eight years old in 1941, had already suffered at least one stroke, and by all reports had lost much of his mental acuity. Harry Bennett (1892–1979) had been in charge of personnel and labor relations at Ford since the 1920s and was Henry's right-hand man. Bennett ran the notorious Ford Service Department in the 1920s and 1930s and prevented the unionization of Ford's workers until 1941. Opposed to Henry Ford and Bennett was Edsel Ford (1893–1943), Henry's only son, whom Henry Ford never granted any real authority within the company. Edsel was the titular president of the company, but following his death from stomach cancer in May 1943, Henry Ford assumed the presidency. Edsel's ally in most disputes was Charles Sorensen (1881–1961), a Danish immigrant who first worked for Ford in 1905, managed production at the Highland Park plant, and later ran the River Rouge plant. His work in casting engines earned him the nickname "Cast Iron Charlie." Sorensen was executive vice president at Ford by the start of the war. He successfully organized the production of Pratt & Whitney aircraft engines at the Rouge plant before taking on the overall management of the Willow Run plant. By all accounts Sorensen was a production genius.[52]

Several incidents illustrate the divisions within the Ford management team. On 18 September 1941, President Roosevelt visited the Willow Run plant as part of a nationwide secret tour of defense plants. He was accompanied by Eleanor Roosevelt, Donald Nelson, and other government officials. When the president's party arrived at the plant, Henry Ford was nowhere to be seen and was discovered out in the plant looking at a new piece of machinery. The president's party arrived at the plant in a private railroad car and then drove through the plant in Roosevelt's presidential limousine. Henry Ford was relegated to sitting in the back seat between the two Roosevelts, two people he detested. Edsel Ford sat in front of Eleanor Roosevelt and Sorensen sat in front of the president, with Nelson next to the driver. Edsel talked nonstop with Mrs. Roosevelt, while Sorensen explained the operations to the president. Henry Ford sat silently throughout the two-hour tour while the plant workers loudly cheered the president. Sorensen commented on Henry Ford's mood:

> It was one of the worst days, up to that time, that I had ever spent with Henry Ford. Even during the hard days of the battles with his stockholders he had not been so gloomy or mean. He had spent a few hours with the man who was running the country and a war. Ford hated him, and he was furious because Edsel and I were giving all we had to a cause that was not his own. From then on he became even more difficult to work with.

President Roosevelt visited when Willow Run had completed only one bomber, and he noted the slow progress made up to that point in an off-the-record statement at a press conference following his return to Washington.[53]

An incident in early May 1943 illustrates the destructive nature of these internal conflicts. Roscoe Smith, who was the manager of Ford's factories outside of the Rouge, spent much of the first half of 1941 in San Diego studying Consolidated's manufacturing operations. He was put in charge of running the Willow Run plant, which was still under construction. Smith and Harry Bennett clashed over authority to run the plant. At one point, Bennett ordered partitions installed on the factory floor, which Smith then removed. In early May 1943, Smith, Sorensen, and Bennett argued and Bennett punched Smith in the eye, knocking him to the ground. Smith went back to his old job running "small plants" and Meade Bricker, who supervised aircraft engine production at the Rouge plant, took over as general manager at Willow Run. Logan Miller, a machinery expert who had also spent time at the Consolidated plant, became plant superintendent and conflicts with Bennett became less frequent.[54]

Dysfunctional management at Willow Run contributed to the slow start of production, which was evident to military and civilian observers. Seven members of the U.S. Senate's Special Committee Investigating the National Defense Program (the Truman Committee) visited the Willow Run plant in mid-April 1942, a time when the plant was still well behind its scheduled production of bombers. Publicly the committee members, including Truman, praised what they saw at Willow Run and were optimistic that bombers would soon be rolling off the assembly line in large numbers. Charles E. Wilson, the vice-chair of the WPB, also visited Willow Run in April and predicted that the plant would be producing 500 planes a month by winter. The Truman Committee issued its written report on Willow Run on 10 July 1942 and praised the Ford Motor Company for the progress already made there. At the same time, however, the committee criticized Ford for ignoring the advice of the aircraft companies and insisting on assembly-line production at Willow Run. The report also blamed Ford for the problems Consolidated had in meeting its production schedules at its Fort Worth plant. The Truman Committee did not acknowledge Consolidated's liability for many of Ford's problems.[55]

The Army Air Force and the Roosevelt administration remained disappointed with Willow Run's slow start-up. In September 1943, the Army Air Force Materiel Command proposed that the government take over the management of Willow Run from Ford. This threat was probably made to put more pressure on Ford to increase production of the B-24. When production improved dramatically in the last quarter of 1943, this threat vanished. According to Sorensen, President Roosevelt decided in March 1944 to remove Henry Ford as the head of the Ford Motor Company and take from him any authority relating to war production. Roosevelt's advisors proposed that Sorensen run Ford. Sorensen had a day-long meeting with Merrill Meigs, who was in charge of the Aircraft Section of the WPB, to discuss this plan. Sorensen successfully argued that the Ford Motor Company was now meeting its production schedules despite Henry Ford's presence. Henry Ford II, Edsel's oldest son, was now waiting in the wings at Ford ready to take over the company.[56]

Sorensen's departure from the Ford Motor Company early in 1944 illustrates how chaotic the top Ford management had become. Sorensen told Henry Ford in November 1943 that he wished to resign from the company effective the first of the new year. Even though the two men had previously agreed to this, Ford seemed not to understand Sorensen's request. Sorensen went to Florida and remained there all of January and February 1944 and continued to press Henry Ford to accept his resignation. In early March, Henry Ford instructed Frank Campsall, Ford's secretary, to send Sorensen a letter demanding Sorensen's resignation, accusing him of plotting to become Ford's president. Henry Ford, clearly in physical and mental decline, apparently wanted the pleasure of firing Sorensen rather than allowing him to resign on his own.[57]

The Ford Motor Company never fully resolved the problems created by an inadequate workforce at Willow Run or its own dysfunctional management; even so, Ford eventually reached the production goal of one plane an hour that Sorensen had proclaimed in early 1941. Ford continued to struggle with the constant design changes made to the B-24, but in time, Ford, Consolidated, and the Army Air Force achieved a compromise solution. Ford was allowed to freeze the B-24 design for a batch of airplanes to facilitate production. The need to alter the design of an aircraft already in production was horrifying to Ford's production engineers and managers. The first 400 planes completed at Willow Run incorporated 372 master changes that required more than 48,000 engineering hours and 290,000 retooling hours to complete. The design modifications continued throughout the life of the aircraft such that the last B-24 to leave the Willow Run plant was almost an entirely different aircraft than the first. With the addition of heavily armored, powered gun turrets and other new equipment, the gross weight of the B-24 ballooned from 41,000 to 60,000 pounds. The design changes remained a constant source of friction between Ford and Consolidated, which merged in 1943 with the Vultee Aircraft Corporation to become Consolidated-Vultee Aircraft Corporation, also known as Convair. Consolidated's ongoing failure to deliver the blueprints Ford needed to make the needed design changes forced Ford to engineer a good deal of the changes on its own, a practice vigorously opposed by Consolidated. For example, in March 1943, the Army Air Force authorized Ford to complete the engineering for a new nose gun turret independent of Consolidated.[58]

The disruptive effect of the constant design changes was greatly reduced through a compromise: the "block system" of manufacturing. Under this system, Ford would produce a block of B-24s without making any changes to its tooling or fixtures and then make wholesale changes all at once on the next block. The block grew larger over time, but 400 planes to a block became the standard by 1943. Willow Run completed 1,980 B-24s between 30 June 1943 and 17 March 1944 in seven blocks, with 273 master changes made during that stretch. These design changes were occasionally major ones involving enormous expenditure of time. In March 1943, for example, the nose gun turret was completely redesigned to house new machine guns. The new turret involved sixty-seven changes requiring 53,456 engineering hours and 208,271 hours to change the tooling needed to produce the new turret. Ford completed the engineering on its own. The block system allowed Ford to maintain high levels of production and to incorporate the design changes smoothly. Aircraft produced in a block that needed alterations were sent to one of several modification centers, where these changes were made without disrupting production at Willow Run.[59]

Charles Sorensen's grandiose goal of one plane an hour from Ford's B-24 assembly line took a long time to become a reality. Although the Army Air Force had issued Ford Motor Company a letter of intent in early June 1941 for Ford to build 800 complete airplanes, the air force did not accept the first plane from Willow Run until 30 September 1942. Production for all of 1942 was only 56 aircraft. The air force initially set a monthly production goal of 405 planes for 1943; in late February

1943 they increased that target to 535 planes a month. Struggling with all of the problems mentioned earlier, Ford slowly ramped up production from 37 bombers in January 1943 to 146 units in April, 254 in September, and 365 in December. By the end of 1943, Ford was meeting its production goals, which the air force had adjusted downward. In six days in April 1944, Ford built 453 bombers, one every 62 minutes. The Willow Run plant assembled nearly 5,000 planes in 1944. As Ford was ramping up production, the government reduced the schedule for December 1944 to a mere 215 bombers. By then, the three plants turning out B-24s were producing more planes that the air force could deploy and resources were being diverted to the production of the longer-range B-29. By the time production of B-24s ended at Willow Run in June 1945, Ford had built 6,792 "flyaway" planes and 1,894 knock-down aircraft, for a total of 8,686. The spare parts manufactured at Willow Run were the equivalent of an additional 364 bombers.[60]

Evaluating Ford's performance at Willow Run is difficult at best. An August 1946 Army Air Force Materiel Command analysis of Willow Run's performance noted the severe shortages of skilled labor as a major source of Ford's problems in getting the plant into full production. The report placed much of the blame on the Ford Motor Company, citing Ford's rigid opposition to the use of soft dies, its failure to clearly define the management structure at Willow Run, and its insistence on running the plant as a branch of the River Rouge factory. It also faulted Ford for allowing the rivalry and animosity between Sorensen and Bennett to divide Ford management into two rival camps. Sixteen months elapsed between the time the government made its commitment to Ford to build complete aircraft and the acceptance of the first bomber. Given the complexity of the airplane, Ford's inexperience in aircraft production, and the problems Ford had working with Consolidated, the delay was understandable. Willow Run needed thirty-eight months to reach full scheduled production, in contrast with the three other plants making the same aircraft, which had time lags ranging from twenty-five to thirty-two months. Once Willow Run solved its initial production problems, its achievements were impressive. In 1944, when the plant was one of four building B-24s, it accounted for 48.5 percent of total production. For 1945, its share was 70 percent. By the end of the war, Ford was eighth among aircraft manufacturers in terms of the total airframe weight it produced, with 6.2 percent of the total. Each of the seven that outproduced Ford had at least three assembly plants in operation for most of the war.[61]

After a long learning process, the Willow Run plant did save considerable labor in producing B-24s. One measure is the number of direct man-hours per airframe pound accepted. In January 1943, Ford needed 5.03 hours versus only 1.11 hours at Consolidated's San Diego plant. By November 1943, Ford was nearly on par with Consolidated (.70 hours versus .67 hours). By September 1944, Ford's direct labor requirements were half of Consolidated's (.32 hours versus .64 hours). However, these comparisons are incomplete and misleading because they do not take into consideration Ford's much larger expenditures on tools and fixtures. The Willow Run plant achieved cost savings by replacing labor with precision machinery. Willow Run outproduced Consolidated's San Diego plant and supplied the Army Air Force with an enormous number of B-24s with interchangeable parts. In 1944, Ford delivered Liberators to the Army Air Force at an average price of $137,000 versus $238,000 two years earlier. Ford's accomplishments are remarkable for a company with no experience in mass-producing aircraft.[62]

Over the course of the war, Convair and the other aircraft companies followed Ford's lead in using (automotive) mass-production methods to fabricate and assemble aircraft. They were under extreme pressure from the Army Air Force to sharply increase production, especially of heavy bombers, an impossibility if they maintained their prewar production methods. The airframe manufacturers adopted interchangeable parts as a necessary prerequisite to large-scale production. They followed Ford in developing specialized fixtures to speed assembly and reduce the number of skills workers needed. They adopted the automotive-style moving assembly line, with components and subassemblies moved by conveyors and brought together in a straight-line assembly operation. Out of necessity, the aircraft industry, especially the manufacturers on the West Coast, adopted many of Ford's methods introduced at Willow Run. In the case of the General Motors-Grumman partnership outlined in the next section, some production expertise and techniques flowed from the aircraft manufacturer to the automaker, but there was a considerable flow in the opposite direction as well.[63]

What impact did Ford's production of B-24 Liberator bombers have on the outcome of the war? Ford accounted for 45 percent of the total production of 19,204 Liberators during the war but also taught the other B-24 manufacturers advanced fabricating and assembly practices. The B-24 Liberator and the Boeing B-17 Flying Fortress did the bulk of the heavy bombing in the European and North African theaters. The Liberator also saw notable service in the Pacific, but the Boeing B-29 Superfortress carried out virtually all of the massive, devastating bombing of Japan proper. Boeing and its partners produced 12,962 Flying Fortresses during the war, bringing the total number of American heavy bombers used in Europe and North Africa to 31,900. Ford production accounted for more than a quarter of that total. In contrast, the combined production of the Boeing B-29 Superfortress by Boeing and others stood at 3,898 planes at war's end.[64]

The impact of strategic bombing on the war in Europe, especially on German armaments production, is disputed among World War II historians. Strategic bombing was not particularly effective in the first years of the war but became more important from early 1944 onward, as the size and scope of the bombing raids increased and German defenses weakened. The first use of U.S. bombers for a substantial strategic attack came on 11–12 June 1942 when thirteen B-24s raided the Nazi-controlled Ploesti oil fields in Rumania. They took off from a Royal Air Force base in the Egyptian Canal Zone and flew across the Mediterranean, Greece, and Bulgaria. They hit their target but did little damage. A much larger raid on 1 August 1943 was a disaster for the U.S. Army Air Corps. A force of 177 Liberators flew from bases in Benghazi, Libya, without fighter escorts, for the 2,700-mile round-trip. They faced intense ground fire at their target, resulting in the loss of 57 aircraft. This mission, dubbed Operation Tidal Wave, set off multiple fires and caused some damage, but the Ploesti oil fields remained operational. Subsequent raids failed to shut down the oil field and refineries. The Red Army finally accomplished that goal in August 1944 when it occupied Ploesti.[65]

The sheer volume and effectiveness of bombing increased dramatically in the spring of 1944 when the American bombers for the first time had long-range fighter aircraft, mainly P-51 Mustangs, to accompany them to their targets and back. The combined Anglo-American bomber force, roughly 1,000 aircraft in March 1943, tripled by February 1944 and totaled 5,250 bombers by July 1944. The U.S. Eight Army Air Force carried out a single raid against Berlin in early February 1945 with 1,000 heavy bombers. After dropping nearly 54,000 tons of bombs on European targets in 1942, the combined British and American bomber forces dropped 226,513 tons in 1943 and nearly 1.2 million tons in 1944. The bombing raids were costly: the British and American forces combined lost a total of 140,000 airmen and 21,000 bombers. The impact of bombing on the German war effort cannot be measured by looking at overall industrial production alone. Richard Overy has pointed out that an increasing share of German industrial capacity and manpower had to be devoted to producing anti-aircraft guns and ammunition, and more soldiers were assigned to defending German cities against the attacks from the air. Fewer tanks, aircraft, guns, and soldiers were available for the war. In the last year of the war, the bombing attacks also crippled German transportation, communication, and electricity networks. There is also little doubt that in the final year of the war, the endless bombing, including firebombing, severely eroded the morale of German civilians.[66]

The General Motors-Grumman Partnership

In contrast to the enormous attention and publicity generated by the Ford Motor Company's production of B-24s at its Willow Run plant, the highly successful wartime partnership of the General Motors Corporation and the Grumman Aircraft Engineering Company is largely unknown. The two companies manufactured the majority of naval aircraft during the war (34,234 out of 57,300 planes) using a production model entirely unlike the one used by Ford. The GM-Grumman achievement has been largely ignored by historians, in large part because Henry Ford generated enormous publicity for his Willow Run plant and Grumman and GM were reticent about discussing their achievements. Grumman was a bit of a corporate misfit in the aircraft industry and did not join the East Coast Wartime Production Council. GM was also reluctant to publicize its wartime accomplishments. In his autobiography, *My Years with General Motors*, Alfred P. Sloan Jr. devotes exactly eight pages to GM's war work and makes no mention of the Grumman partnership. GM's aircraft contracts of all types amounted to $4.9 billion, 40 percent of the value of GM's war contracts. Nearly half of the value of the automaker's aircraft contracts involved engine production, but the other half came from work on complete aircraft and components.[67]

Grumman's founder, Leroy R. Grumman, earned a degree in mechanical engineering from Cornell, became a naval aviator in 1918, and worked as a project engineer and test pilot at the Naval Aircraft Factory in Philadelphia. He then held several positions, including general manager for Grover Loening, a successful New York City aircraft manufacturer. Grumman and six investors launched the Grumman Aircraft Engineering Company in December 1929, setting up shop in a large garage in Baldwin in the southwest part of Long Island. This was not a propitious time to start an aircraft manufacturing company. The company survived and grew during the tumultuous 1930s by producing military aircraft for the U.S. Navy. From its foundation, Grumman worked closely with the navy in developing new aircraft, and the navy in turn became Grumman's primary customer. Because Grumman needed more manufacturing space to fulfill its navy contracts, the company took over a former aircraft factory in nearby Farmingdale in November 1932 and enlarged the facility in 1936. By the mid-1930s, Grumman was manufacturing a single-seat fighter, a scout plane, and three versions of amphibious aircraft, which could operate from water or land, all for the navy.[68]

As orders for navy aircraft increased, Grumman prepared to expand production by opening a new factory. In 1936, the company purchased a 120-acre parcel in Bethpage, also in southwestern Long Island. The new plant opened on 8 April 1937, and in late 1938 Grumman acquired another 100 acres at the same location. Bethpage would become Grumman's principal engineering and assembly center during the war, encompassing 2,650,000 square feet of floor space. Grumman and the navy worked together to develop a new carrier-based fighter, the F4F, later known as the Wildcat. The navy ordered 54 Wildcats (designated the F4F-3) from Grumman in August 1939, 759 more in 1940, and 472 more in 1941. After overcoming multiple problems with the Wildcat prototypes, Grumman delivered the first F4F Wildcat to Britain's Fleet Air Arm on 27 July 1941. Grumman modified the airplane's design by giving it folding wings, which saved space on carrier and hangar decks. On 14 June 1942, the company delivered its first folded-wing Wildcat (designated the F4F-4) to the navy. Grumman's second major naval aircraft was the TBF-1 Avenger, a carrier-based torpedo bomber. In December 1940, the navy placed its initial order for 286 of these aircraft.[69]

Grumman was operated quite differently than the larger airframe manufacturers such as Curtiss-Wright, Boeing, or Douglas, which typically grew by building massive new plants, often paid for by the DPC. Grumman grew by building components in small factories on Long Island. Grumman opened five small plants on Long Island in the first five months of 1942, employing 3,000 workers. By the end of the war, they operated scores of small factories. Although Grumman's labor force jumped from 2,000 to 7,000 in 1941 alone and peaked at 25,527 in September 1943, it remained a relatively small company. The top management, especially Leroy Grumman, provided workers with a lot of amenities, including day care facilities in the factory. The company was never unionized, labor turnover rates were much lower than at other aircraft companies, and worker morale was generally high. Part of Grumman's wartime expansion came through an innovative partnership forged in January 1942 with the Eastern Aircraft Division of the General Motors Corporation.[70]

Two weeks after Pearl Harbor, GM ended automobile assembly at its plant in Linden, New Jersey, which had produced Buicks, Pontiacs, and Oldsmobiles. The automaker offered the plant to the Office of Production Management (OPM) for use in aircraft subcontracting, which showed no interest at first. The navy then asked GM to build two Grumman aircraft under license, and the automaker created the Eastern Aircraft Division for that purpose on 21 January 1942. Four additional plants came under Eastern's control: Fisher Body plants at Tarrytown, New York, and at Baltimore; a Delco-Remy plant at Bloomfield, New Jersey, which had made electrical equipment for the cars assembled at Linden; and its Trenton-Ternstedt Division plant in Trenton, New Jersey. The Trenton plant made up to 750,000 automobile hardware and trim pieces per day, such as door handles, mirrors, and exterior trim items. In early February, the navy sent letters of intent to Eastern Aircraft offering contracts to build Grumman's fighter plane (the Wildcat) in Linden and its torpedo bomber (the Avenger) in Trenton. The building of Avenger components would be done at Tarrytown and Baltimore, Wildcat fabrication and assembly would take place at Linden, and electrical components for both planes would be built at the Bloomfield plant. Contracts for the torpedo bomber and the fighter followed on

2 and 25 March, respectively. All five plants were reasonably close to each other and to Grumman's engineering facilities in Bethpage.[71]

Eastern Aircraft had two daunting restrictions to overcome in starting production of the two Grumman aircraft. The agreements with the OPM and the navy forbade Eastern from luring personnel from Grumman or from other aircraft manufacturers. They were forced to find their own labor force but were able to train workers through a series of joint training programs with Grumman and others. Eastern was also forbidden from ordering parts or components from Grumman's existing stable of suppliers. In 1942, Eastern created its own supply network of more than 3,000 firms to provide over 10,000 parts it needed. In 1942 alone, the GM subsidiary placed orders with suppliers for more than $80 million.[72]

Before General Motors established Eastern Aircraft, their production engineers visited Grumman's Bethpage plant. Much like Ford's experience with Consolidated Aircraft, GM found Grumman's production techniques and culture to be radically different from theirs. Some of these differences reflected the fact that automobiles and aircraft were very different pieces of machinery. The outer body of an automobile has almost no bearing on its performance and is mainly decorative, but on aircraft, the shape and finish of the exterior sections are vital to performance. Grumman's production operations were largely unchanged from the 1930s, that is, they used "batch production" methods. Their blueprints were incomplete and outdated, and they expected their skilled workmen to interpret and modify the designs when needed. Grumman could not supply GM with parts lists or bills of materials needed for a particular aircraft, much to the horror of the automotive engineers. The two engineering staffs battled initially, but the Eastern engineers concluded that they could not adopt automobile industry mass-production methods if they were going to quickly produce the aircraft the navy desperately needed. Instead, GM's engineers spent an enormous amount of time at the Bethpage plant learning Grumman's methods in order to copy them. The Eastern Aircraft plants adopted general-purpose machines that could be easily altered to make new parts. They developed a more flexible manufacturing system that was better suited to the changing manufacturing requirements for aircraft than was Ford's system at Willow Run.[73]

Eastern Aircraft engaged in what is sometimes called "reverse engineering." Grumman supplied Eastern Aircraft with ten planes, both Wildcats and Avengers, to use to develop their own tooling and fixtures. These were not fully assembled planes, rivets and all, but were held together with Parker-Kalon temporary fasteners so the Eastern engineers could disassemble them, take dimensions, see how they fit together, and then reassemble them. These "PK planes" or "PK ships" were shortcuts that allowed Eastern to get into production quickly. Eastern's engineers would compare the parts of the PK planes with whatever blueprints Grumman gave them and then correct the blueprints to reflect the actual dimensions of the parts. Based on their needs for machine tools and presses, Eastern aircraft placed 2,145 orders for machinery in April 1942 and by October had taken delivery on more than 90 percent of their orders. These were mostly general-purpose machine tools. In another break with automotive mass-production tooling, Eastern used the less expensive and more flexible soft kirksite dies for stamping. GM's subsidiary did, however, install conveyors for final assembly at their plants.[74]

The willingness of the engineering staffs of Eastern and Grumman to fully cooperate to meet a common goal and the close proximity of the plants of Eastern, Grumman, and their suppliers enabled a remarkably fast ramping-up of production. The first Wildcat manufactured at the Linden plant flew successfully on 31 August 1942, and the first Avenger assembled at Trenton completed its first test flight on 11 November 1942. By the end of 1942, Eastern Aircraft had delivered thirty-one Wildcats and three Avengers to the navy, well ahead of schedule. This quick ramping-up of production by Eastern Aircraft stands in sharp contrast to the long gestation period needed by Ford at Willow Run. Grumman developed a new and superior fighter aircraft, the F6F Hellcat, which had its first test flight on 31 July 1942. The Hellcat went into production at the Bethpage plant later in the year, and in January 1943 all Wildcat production was shifted to Eastern Aircraft. Similarly, in December 1943, Grumman shifted all production of Avengers to Eastern Aircraft. By the end of the war, Eastern Aircraft had manufactured 13,466 planes for the navy (5,920 Wildcats and 7,546 Avengers), and Grumman had completed 17,478 aircraft. Although fighters and torpedo bombers are simpler aircraft than bombers, this was an impressive achievement.[75]

The Avenger and Wildcat aircraft played significant roles in naval warfare, particularly in the Pacific. The first combat mission for the Avenger was the Battle of Midway on 4 June 1942, although the Avengers used there were not built by Eastern Aircraft. Midway was one of the early U.S. naval victories in the Pacific theater, significant because of the destruction of four Japanese aircraft carriers. The F4F-4 Wildcat was the standard ship-based fighter aircraft by the end of 1942 but was inferior to the Japanese Zeros it faced with respect to speed and climb rate above 1,000 feet, as well as range and service ceiling. Grumman's heavier and more powerful Hellcat replaced the Wildcat as soon as it was available. The Wildcat, however, had better firepower and armament than the Zero, and the navy devised a fighting strategy that used two Wildcats acting in tandem to fight the Zeros. The U.S. Navy credited the Wildcat with the destruction of 905 enemy aircraft in 1941–43, while losing only 178, a kill ratio of 5 to 1. For the entire war, the Wildcat achieved a kill ratio of 7 to 1, not too bad for a fighter with inferior performance. The Wildcat fought with distinction in all the major Pacific battles, including Wake, Midway, Guadalcanal, Coral Sea, and the Solomons.[76]

Ford's Wooden Gliders and Nash-Kelvinator's Helicopters

Ford Motor Company emerged as a major supplier of gliders to the Army Air Force in the course of the war. After the German army successfully used gliders in their invasion of Crete in May 1941, the army and marines became interested in their potential as a way to move troops into battle. The United States had no gliders capable of carrying troops or equipment, but the Waco Aircraft Company of Troy, Ohio, had several models under development. On 8 March 1942, Lieutenant Colonel Kenny from the Army Air Corps began discussions with Ford about producing a glider that could carry men or cargo. Ford dispatched a team of engineers to Wright Field and to the Waco plant to examine the aircraft more closely, with mass production in mind. Ford had a substantial sawmill and wood-processing plant in Iron Mountain, located in Michigan's Upper Peninsula, sitting idle, so Ford and gliders seemed like a good fit. The army approved the project in principle on 27 March 1942 and sent Ford a letter of intent on 21 April providing for the manufacture of 1,000 gliders. Designated the CG-4A model, with "CG" standing for "Cargo Glider," they were capable of carrying fifteen men, or a howitzer, or a jeep. The estimated cost was $19 million, but this did not include the cost of converting the Iron Mountain plant. Waco Aircraft was suspicious of Ford's production plans for its glider but nevertheless agreed to license Ford to produce it at a cost to Ford of $20.05 for each glider.[77]

The wooden gliders, built largely of pieces of Sitka spruce from the Pacific Northwest glued together, might appear to be worlds apart from the giant B-24 Liberators Ford built at Willow Run, but Ford ran into similar production challenges and used similar solutions. Although the glider design seemed simple at first glance, it consisted of 70,000 parts. As they had with Consolidated's designs, Ford engineers had to redo Waco's blueprints, which were done at half scale, were full of errors, and did not reflect recent design changes. Ford also made more than 10,000 alterations to the original design to strengthen and simplify the aircraft. Ford's modified design became the standard used by Waco and its other licensees. The glider had a steel frame, but the rest of the fuselage and wings consisted of wooden ribs made from hundreds of pieces glued together and then covered with cotton fabric. Ford designed specialized fixtures and jigs for the manufacture of the parts and for the final assembly of the glider. One of the fixtures reduced the drying time for the glue from eight hours to ten minutes.[78]

Ford-built 15-passenger gliders, Iron Mountain (MI) plant *(ACWP)*.

The first Ford-built glider was assembled at the former Ford Trimotor aircraft factory building at the Ford Airport in Dearborn. It was fifty feet long, had a wingspan of eighty-four feet, and weighed 8,400 pounds fully loaded. On its first test flight (16 September 1942), two army officers were at the controls and two Ford engineers were onboard. The glider was towed to an elevation of 8,400 feet, and the successful test flight lasted forty-five minutes. The Army Air Force accepted the test model and Ford began to prepare the Iron Mountain plant for full production. Ford started final assembly in December 1942 and finished twelve gliders by late January 1943. After Ford turned out 130 gliders in June 1943, the air force asked the automaker to design a larger model (CG-13A) capable of carrying thirty men and a jeep and a howitzer or two jeeps. Ford agreed and its initial model was accepted in January 1944. Although Ford produced only eighty-seven of the larger versions, this was three-quarters of the total number of gliders built. When production ended at Iron Mountain in August 1945, Ford had produced 4,202 of the CG-4A gliders, or 30 percent of the total built during the war. In 1945, Ford produced half of the gliders delivered to the Army Air Force. Over the course of the war, Ford sharply lowered the cost of the CG-4A glider from $21,391 to $12,159 per unit.[79]

Ford revolutionized the production of gliders by applying mass-production methods to manufacturing and assembly, and their efforts were well received by those who flew the aircraft. Army Air Force pilots such as R. R. Hansen praised their handling characteristics: "The Ford glider is still the best, the cleanest, the easiest to fly, quickest to trim, smooth in free flight, a good glider." Ford quickly established the standard for interchangeability of glider parts, and as a result a Ford-built glider was sent to all the other manufacturers to use as a standard for accuracy. Once Ford tested its first 100 gliders, the Army Air Force required no additional testing. Gliders built at Iron Mountain were disassembled and shipped to their final destination in crates on railroad flat cars or in the haul-away trailers first designed to deliver knock-down B-24s. To be certain that no parts were missed, Ford completely assembled each glider and then disassembled it for shipping. The Army Air Force required the other manufacturers to follow the same practice.[80]

An even more obscure aircraft contract went to Nash-Kelvinator to produce helicopters under license by the Sikorsky Division of United Aircraft Corporation. In early 1943, Sikorsky was producing two models, the R-4 and the R-5, while starting development of a third model, the R-6. The Army Air Force wanted to place an order for the R-6, but Sikorsky was not able to satisfy the demand and instead suggested Nash-Kelvinator as a contractor. On 28 May 1943, the Army Air Force authorized Nash-Kelvinator to build 800 R-6 helicopters. The government would supply the engines. Because of labor shortages in Kenosha and Milwaukee, the Army Air Force specified that helicopter production take place elsewhere. The company made the fuselage in Grand Rapids but relied on many subcontractors, including Sikorsky, for most of the drivetrain components including the rotor blades. Nash-Kelvinator would complete final assembly at its plant on Plymouth Road in Detroit. The formal contract with Nash-Kelvinator came on 28 August 1943 and called for 900 helicopters.[81]

In June 1943 Nash-Kelvinator sent twenty engineers to the Sikorsky factory in Bridgeport, Connecticut, to study helicopter manufacturing and to help Sikorsky engineers produce the necessary drawings. In August 1943, the government gave Nash-Kelvinator permission to develop a tiny (4.5-acre) parcel behind its Detroit plant as a testing airfield. By the end of 1943, the automaker had produced a mahogany model of the R-6 helicopter in its Detroit engineering laboratories. Nash-Kelvinator would make the tools and fixtures needed for quantity production from this model. The company's engineers developed a time-saving method for testing helicopter rotor blades. Rather than testing the blades on an actual helicopter, they tested blades before installation in a testing facility built on the tiny landing field

Helicopter final inspection, Nash-Kelvinator Detroit plant (*CKH*).

behind its Detroit plant. They removed the blades from the test building in sets of three, ready for installation on a helicopter.[82]

Production was slow in coming, mainly because Sikorsky made countless changes (approximately 20,000) to the original design, which delayed the delivery of drawings. As a result, Nash-Kelvinator did not test its first production model until mid-September 1944 and did not receive Army Air Force acceptance of its first helicopter until 23 October 1944. Approval of its third machine did not come until 24 December 1944. When the Army Air Force canceled the helicopter contract on 16 August 1945, Nash-Kelvinator had completed 262 helicopters and had 20 more partially finished. The government paid Nash-Kelvinator more than $17 million for its helicopter work.[83]

The Overall Achievement

The case studies presented in this chapter— are all success stories, hiccups and all. Automobile companies made large quantities of high-quality aircraft or aircraft components. None of the automobile manufacturers was accused of price-gauging, dishonest practices, or fraud. It is noteworthy that the only aircraft manufacturer accused of fraud by the Truman Committee was the Wright Aeronautical Corporation for its operation at Lockland, Ohio, which built aircraft engines.[84]

Over the course of World War II, both the aircraft manufacturers and the automobile companies usually met and sometimes exceeded the grandiose production goals for aircraft set by Franklin Roosevelt and the military services *after* modification of the original goals. After solving initial problems related to the unique problems of fabricating airplane components and assembling complete aircraft, the automakers successfully accomplished both tasks. No other industry could have supplied the engineering talent, production expertise, and workforce that the auto industry contributed to this joint venture. The case studies provided in this chapter demonstrate that a variety of manufacturing approaches worked. The aircraft production miracle of World War II was possible only because of the cooperation of all the parties involved: the military services, the aircraft companies, and the automobile companies. During normal peacetime conditions, the aircraft companies would not have cooperated with each other, much less with the automakers, but patriotism changed their outlook and their behavior. The results were remarkable.

The accomplishments are worth repeating. Between July 1940 and December 1945, the combined aircraft-automobile industry produced over 802,000 aircraft engines, more than 708,000 propellers, and almost 300,000 military aircraft of all types. Production had grown from about 13,000 aircraft in 1940, half of these civilian planes, to 96,000 military aircraft in 1944 before falling off in the final year of the war. In 1940, approximately 13 million square feet of factory space was devoted to the production of airframes, aircraft engines, and propellers. By the end of 1944, the floor space had increased thirteenfold to 167 million square feet. Most of this expansion was financed by the government, and much of it took place in plants operated by the automobile industry. The six corporations that received the most government funding to expand aircraft production were, in descending order, General Motors, Curtiss-Wright, Ford, Chrysler, United Aircraft, and Douglas. The three automakers received $922 million in government funds, while the three aircraft companies received $828 million. Over the course of the war, the aircraft industry substantially reduced the cost of the aircraft it delivered to the Army Air Force. For example, the unit cost of B-17 Flying Fortress fell from $301,000 in 1939–41 to less than $188,000 in 1945; the price tag on a B-24 Liberator went from $379,000 in 1939–41 to $215,500 in 1944; and, finally, the unit cost of a B-29 Superfortress, roughly $894,000 in 1942, fell dramatically to $509,000 in the final year of the war.[85]

The contrast between American aircraft production and that of the other combatants is striking in many respects. The automobile industries of the United States and

Great Britain played a much larger role in aircraft production than did the German auto industry. The automobile industries of Japan and the Soviet Union were so small at the outset of the war that their contributions were negligible. The U.S. government was willing to use resources outside the aircraft industry to produce aircraft and naturally turned to the automobile industry, with its manufacturing experience, engineering expertise, and large stock of machine tools. By the end of the war, the auto industry had produced two-thirds of the aircraft engines used in combat and 40 percent of all airframe production by weight. At its peak production, the Ford Willow Run plant turned out half the weight of airframes of the entire German aircraft industry. The British had initiated a similar plan as early as 1936, when British automaker Herbert Austin began to organize the auto industry for future aircraft production. British automakers like Morris Motors, Austin, and Rolls-Royce became heavily involved in aircraft manufacturing. Over the duration of the war, British firms not previously involved in aircraft production accounted for 45 percent of the heavy bombers built (by weight), two-thirds of light bombers, and one-fifth of all aircraft.[86]

In contrast, the German government failed to harness their auto industry to increase aircraft production. It relied heavily on a small number of existing aircraft manufacturers, namely Junkers, Heidel, Dornier, and Messerschmitt. The Nazi government nationalized Junkers in April 1935, but the remaining firms remained fiercely independent. Each wanted to design and manufacture its own version of every military aircraft in service. In 1943, German manufacturers produced fifty-three types of aircraft. They rarely cooperated with each other and did not unite to produce aircraft in common, as the American companies did for the B-17, B-24, B-29, and others. For example, none of the companies other than Messerschmitt would agree to make Messerschmitt aircraft during the war. The German aircraft companies, as well as the government, had little interest in involving the automobile industry in aircraft manufacturing until 1944, by which time it was too late. According to one estimate, only half of the manufacturing capacity of Germany's largest automakers, Volkswagen and Adam Opel, was used for war production. From 1939 through 1942, German military aircraft production doubled, while British output tripled and U.S. production increased twentyfold. German aircraft output increased substantially from 15,556 units in 1942 to its wartime peak of 39,807 aircraft in 1944, the only year the Germans outproduced the British during the war. American production of more than 96,000 aircraft in 1944 dwarfed the German achievement.[87]

The Japanese aircraft industry faced many of the same challenges that its German counterpart encountered but had no automobile industry to mobilize. Three large companies (Nakagima, Mitsubishi, and Kawasaki) accounted for three-quarters of the combat aircraft produced in 1941–45. Japanese aircraft companies had to produce a bewildering variety of aircraft because of the demands made by the military. Over the course of the war, the navy developed 53 basic models, with 112 variations, while the army ordered 37 basic models with 52 variations. The Japanese government encouraged the concentration of the industry near Tokyo, Osaka, and Nagoya, but in 1944 the government ordered the industry to disperse. As one historian observed, "rarely in the annals of history has a group of military planners . . . ever exhibited greater stupidity." Because of a lack of materials, the industry had a serious shortage of engines by 1944, but a shift from multi-engine bombers to single-engine fighters reduced this bottleneck. Japan's aircraft production, a mere 5,088 units in 1941, climbed in a spectacular fashion to reach 28,180 aircraft in 1944, slightly higher than British output but less than one-third of American production. By mid-1944, Japan's aircraft industry could barely replace the aircraft lost in battle, and circumstances worsened as production fell and losses increased for the rest of the war. Between January 1943 and July 1945, Japanese front-line aircraft actually increased from 3,200 to 4,100, but American combat strength jumped from 3,537 to 21,908 aircraft.[88]

The next chapter of this book examines the wartime production of armored vehicles: tanks, tank destroyers, universal carriers, and armored cars. Although these vehicles share some features with automobiles, trucks, and tractors, they are significantly different in many ways. None of the automobile companies had prior experience in making tanks, but they nevertheless dominated the manufacture of this important weapon.

FIVE

Tanks and Other Armored Vehicles

At first glance, the automobile manufacturers would appear well positioned to fabricate and assemble tanks and other armored vehicles for the war effort. Tanks, after all, have a mechanical drivetrain much like that of a car or truck, with an engine, transmission, driveshaft, and the like. However, the differences between tanks and standard motor vehicles are in fact more significant than their similarities. They are all-terrain vehicles driven by moving tracks rather than by wheels and thus often referred to as "track-laying vehicles." They are covered by thick armored steel plate, which presents very different fabrication and assembly challenges than do stamped steel bodies found on cars and trucks. Tanks typically are equipped with several guns, usually mounted in rotating turrets. Most tanks manufactured during the war were much heavier than the largest trucks and usually required much larger engines to power them. While not as complex as aircraft, tanks consist of many more parts and components than do cars and trucks.

Despite these major differences, the U.S. Army Ordnance Department viewed the automakers as the logical candidates to make tanks, but they needed to be convinced. The barriers the auto companies faced in producing tanks were in some ways greater than those they faced in producing aircraft components and complete aircraft. In the late 1930s, the U.S. Army was not using tanks in any capacity, and there were no manufacturing facilities in the United States to make them, even in small quantities. There were no tank designs ready to go into production and no one to design tanks other than the Army Ordnance Department. Considering these severe challenges at the start of defense production, the automobile industry's contribution to tank production is impressive. Out of the 88,410 tanks produced in 1940–45, manufacturers of automobiles and automotive components assembled 49,676 of them (56 percent of the total).[1]

The U.S. Army Ordnance Department was even less prepared to start large-scale production of tanks in the late 1930s than the Army Air Force was to get aircraft production under way. There were no substantial private enterprises or government arsenals primarily devoted to tanks. Between 1919 and 1935, the United States produced no more than thirty-five tanks, each of which was a different model. This seems peculiar in light of the (apparent) value of tanks to the British and French in ending the battlefield stalemate of World War I. By the end of that conflict, the British and French had produced roughly 6,500 tanks, the United States only 84, and Germany a mere 20. None of the American tanks saw battle. The U.S. Army's leaders did not foresee the tank as a central element in future battlefield tactics and took steps to guarantee this would not happen. The Army General Staff convinced Congress to abolish the World War I Tank Corps as a separate entity as part of the National Defense Act of 1920. Tanks used in combat were placed under the control of the infantry, which envisioned using tanks exclusively in support of advancing foot soldiers. The Army Ordnance Department, which had the responsibility of developing new tank designs, put tanks and all motorized vehicles into its Artillery Division until 1941. Between 1920 and 1935, individual experimental tanks were hand-built at the Rock Island (Illinois) Arsenal. The first time the Rock Island Arsenal made multiple copies of any tank was in 1935–36, when the arsenal made sixteen medium tanks.[2]

Even as war appeared on the horizon, the army moved at a glacial pace to launch tank production. When hundreds of educational orders were granted to private industry in 1939–40, the Ordnance Department issued only two related to tanks: one to the Baldwin Locomotive Works in Philadelphia for ten light tanks (M2A4 model) and a second one to the Van Dorn Iron Works for light tank hulls. In awarding contracts, the Ordnance Department favored railroad locomotive and equipment manufacturers, largely because they had experience in fabricating and assembling large castings and other components. Since the sales of locomotives had declined sharply throughout the 1930s, locomotive manufacturers were able to take on new work. In most other respects, locomotive manufacturers were not a good choice to produce tanks in quantity. Locomotives were custom-built to meet the requirements of the railroad making the purchase and were assembled one at a time by highly skilled workers.

In October 1939, following competitive bidding, the Rock Island Arsenal awarded the first tank contract of the World War II era to the American Car and Foundry Company (ACF). This was a fixed-price contract for 319 light tanks (M2A4) to be built at ACF's plant in Berwick, Pennsylvania. This 12-ton tank consisted of 14,000 parts, not including the engine, and required more than 2,000 blueprints. Continental Motors of Detroit supplied the aircraft-type radial engine. ACF delivered its first tank to the Ordnance Department in April 1940 and completed 325 by the end of the year. Over the course of the war, ACF built 15,524 light tanks for the Ordnance Department. Other notable railroad equipment manufacturers that produced tanks in quantity included the Pressed Steel Car Company of Chicago (8,648 medium tanks); the Pullman-Standard Car Manufacturing Company (3,926 medium tanks); American Locomotive Company (ALCO) (2,985 medium tanks); Baldwin Locomotive (2,515 medium and heavy tanks); Lima (Ohio) Locomotive (1,655 medium tanks); Montreal Locomotive, the Canadian division of ALCO (1,144 medium tanks); and Pacific Car and Foundry (926 medium tanks). Locomotive and railroad equipment manufacturers combined produced 35,919 tanks or 41 percent of the total.[3]

The experience of the railroad equipment manufacturers in making tanks stands in sharp contrast with that of the automakers that began making tanks a bit later. ACF, the first major tank manufacturer, continued to build railroad cars in the same plant in which it built tanks. When the company found that steel mills were unable to supply the required armor plate for the tank in a timely manner, ACF installed its own heat-treating furnaces to make its own armor plate. As a result, it became the largest producer of armor plate in America and over time provided armor plate to other firms making armored vehicles. ACF had no government assistance in expanding their factory or in buying the 621 machines needed for tank production. This company already used an assembly line in building railroad cars, so they easily applied the same approach to tanks.[4]

ALCO received a letter of intent to build the M4 medium tank from the OPM in July 1940, but production was already well under way before the formal signing of a contract in November 1940. The company delivered its first "pilot" tank in mid-April 1941, and the tank was in regular production by June at its plant in Schenectady, New York. ALCO also continued building locomotives after they took on the tank contract, so work on tanks was scattered throughout their plant. They did not have an assembly line but utilized "station assembly" instead, the method used to build locomotives. As the name suggests, the product, in this case a tank, was assembled at a fixed station, with parts added until the tank was completed, similar to the way in which automobiles were built before the assembly line. ALCO bought roughly 200 machine tools for its tank work, but most of their tools worked on both tank and locomotive parts. As a result, integrating locomotive and tank production, especially machining operations, was challenging. ALCO would machine each tank part in lots of thirty-five and then switch the machine tools to work on another part. This approach was similar to the prewar production methods used in the aircraft industry.[5]

In July 1940, the Ordnance Department contracted with three companies to build M3 medium tanks: ALCO, Baldwin, and the Chrysler Corporation. In the spirit of "friendly competition," all three manufacturers delivered their first pilot tanks to the army in April 1941. Following the Nazi invasion of the Soviet Union in July 1941, tank production suddenly became one of the top priorities of President Roosevelt and the army. That month, the Ordnance Department created a separate Tank and Combat Vehicle Division headed by Lieutenant Colonel John K. Christmas, removing tanks from the Artillery Division of Ordnance. Army planners estimated that about 1,600 medium tanks would be produced in 1941 and that a maximum achievable goal would be 1,000 medium tanks a month. President Roosevelt shocked his military advisors by demanding production of 2,000 medium tanks and 400 light tanks per month, or a projected annual output of 28,000 tanks. Actual production for 1941 was 2,591 light tanks and 1,461 medium tanks, for a total of 4,052. Once tanks became a high priority within the procurement system, tank production jumped dramatically. In 1942, output reached 24,997 units (10,948 light tanks and 14,049 medium tanks). Over the course of the war, the medium tank served as the army's main battle tank, although they eventually built some heavy tanks and continued to use light tanks. Of the 88,410 tanks built during the war, 57,027 were medium tanks, some 65 percent of the total.[6]

Once the higher tank production targets were established for 1942, the Ordnance Department out of necessity turned to the auto industry to achieve these goals. The Detroit Tank Arsenal operated by Chrysler became by far the largest tank manufacturer, producing 22,234 tanks by the end of the war. A detailed case study of the Chrysler Tank Arsenal will be presented in the next section. General Motors was also a major tank producer, with its Cadillac Division in Detroit producing 10,142 light tanks. GM's Fisher Body Division built 13,137 tanks, mostly M4 General Sherman medium tanks, at its new plant in Grand Blanc, Michigan, south of Flint. Ford Motor Company also built 1,690 Shermans at its River Rouge complex, as well as tank destroyers and over 25,000 tank engines. The final automotive industry tank manufacturer was the Massey-Harris Company, which built farm implements. Massey-Harris converted the former Nash-Kelvinator assembly plant in Racine, Wisconsin, to produce light tanks. With the assistance of the Cadillac

Division of GM, Massey-Harris assembled the necessary machine tools and built 2,473 light tanks at Racine.[7]

The Army Ordnance Department recognized the need to forge a close working relationship with the auto industry to ensure adequate production of tanks and other motorized vehicles. After responsibility for trucks and other transport vehicles was transferred from the Quartermaster Corps to Ordnance in July 1942, General Levin H. Campbell Jr. combined tank and truck procurement into a single office, which he relocated to Detroit. Named the Detroit Tank-Automotive Center (T-AC), later renamed the Office Chief of Ordnance-Detroit (OCO-D), the new operation occupied space in the Union-Guardian Building in downtown Detroit. Campbell named General Alfred R. Glancy, former president of the Pontiac Division of General Motors and vice president of General Motors, as the first head of the Tank-Automotive Center. By the end of 1942, the Center employed 400 officers and 4,200 civilian workers in Detroit.[8]

The Detroit (Chrysler) Tank Arsenal

William S. Knudsen, codirector of the OPM, first contacted K. T. Keller by telephone on 7 June 1940 to discuss a possible tank contract. Knudsen came to Detroit two days later to confer with Keller, who agreed in principle that Chrysler would produce a tank but only in a government-owned plant. Keller agreed to make the tanks but only on a cost-plus basis, since his company had no experience with tanks and had no idea what it would cost to make them.[9] Within days, the War Department made its first commitment to build tanks and set aside $20 million to get started. The army would supply Chrysler with the guns, and the Continental Motors Corporation of Detroit would supply the engines. Keller and a group of Chrysler engineers went to the Rock Island Arsenal on 12 June to see a pilot model of this 18-ton tank, designated as the M2A1. Rock Island had built three pilot models and the army wanted 1,500 produced as soon as possible. Keller brought some of the tank blueprints back to Detroit and the army sent the rest. The complete set of blueprints, weighing 186 pounds, arrived in Detroit on 17 June. A team of 197 men worked for four and a half weeks, seven days a week, to complete an estimate of the cost of producing the tank. Chrysler also had its pattern shops produce a full-scale mock-up of the M2A1 tank in wood and shellacked each part to check on the fit of the components.

On 19 July 1940, Chrysler presented the army with a contract proposal: it would produce either 1,000 tanks at $33,500 each or 2,000 tanks at $31,500 each over the next two years. The army chose the smaller order and on 15 August 1940 awarded Chrysler a contract to build the tank plant at a cost of about $200 million. Chrysler had already selected a 113-acre site for the tank arsenal in Warren Township, roughly seventeen miles from downtown Detroit.[10]

On 28 August 1940, just as Chrysler was starting to collect the machinery and tooling for the M2A1 tank, the army dropped that design, declaring it obsolete, and proceeded to develop an entirely new model, the 28-ton M3 tank. The army told Chrysler it would modify the original contract once the design was complete and Chrysler could generate new cost figures. Chrysler moved ahead on tank plant construction, with groundbreaking on 9 September, not knowing exactly what it was going to build there. By mid-October Chrysler had ordered more than half the required machinery and tools, even though the army had not finished the M3 tank design. As was frequently the case with tanks that the United States supplied to its allies under Lend-Lease, the M3 had more than one name: the U.S. Army dubbed it the General Grant, while the British called it the General Lee.[11]

The Army Ordnance Department assigned the design of the M3 to its Aberdeen Proving Ground in Maryland because Aberdeen had superb testing facilities and an experienced engineering and testing staff that had developed a variety of armored fighting vehicles. Work began on the tank design in September 1940 and extended into late February 1941. The army transferred experienced draftsmen from the Rock Island Arsenal to Aberdeen to work on the new tank. They produced general lay-out blueprints, converted them into full-size wooden mock-ups, and then produced more detailed drawings and more detailed wooden models. The draftsmen in turn created the detailed working drawings used to fabricate full-size metal parts.

During the entire process, Army Ordnance provided the prime contractors for the M3 with preliminary drawings to help them plan production. Engineers from the prime contractors, in this case Chrysler, ALCO, and Baldwin, as well as engineers from the major subcontractors, were constantly at Aberdeen interacting with the engineers designing the M3. Their input significantly altered the design of the new tank. As the engineering and drafting staff at Aberdeen completed drawings, they sent them directly to the contractors. Aberdeen generated roughly 6,000 drawings to cover the entire tank and provided the prime contractors and subcontractors with more than 75,000 prints, along with thousands of sheets of specifications and parts lists. This was an unprecedented case of cooperation between the army and private industry.[12]

Plant construction and tooling up for production moved ahead at a feverish pace. Chrysler put its master mechanic Edward J. Hunt in charge of planning production, including the choice and layout of the machine tools that were needed, as well as more than 8,500 fixtures and jigs. Hunt headed a team of about 380 machinists and master mechanics who planned the entire production system at the new plant.

In contrast with automobile manufacturing plants, where single-purpose, highly specialized machines were used, the Chrysler tank arsenal used general-purpose machine tools, such as drill presses, lathes, milling machines, planers, and borers. This arrangement allowed Chrysler to purchase machinery before the design of the M3 was finalized and gave the automaker greater flexibility in switching over to a new tank design altogether.[13]

Despite a cold Detroit winter, the plant's steel structure was finished on 28 January 1941. At that point, Chrysler partitioned off part of the main building with windows, about one-third of the total, and operated a steam locomotive inside the building to provide heat. This allowed machinery to be installed before the permanent heating plant went into service. The contractor finished all glass installation by 1 March 1941 and the concrete floors shortly thereafter. The main assembly building, a single-story, steel-framed building encased in glass, measured 500 feet by 1,380 feet, and enclosed 690,000 square feet. The facility included a one-mile figure-eight test track.[14]

Even after the army had settled on the final design, getting all the necessary tools and equipment in place in the tank plant was no easy task. Aberdeen did not produce final blueprints for all the parts and a final parts list until early March 1941. Chrysler had already ordered a majority of the machine tools it would need by mid-October 1940, but orders and deliveries were two different matters. The first production castings arrived at the plant on 12 February 1941 and machinery installation continued throughout March. The plant completed the first pilot tank on 12 April, and after nearly two weeks of performance tests, Chrysler delivered the first M3 tank to the government on 24 April 1941. The tank plant employed only 230 hourly workers in mid-April 1941, with full-scale production not planned until late summer.[15]

The tank arsenal went into full-scale production gradually, completing only seven tanks in July 1941. The tank plant workforce, already 2,107 strong on 24 July 1941, shot up to over 5,000 a month later. The plant turned out 192 tanks in November, 237 in December, and a total of 729 for the first six months of operations, well above the original target.[16]

Production of the M3 tank was barely under way when the army deemed it obsolete due to two major design flaws. Although the turret was a steel casting, the hull consisted of steel armor plates riveted together. If the tank suffered a direct hit in battle, flying rivets would endanger the tank crew and nearby soldiers. Versions of the M3 tank made by ALCO and Baldwin had cast steel or welded hulls, which greatly reduced the danger. The second design flaw was a main gun (75-mm) mounted into one side of the hull in a rotating sponson, giving it limited field of fire.[17]

First pilot M3 tank from Chrysler Tank Arsenal, 12 April 1941 (*TACOM*).

The replacement for the M3 was the 32-ton M4 General Sherman tank, which had an all-welded body and its main gun, a 75-mm cannon, mounted on a turret that rotated a full 360 degrees. The M3's second largest gun, a 37-mm cannon, was not in the M4 design. In early October 1941, the Aberdeen Proving Ground sent the drawings for the M4 to Chrysler. By mid-November Chrysler had agreed in principle to make the M4 tank and to expand production at the tank arsenal to 750 tanks per month. In late March 1942, Chrysler signed supplemental agreements with the army for the production of 1,000 M4 tanks per month. The army authorized Chrysler to buy another forty acres of land at the tank arsenal and build an additional 500,000 square feet of floor space. The total cost of the new plant, including dies, jigs, tools, and machinery, was roughly $23 million. Chrysler completed the first handmade copy of the M4 on 27 June 1942 and the first production version on 22 July. The tank plant finished the last M3 on 3 August 1942, having produced 3,352 of them during the plant's first year of operation.[18]

The first batches of General Grant tanks used by British general Bernard L.

Montgomery against General Erwin Rommel's Afrika Corps helped stall Rommel's offensive designed to seize the Suez Canal. The initial shipment of General Grants arrived in North Africa in July 1942 and by mid-September 300 Shermans had arrived. By then, Rommel's offensive had stalled. Montgomery decisively defeated Rommel at the Second Battle of El Alamein on 23–24 October 1942 largely because he commanded a tank force that was vastly superior in numbers and quality to Rommel's. Montgomery had 1,200 tanks and more than half of them were Grants and Shermans. Rommel, in contrast, had about 500 tanks, but more than half were obsolete Italian models. He had 210 medium German tanks, but only thirty of the new Panzer IVs, which could match the American tanks in firepower and armor. The rest were outdated Panzer IIIs. Rommel's standard 50-mm antitank guns were not able to penetrate the armor of the American tanks or the British Valentine tank. By the time Rommel began his retreat in earnest, he had lost all but thirty of his tanks.[19]

Before putting the M4 Sherman tanks into production, Chrysler also designed a new tank engine. A modified 9-cylinder Wright radial aircraft engine made by Continental Motors had powered the M3 tanks. The Army Air Force needed these Wright engines for aircraft production, so the army asked Chrysler to develop a new engine for the M4. Rather than try to design an engine from scratch, Chrysler's engineers developed an innovative design using existing automobile engines. They took five 85-horsepower, 6-cylinder Chrysler engines, yielding 425 horsepower in total, installed an engine drive gear at the end of each crankshaft, and then meshed the gears together with a single large gear that turned the tank's driveshaft. Chrysler installed the first of these engines in a tank in mid-November 1941 for extensive testing and the engine was in full production by spring 1942. The first 109 of the new engines went into the last M3s produced by Chrysler. This "multibank" engine eventually powered 7,499 Sherman tanks.

In a 4,000-mile endurance test (11 October 1943 to 10 February 1944) against twelve tanks equipped with other engines, three of the four Chrysler tanks completed the full course while only one of the twelve competitors finished. One drawback of Chrysler's multibank engine was its larger size compared to other engines installed in tanks, leaving less space for ammunition and supplies. In October 1942 and again in December 1942, the Ordnance Department ordered Chrysler to switch back to Continental engines but then rescinded the order because those engines were needed elsewhere.[20]

American military and civilian leaders alike quickly recognized Chrysler's achievements at the tank arsenal. The army awarded the plant the Army-Navy "E" Pennant for production excellence on 10 August 1942, the first awarded to a defense plant. In September 1942, President Roosevelt made a secret twelve-day, cross-country tour of defense plants; no information about the tour was released until after he returned safely to Washington. The first stop on the tour was the tank arsenal, which Roosevelt visited on 18 September. The presidential train pulled into the arsenal complex at 1:30 P.M. and Roosevelt got into a seven-passenger Chrysler parade car for a drive through the plant and to the adjacent test track. Roosevelt observed gear-cutting, an engine and transmission being dropped into a tank, and about fifty tanks running through their paces at the test track. Roosevelt's train left after about an hour and continued on to the Willow Run bomber plant.[21]

After clamoring for 1,000 tanks a month from the plant, in September 1942 Army Ordnance cut tank production scheduled for the rest of the year by 40 percent because of steel shortages. The cutback in orders was moot, because the WPB never supplied Chrysler with enough machine tools to produce the larger volume. Still, the tank arsenal delivered 896 tanks in December 1942, its highest monthly output during the war and three times the number produced in January 1942.

Chrysler increased output at the tank arsenal by shifting most parts manufacturing to other plants, thereby converting the tank plant into an assembly operation. By June 1944, Chrysler was running five parallel tank assembly lines at the plant. Peak employment there was 6,212 in 1942 and for the rest of the war ranged between 4,500 and 5,500 workers. The automaker's work on tank production went well beyond the tank arsenal. In June 1944, Chrysler devoted 3,200,000 square feet of space at twelve plants to tank production, only 1,300,000 square feet of which was at the tank arsenal. About 14,000 employees worked on tank production in these other facilities, where Chrysler used more than 5,000 machine tools. For the assembly of M4 Sherman tanks, Chrysler supplied 1,269 components and relied on subcontractors for 3,268 parts.[22]

Over the course of the war, the Chrysler Tank Arsenal assembled a grand total of 22,235 tanks. The M3 accounted for only 3,352 of the total. The vast majority, a total of 17,948, were six different versions of the M4 tank, differentiated either by the engine or by the size of the main gun. Chrysler's tank production was nearly half of the auto industry's tank output of 49,676 units and more than one-quarter of combined U.S. production of 88,410 tanks from all sources.

The largest runs of tanks were the Shermans equipped with a 75-mm gun and the Chrysler multibank engine (7,499 produced) and Shermans powered by Ford engines (7,050). At the very end of the war, the arsenal produced the 45-ton M26 General Pershing tank, with 90-mm guns (500) and 105-mm howitzers (185). Chrysler also built two tanks that never saw battle: the T23, equipped with a Ford V-8 engine that powered an electric drive system developed by General Electric, and a model powered by a Caterpillar radial diesel engine. Chrysler also designed and built another dozen pilot and experimental models that never went into production.[23]

Assembly of M26 General Pershing Tanks at the Chrysler Tank Arsenal, 1945 *(CKH)*.

The end of the war brought an instant cancellation of the tank contracts and a quick end to work at the tank arsenal. The last Sherman tanks came off the line on 7 June 1945, but production of the General Pershing tank continued into late September. Employment at the tank plant, 5,074 workers on 1 June 1945, dropped to 3,446 a month later, slid further to 1,999 by 19 September, and by 19 October 1945 was down to a mere 520. Finally, on 26 October 1945, Chrysler Corporation officially turned the tank arsenal over to the Detroit Ordnance District.[24]

Fisher Body Tank Production

The U.S. Army Ordnance Department met with Fisher Body officials in Washington, D.C., in early September 1941 to begin preliminary discussions regarding the involvement of the Fisher Body Division of General Motors in building the (not-yet-designed) M4 medium tank. In late September the army asked Fisher Body to present proposals to build this tank model and Fisher submitted several proposals in October. The government officially accepted one of Fisher Body's proposals on 4

November 1941 and issued an initial letter of intent on 6 February 1942 covering 349 tanks. Additional letters of intent followed, and the Ordnance Department issued a formal contract on 6 April 1942 providing for the delivery of 4,324 M4A2 (General Sherman) tanks at a total contract price of $287,844,356 or $66,569 per tank. The designation M4A2 indicated that it was powered by GM twin diesel engines.[25]

Before Fisher Body had submitted its first proposal to the Ordnance Department, it had taken options on a 320-acre parcel of land in Grand Blanc, Michigan, just south of Flint. In mid-November 1941, the DPC agreed to provide $37,907,000 to Fisher Body and to the Buick Division of General Motors to build the facilities and acquire the machinery and tools needed for the tank program. Buick was to build the transmissions and final drives for the tanks. The bulk of the funding was for the Grand Blanc plant, but additional Fisher Body plants and several Buick plants received funding as well. Fisher Body's existing plants would provide 534,000 square feet for tank production and the new Grand Blanc plant an additional 526,000 square feet. The cost of more than 3,700 fixtures, jigs, dies, and special tools were included in the $38 million price tag. Among the machines was a 37-ton fixture used in welding steel armor plates to form the hull and a 40-ton fixture used for final assembly of the hull. Because the Ordnance Department had not supplied complete drawings for the all-welded hull, Fisher Body engineers had to redesign the hull and build the needed fixtures and jigs in the Fisher tool shops. Motive power for the Fisher-built M4A2 was provided by twin 210-horsepower diesel engines supplied by the Detroit Diesel Engine Division of General Motors.[26]

Construction was under way on the Grand Blanc tank plant in early January 1942, but Fisher Body went ahead with tank production in its other Flint plants well before the Grand Blanc plant started production in early June. The first completed tank drove out of a converted body plant in Flint on 7 March 1942. Before starting production at the new tank arsenal, Fisher Body delivered twenty Sherman tanks to the Ordnance Department starting in April 1942 and had another sixty-six partially completed. By the end of July, Fisher Body delivered 180 tanks to the Ordnance Department. By May 1943, thirteen months after production started, Fisher Body had completed 2,889 Sherman tanks. M4 tank production at Grand Blanc reached 2,240 units in 1943 and then peaked at 5,627 tanks in 1944 before falling off to only 2,148 units in 1945. The Ordnance Department approached Fisher Body in April 1943 about producing a new heavy tank weighing 44 tons and armed with a 90-mm main gun. This heavy tank was designated as the M26 or the T26 and was commonly known as the General Pershing. Fisher Body produced the first pilot heavy tank in May 1944 and the first production model in November 1944. By the end of the war, Fisher Body had built 1,542 M26 Pershing tanks and 11,595 M4 Sherman tanks, for a total production of 13,137 tanks. The Fisher Tank Arsenal was the third-largest tank producer during the war, after Chrysler and American Car & Foundry.[27]

Fisher Body also produced the M10 series 3-inch Gun Motor Carriage, better known as the M10 tank destroyer, at Grand Blanc. Tank destroyers were specifically designed to knock out enemy tanks and were not used in any other combat situations. The M10 was a clone of the M4A2 Shermans, with the same chassis and drivetrain. Both weighed roughly the same and could achieve a maximum speed of 25 mph. The M10 had a different turret than the Sherman tank and a 3-inch cannon as the main armament. The main gun had a firing range substantially greater than the M4 Sherman's 75-mm gun, making it a tank destroyer rather than a battle tank. Fisher Body received a letter contract from the Ordnance Department on 23 June 1942 to make 1,800 M10 tank destroyers. Fisher Body delivered the first tank destroyers to the army in September 1942, and when the contract expired in December 1943 the Grand Blanc plant had completed 5,668 M10s, including 375 equipped with Ford-built V-8 engines and 300 without turrets. Tank destroyer production, although it continued for only sixteen months, was a major part of Fisher Body's war work. As of June 1944, Fisher Body tank contracts in place (not all of which had been fulfilled) amounted to roughly $1,152,800,000. Contracts for the M4 Sherman tanks totaled $558 million or 48 percent of the total; T26 Pershing tank contracts amounted to $257 million or 22 percent of the total; and work on the M10 tank destroyer, already completed, came to $225 million or 20 percent of the total.[28]

Fisher Body also built two vital components for armored vehicles built by the Cadillac and Buick divisions of General Motors: turrets and hulls. In May 1942, the Ternstedt Manufacturing Division of Fisher Body, with plants in Detroit, began delivery of turrets for the M5 light tank, previously designated as the M4, built by Cadillac in Detroit. Through October 1943, Fisher Body delivered 3,681 M5 turrets to Cadillac and had orders for another 1,271. In August 1942, Ternstedt began production of turrets for the M8 Howitzer Gun Carriage, also built by Cadillac in Detroit. By October 1943, they had completed 1,633 M8 turrets and had orders in place for 482 more. At Grand Blanc, Fisher Body also built hulls and turrets for the T70 (Hellcat) tank destroyer (later renamed the M18), assembled by Buick in Flint. Fisher Body had orders in hand in October 1943 for 2,800 turrets and 1,800 hulls for the M18 Hellcat tank destroyer. At that point, Fisher Body had already delivered 462 turrets and was starting hull production.[29]

In January 1942 the Ordnance Department asked General Motors to design a lightweight, high-speed, track-laying tank destroyer. GM assigned the project to Buick, which fundamentally altered the original design. The Ordnance Department awarded Buick a contract for the Hellcat in January 1943 and the GM division

M18 Hellcat tank destroyer
production, Buick plant,
Flint, Michigan (*ACWP*).

began deliveries in June. The Hellcat, powered by a Continental air-cooled, 9-cylinder radial engine that developed 400 horsepower, could reach speeds of 50 mph. The Hellcat weighed less than 19 tons, in contrast to the M4, which weighed 30 to 34 tons. The lower weight was achieved by fitting the Hellcat with thin armor only one-inch thick compared to the normal four-inch armor found on battle tanks and by giving it an open-topped turret. The Hellcat came with a long-range 76-mm main gun, which, combined with the tank's speed and agility, allowed it to kill off enemy tanks while staying out the range of the enemy's guns. Buick eventually built 2,507 Hellcats in Flint.[30]

Cadillac Tank Production

While the Fisher Body Division of General Motors specialized in the production of medium and heavy tanks, Cadillac produced 10,142 light tanks during the war. On 29 May 1941, the Cadillac Division submitted a proposal to the Ordnance Department to build a light tank powered by twin Cadillac V-8 engines developing 296 horsepower in total and equipped with two Hydra-Matic transmissions connected through a transfer gear box (transfer case). The army's light tank at the time was the M3 Stuart tank, powered by a Continental air-cooled, 7-cylinder radial engine producing 262 horsepower. The Ordnance Department preferred to use the familiar air-cooled engine and manual transmission but had such a desperate need for tank engines that it was willing to compromise.

At the end of June 1941, the army sent Cadillac an M3 light tank to be fitted with a Cadillac drivetrain. The first experimental tank was completed on 18 September 1941 and successfully underwent exhaustive testing at the General Motors Proving Ground in Milford, Michigan, in late September. The Cadillac-powered tank could start and stop on a 60-degree grade and had improved hill-climbing ability, while the automatic transmission allowed for faster acceleration and higher speeds. Eliminating the pause when shifting gears also reduced the tank's vulnerability to enemy fire. The Ordnance Department endorsed the new design after the experimental tank proved its durability during a 500-mile drive under its own power from Detroit to the Aberdeen Proving Ground in Maryland in late October 1941.

Cadillac substantially redesigned the M3 light tank to accommodate the new drivetrain and made dozens of additional design improvements. Because of these changes, the Ordnance Department renamed the Cadillac version the M4 but quickly changed it to M5, also known as the Stuart, to avoid confusion with the General Sherman medium tank. The M5 weighed 17 tons, had a 37-mm gun as its main armament, and could achieve a maximum speed of 36 mph. It was the first combat vehicle with an automatic transmission, which quickly gained widespread acceptance.[31]

On 7 October 1941, Cadillac submitted a proposal to the Ordnance Department to deliver a pilot production tank four months after receipt of complete specifications and to start full production two months later. Cadillac received a letter of intent from Ordnance in early November initially calling for the production of seventy-five tanks. Converting plant space intended for automobile assembly to tank production was a challenge, but finding the needed machine tools, jigs, and fixtures was an even greater problem for Cadillac. Even before the tank design was complete, the company ordered 494 machine tools, mostly special-purpose ones that needed to be designed from scratch. In desperation, Cadillac sent three men to scour the country for used machine tools. The automaker assembled many of the early tanks by hand until the machine tools, jigs, and fixtures arrived. It also needed to find outside firms to supply many of the tank parts that it did not plan to manufacture. In January 1941, Cadillac created an exhibit of 189 tank parts in its new-car showroom and invited outside suppliers to examine the parts and to submit proposals to supply materials ranging from axle housings to oil pumps. Over the course of the war, Cadillac relied on thirty-nine major suppliers for its armored vehicle production and twelve of these were various divisions of General Motors.[32]

The M3 General Stuart had a riveted hull, but the Ordnance Department notified Cadillac early in its redesign of the M3 that the new version would have a welded hull. This presented Cadillac with several problems, including finding a source of homogeneous armor plate, which could be welded, versus the previously standard face-hardened armor plate, which was nearly impossible to weld. Cadillac helped establish the Standard Steel Spring Company, which had a plant in Detroit, as a supplier of armor plate for Cadillac and for other manufacturers of armored vehicles. Cadillac had no experience in welding armor plate, so it fine-tuned electric arc welding to prevent buckling of the armor plates. The automaker needed to design fixtures capable of holding armor plates weighing up to two tons. Cadillac also established a welding school to train workers in the fine art of arc welding.[33]

Cadillac's tank contract, based on the original letter of intent of 6 November 1941, called for the production of 3,266 M5 tanks; a supplemental contract of 27 April 1942 included an additional 6,000 M5s, bringing the total to 9,266. Cadillac completed its first pilot tank in early March 1942 and the first production tank at the end of the month. To meet the demand for the M5, the Ordnance Department awarded contracts to the Massey-Harris Implement Manufacturing Company to assemble Cadillac-designed M5s in Racine, Wisconsin, and to Cadillac to build them at its assembly plant in South Gate, California, near Los Angeles. By July 1942, M5s were coming off the production lines in Racine and in South Gate. By the end of the year, Cadillac's Detroit plant shipped 2,174 M5s, the South Gate plant completed 427 units, and Massey-Harris another 254 units.[34]

The Ordnance Department also asked Cadillac to produce a companion model to the M5, the M8 75-mm Howitzer Motor Carriage. The two vehicles shared the same power train, chassis, and hull but had different turrets. With its open-topped turret, the M8 was not really a tank in the usual sense but a self-propelled gun. On 23 May 1942, the Ordnance Department awarded Cadillac a contract for 2,116 M8 Howitzers and a supplemental contract in early September for an additional 2,127 units, for a total of 4,243. Cadillac shipped its first production M8 on 3 September 1942 and a total of 373 in 1942. Shipments of the M8 peaked at 1,330 units in 1943, and following the termination of the Ordnance contract in mid-January 1944 Cadillac shipped only 75 M8s in 1944, for a grand total of 1,778 units.[35]

In 1943, the Cadillac Detroit plant turned out 1,772 M5s, the South Gate plant 1,123, and the Massey-Harris factory an additional 756, for a grand total of 4,981. In late August 1943, the South Gate plant stopped assembling M5s and converted to aircraft manufacturing. In the fall of 1943, Ordnance issued contracts for the new M24 light tank, which would replace the M5. In October 1943, Ordnance terminated contracts with Cadillac for 2,125 M5s, reducing the contracts in place from

8,675 units to 6,550 units. Cadillac shipped its last M5 on 31 May 1944, for a total of 1,054 for the year, and focused its efforts on the M24.[36]

The last tank Cadillac produced in quantity during the war was the M24 Chaffee light tank, which weighed twenty tons, carried a 75-mm gun, and was powered by the same Cadillac drivetrain used in the M5. Preliminary design work began on the T24 (later the M24) light tank in mid-December 1942 at the request of the Ordnance Department. Cadillac received its first contract (for 1,000 M24s) on 26 November 1943, with supplemental contracts in April and May 1944 for an additional 2,098 units, for a total of 3,098. By mid-March 1945, Cadillac had orders in place for 7,926 M24s, but the end of the war meant the cancellation of most of those orders. The company shipped the first production M24 to Fort Benning, Georgia, on 13 April 1944. Cadillac and Massey-Harris became the exclusive manufacturers of the M24: the two firms shipped 1,740 and 190 M24s, respectively, in 1944. After a spate of contract cancellations that began on 11 May 1945, three days after V-E Day, Cadillac delivered a total of 3,592 M24s to the Ordnance Department and Massey-Harris completed 1,139 units.[37]

The Ford Motor Company

Although the Ford Motor Company built a relatively small number of tanks (1,683 M4A3s) and tank destroyers (1,038 M10A1s), it was a substantial contributor to tank manufacturing nationally as a result of its production of armored plate and tank engines for other manufacturers. Because of this, and because much of its production was never covered by formal contracts, the company's relationship with the Ordnance Department was more complex and confusing than was the case for other tank manufacturers.

Ford and the Ordnance Department began discussions in mid-August 1941 about the possibility of the automaker producing tanks. On 17 September 1941 Edsel Ford, Charles Sorensen, and other Ford officials discussed possible tank production with Ordnance representatives in Washington, D.C. The army asked Ford to submit a proposal to build 400 tanks a month, 2,350 tanks in total. Five days later, Ford engineers went to the Aberdeen Proving Ground to view a pilot tank and to work with Ordnance to help complete the blueprints for the M4 tank. On 10 October 1941 Edsel Ford informed the army that Ford would manufacture the M4 tank, and five days later the War Department issued a letter of intent to Ford authorizing the company to spend $2 million to get started before a contract was issued. Ford submitted a proposal on 23 October to supply armor castings and armor plate and to assemble the tanks in facilities that would cost $45,190,000.

Ford and the Ordnance Department exchanged a series of proposals and counterproposals from October through early December 1941. Finally, the Ordnance Department offered Ford a contract on 9 December 1941 authorizing the construction of manufacturing facilities costing no more than $38,364,949 to build 400 M4 tanks per month. This was a CPFF contract that would pay Ford $59,000 per tank, including a fixed fee of $3,540 (6 percent). Ford signed the agreement on 15 December 1941, but the two parties did not sign the definitive contract, which included supplemental agreements, until 5 May 1942. The M4 medium tank was designated as the M4A3 when equipped with Ford's V-8 tank engine.[38]

Although Ford received its first order for tanks from the Ordnance Department on 15 November 1941 (1 pilot model and 349 tanks), the company did not finish the pilot model until 13 May 1942 and the first production tank did not roll off the assembly line until 4 June 1942. There were several reasons for this delay. The final design of the M4 was not settled until late January 1942, but more important, Ford had to first start the production of armor plate, armor castings, gun mounts, and tank engines.[39]

Tanks built before World War II typically were constructed with one-inch steel plates to protect against small arms fire. World War II tanks were fitted with three- or four-inch armor plate to protect against artillery fire, and the armor accounted for more than half of the tank's weight. Face-hardened armor plate, that is, plate hardened on only one side, was used extensively early in the war, but the alloy steel used to make it included a lot of nickel, which was in short supply. Homogeneous armor plate, which was uniformly hard throughout its depth, used little nickel and was easier to machine, weld, and cast. It quickly became the Ordnance Department's preferred armor.[40]

Although several versions of the M3 medium tank used riveted plates to form the hull, the design of the M4 used a cast steel armored turret and a hull consisting of welded plates. Even before Pearl Harbor, the existing plants capable of making steel armor castings or rolled armor plate were woefully inadequate to meet the Ordnance Department's projected armored vehicle needs. Starting in September 1941, the Ordnance Department and the DPC authorized the expansion of nearly all of the existing plants that made steel armor castings. Ford produced steel armor castings for its tanks on a temporary basis in several of its foundries at the Ford Rouge plant until it opened its Ordnance Foundry, with a capacity of 10,000 tons of castings per month, in mid-September 1942. Ford also developed an improved method to prevent armor plate from warping while it was being rapidly quenched after the initially rolling. By holding the rolled plates in fixtures, the company prevented warping and reduced production costs to about three cents per pound of armor plate. The same armor plate from other manufacturers typically cost thirty-five to fifty cents per pound. Ford not only saved the government a significant sum on the production of the tanks it built but also supplied armor plate to c   tank manufacturers.[41]

By June 1940 Ford had begun to develop a li   cooled V-12 engine for use in aircraft entirely on its own, with no government contract or assistance. Cornelius Van Ranst, the engineer who designed the engine, used an aluminum cylinder block and crankcase in a single unit. Ford converted this design into a tank engine by removing four cylinders, resulting in a V-8 engine producing 450 horsepower. (This engine should not be confused with the puny [75-horsepower] V-8 Henry Ford introduced in 1933.) On 3 November 1941, the Ordnance Department asked Ford to build a sample tank engine, and a month later Ford was preparing the machine tools to make tank engines in quantity. The company finished its first engine in April 1942 and began operating the engine pilot line on 1 May 1942. Ford finally signed a contract with the Ordnance Department on 20 May 1942 to make tank engines.[42]

Once Ford went into production, the government increased the tank engine delivery schedule from twenty engines per day to forty and, in time, to forty-five. Ford devoted 570,000 square feet of factory space to tank engine production, with roughly two-thirds of the space at its Lincoln plant in Detroit, where Ford built an aluminum foundry and carried out final assembly, and the remaining one-third at the Rouge plant. Over the course of the war, Ford received contracts to produce slightly more than 40,000 tank engines, but with revisions and cancellations to their contracts the company completed 26,954 tank engines in four slightly different versions. The largest annual production was 11,208 engines in 1944, with peak monthly output of 1,287 engines in November of that year. Ford installed 1,690 engines in the M4A3 tanks it built and another 1,038 engines in Ford-built M10A1 tank destroyers. The remaining 24,226 engines were installed in tanks built by other manufacturers or became part of the inventory of spare tank engines kept in stock at home and abroad to replace those that failed or were damaged.[43]

The Army Ordnance Department in time awarded Ford contracts to build 4,050 M4A3 tanks and 2,990 of the closely related M10A1 tank destroyer, also called a "Three-Inch Gun Motor Carriage." The tank destroyer used the same chassis and drivetrain as the M4A3 tank but had a different upper hull structure and was equipped with a three-inch cannon. Once the contract for tank destroyers was finalized in October 1942, Ford assembled the two vehicles on parallel assembly lines at its Highland Park plant. Ford devoted more than two million square feet of factory space to produce the two vehicles: nearly 890,000 square feet at the Rouge plant, 790,000 square feet at Highland Park, and 380,000 square feet at the Lincoln plant. Ford also established a tank and tank engine training school at the Lincoln plant in

September 1942 to teach army and civilian mechanics how to operate and repair the equipment. Ford eventually trained more than 7,000 tank and tank engine service men at this school.[44]

Ford successfully produced tanks and tank destroyers but received notice in the middle of 1943 that its contracts would be terminated. In a desperate effort to ramp-up tank production, Army Ordnance had issued tank contracts in 1941–42 to sixteen manufacturers but by the summer of 1943 found itself with excess capacity given the projected needs for 1944. Ordnance ended its contracts with three railroad equipment manufacturers: Pacific Car and Foundry, Lima Locomotive, and Pullman-Standard, and with Ford. The remaining auto plants under contract to make the M4 tanks, Chrysler and Fisher Body, operated government-owned factories, whereas Ford did not. The government also wanted Ford to devote more resources to producing the B-24 Liberator. The Ordnance Department canceled orders for 1,524 tank destroyers on 7 May 1943, orders for 1,814 M4A3 tanks on 14 July 1943, and finally, in August 1943, orders for 974 additional units of both vehicles. The last tanks and tank destroyers rolled off the Ford assembly line in September 1943. The tanks (1,690) and tank destroyers (1,038) that Ford delivered to the government represented less than half of the orders Ford had accepted.[45]

Although ultimately successful in producing large numbers of reasonably reliable tanks, the Ordnance Department's tank procurement system seemed in many respects inefficient and chaotic, especially when contrasted with the system used by the Army Air Force to procure aircraft and aircraft engines. There were too many tank models produced during the war and probably too many manufacturers involved. Seventeen firms manufactured tanks, but five of these (Chrysler Corporation, American Car & Foundry, Fisher Body Company, the Cadillac Motor Car Company, and the Pressed Steel Corporation) built 78.6 percent of the 88,410 tanks produced between 1 July 1940 and 31 December 1945. Three automakers (Fisher Body, Buick, and Ford) manufactured slightly more than half of the 17,944 tank destroyers produced during the same period.[46]

Challenges to the Tank Production Program

The Ordnance Department had to face three persistent challenges throughout the war: drastic shifts in the "mix" of tanks the U.S. Army demanded between light, medium, and heavy types; its own failure to develop standard engines to power American tanks; and the need to modify tanks after they left the factory. Until the middle of 1940, tanks were under the control of the infantry, which viewed tanks merely as a supporting element for advancing foot soldiers. Light tanks would serve that purpose, and in 1940 all but six of the 331 tanks delivered to the army were of the light variety. However, the German army's stunning victories over the French, British, and Belgian forces in May and June 1940 using light and medium tanks, dive bombers, and mechanized infantry caused the U.S. Army to rethink how tanks could be used. The army established a separate Armored Force on 10 July 1940 and accelerated plans to build both light and medium tanks. For all of 1941, American industry managed to deliver 2,591 light tanks and 1,761 mediums to the Ordnance Department, but no heavy tanks. The production of light tanks peaked in 1942 at 10,947 units but had already been surpassed by medium tank production (13,746).[47]

Army Ordnance quickly replaced the badly flawed General Grant with the much-improved General Sherman, which became the mainstay of the American armored forces. The total production of tanks during the war included 28,919 light tanks, 57,027 mediums (6,258 Grants, 50,385 Shermans, and some others), and only 2,464 heavy tanks. The Shermans performed well for the British in the early stages of the 1942 North African campaign, when they were often opposed by outdated German tanks. The Shermans were known for their maneuverability in mountainous terrain and their overall reliability. The engines in German Panther tanks, for example, had a life expectancy of about 600 miles, whereas Sherman tank engines often lasted for 3,000 miles. The German army had frantically developed a new series of heavy tanks after their Panzer II, III, and IV models were practically annihilated by heavily armored and heavily gunned Soviet heavy tanks in the second half of 1940 after Germany invaded the Soviet Union. When the Shermans faced German Tiger (Panzer VI) tanks in North Africa and Panther tanks in Italy and France in 1943, they were outgunned and had much weaker armor. The Tiger had an 88-mm main gun, versus the Sherman's 75-mm gun. In direct tank-to-tank confrontations, the Shermans lost. The American troops derisively called them "Ronsons" after the cigarette lighter because of their tendency to blow up when enemy fire pierced their armor. Later versions known as "wet Shermans" had water jackets that surrounded their ammunition and reduced the incendiary risks. The Armored Force had many more tanks than the Germans and could afford to sacrifice them in large numbers. Armored units avoided head-to-head confrontations with the German tanks and instead surrounded them with superior numbers and launched flank attacks.[48]

Even though the Sherman's inferiority to the heavy German tanks was clear by early 1943, heavy tanks were not produced in significant numbers until 1945 and few ever saw combat. The Ordnance Department aggressively pushed for the development of a heavy tank, while the Armored Force steadfastly resisted its use. In spring 1940, Ordnance began developing a 50-ton tank equipped with a 3-inch gun and powered by a 925-horsepower engine. The Baldwin Locomotive Works received a contract to build this tank, identified as the M6, in August 1940, and the company unveiled a pilot model the day after Pearl Harbor. Roosevelt's ambitious tank program called for 500 heavy tanks to be completed in 1942 and 5,000 in 1943. Baldwin and Fisher Body were contracted to build the heavy tanks, but in September 1942 the army cut the heavy tank orders to a mere 115 units. The Armored Force then announced in December 1942 that it had no need for the heavy tank and urged an end to production. The Armored Force further discredited the M6 as unacceptable for combat use because of multiple design defects. The top army officers took the position that they needed only Shermans and tank destroyers to counter the German tank forces. Baldwin completed only forty heavy tanks in 1942–44. The Ordnance Department worked on an improved heavy tank and in June 1944 won approval to build a new heavy tank, the T26, later renamed the M26 General Pershing. The new tank weighed 46 tons, was fitted with a 90-mm main gun, and was powered by a 500-horsepower engine. The Fisher Body tank arsenal completed 50 M26 Pershing tanks in late 1944 and the Detroit Tank Arsenal and Fisher built a total of 2,374 M26 tanks in 1945, but only a handful ever saw combat.[49]

In addition to fighting wrongheaded thinking from top army officers, Ordnance had to struggle to produce enough tank engines to power the growing armored forces. When the Ordnance Department tried to jump-start tank production in 1940, there were no engines available that were specifically designed for use in tanks. Ordnance had no funds in the late 1930s to develop such engines, and the auto industry had no reason to design engines to produce more than 350 horsepower. Ordnance initially planned to power its tanks with diesel air-cooled radial engines manufactured by the Guiberson Diesel Engine Company of Texas and with gasoline radial engines from the Wright Aeronautical Company. Because aircraft and ships had higher priority, thousands of engines earmarked for tanks were commandeered by the Army Air Force and the navy. Out of desperation, the Ordnance Department supported the development of multiple tank engine designs. By the end of 1942, American industry was building M4 Sherman tanks with five different engines. The lack of a standard engine for medium tanks meant that battlefield maintenance and repairs were difficult, simply in terms of having the correct parts and qualified mechanics available.

In early September 1940, the Ordnance Department awarded Continental Motors Corporation of Detroit a contract to build 200 tank engines a month starting in October 1941. In November 1940, the DPC provided Continental with $8 million to prepare its idled Detroit factory to produce the R-975 air-cooled radial engine under license from the Wright Aeronautical Corporation. In 1941–45, Continental produced 54,104 of these engines for use in tanks. The R-975 engine proved problematic when first installed in the 30-ton M3 General Grant medium tank. It overheated, consumed excessive oil, and produced only 340 horsepower instead of its rated 400 horsepower. Continental tweaked the design, reduced the overheating problem, and increased the engine's output. Despite its shortcomings, the Continental R-975 radial engine was the standard power plant for medium tanks produced in 1940–42 until other tank engines came into production.[50]

Chrysler's multibank engine, which generated 425 horsepower, came into full production in spring 1942 and powered 109 M3 General Grants and 7,499 M4 Shermans, all produced at the Detroit Tank Arsenal. Most of the multibank-engine Shermans went to the British under Lend-Lease. Because the initial multibank engine was simply five engines linked together, the engine had five water pumps, five generators, five distributors, and five of many other components, making maintenance and repairs difficult. Because the engine fit tightly into the tank, some repairs were almost impossible to complete. Chrysler modified the design, by replacing five water pumps with a single one and improving access to areas needing regular maintenance or repairs. In September 1943, after the shortage of tank engines eased, the Ordnance Department discontinued the multibank engine.[51]

The Ordnance Department also encouraged the development of diesel tank engines, but had to confront an about-face from the army regarding the use of diesel-powered combat vehicles. Before March 1942, the Armored Force favored the complete dieselization of tanks and other combat vehicles but then reversed its position and advocated an all-gasoline fleet. There were deep concerns expressed about the availability of diesel fuel in most theaters of operation. Military planners recognized the inherent problems in building and operating dual systems to supply the forces with gasoline and diesel fuel. However, production of diesel engines in quantity was well under way before this policy reversal, so the Ordnance Department kept the orders in place and by the end of the war had installed more than 12,000 diesel engines in American-built tanks. Some of the diesel tanks remained in the United States and were used for training purposes, but the bulk of them went to Great Britain and the Soviet Union through Lend-Lease.[52] The Texas-based Guiberson Diesel Engine Company, which had supplied air-cooled radial diesel engines for light tanks since the mid-1930s, developed a larger engine, the T-1400, which developed 370 horsepower and was intended to power medium tanks. Army Ordnance tested the new design, and in September 1941 the Armored Force Board approved its use in medium tanks as a replacement for the Continental radial engine. American Locomotive Company (ALCO) equipped twenty-eight M3 medium tanks with Guiberson engines starting in February 1942. After awarding Guiberson Diesel an $8 million engine contract and providing a new plant in Garland, Texas, to build the engines, the Ordnance Department soon determined that the engines were unreliable and in April 1942 abruptly canceled the contract. In July, Ordnance turned the Garland plant over to Continental Motors for the production of additional R-975 gasoline air-cooled radial engines.[53]

The second diesel engine used in tanks was a General Motors two-stroke twin diesel engine consisting of two 6-cylinder engines linked though a transfer gear box. The engine, designated as the GM 6046, displaced 850 cubic inches and was rated at 420 horsepower. General Motors delivered a pilot tank with the new engine to the Aberdeen Proving Ground on the final day of December 1941. The Army tested the new engine for four months, running the tank over 4,200 miles in the process. Despite some minor faults, the engine performed well and the Ordnance Department ordered these engines in large numbers. One of the main advantages of diesels over gasoline engines was that they developed more torque at low engine speeds, required fewer gear changes, and achieved greater power and speed. Baldwin Locomotive installed 322 GM diesels in M3 General Grants, but the bulk of these engines went into M4 Shermans. Fisher Body installed 8,053 in Shermans built at the Grand Blanc tank arsenal, while four other manufacturers (ALCO, Baldwin, Federal Machine, and Pullman Standard) used an additional 3,071 GM diesels, yielding a total of 11,124 Shermans powered by these engines.[54]

The third diesel engine was a radial air-cooled design manufactured by the Caterpillar Tractor Company starting in 1943. Caterpillar modified a gasoline-powered Wright Aeronautical Cyclone radial aircraft engine to burn diesel fuel in late 1942. Following successful trials, in late January 1943 the Ordnance Department ordered 775 of these engines from Caterpillar. Chrysler installed these diesel engines, which developed 450 horsepower, in the M4A6 version of the Sherman tank at the end of October 1943, but completed only seventy-five when the Ordnance Department suspended production in February 1944. The reason for this suspension is not known.[55]

The Ford Motor Company's V-8 gasoline tank engine, discussed earlier, deserves another look. Ford reduced the weight of the engine considerably by using aluminum castings extensively in the engine components, including the cylinder block and crankcase. As a result, the Ford GAA engine was 2,825 pounds lighter than the GM twin diesel engine and only 200 pounds heavier than the Continental radial engine. The Ford engine also produced 450 horsepower, the highest output of all the tank engines, which also gave it the best power-to-weight ratio. After undergoing extensive testing at the Aberdeen Proving Ground in July 1943, the Ford GAA engine was approved by the Ordnance Department as the preferred engine for medium tanks. It was also preferred by tank fighting personnel and mechanics alike for its reliability

General Motors Detroit diesel plant, twin tank engines (ACWP).

and ease of maintenance. Were it not for limitations on Ford's production capacity, their engine might have become the standard power plant for medium tanks. Ford produced a total of 26,954 tank engines during the war but used only 2,728 of them for the tanks and tank destroyers it assembled. The rest went to other manufacturers of the M4 medium tank.[56]

Faced with the need to modify tanks after they left the assembly line, Army Ordnance, much like the Army Air Force, developed tank modification centers or tank depots away from the factories. Ordnance faced two problems that led to the creation of these facilities. Completed tanks needed to be fitted with a variety of additional equipment, such as radios, which were the responsibility of the government and not the tank contractor. Thousands of tanks going overseas through Lend-Lease, particularly to Great Britain and the Soviet Union, needed special equipment. British tanks, for example, required sand shields, smoke generators, and smoke bomb throwers. Design modifications ordered after tanks were assembled were also best carried out away from the production line. As was the case with the Army Air Force, the Ordnance Department did not want stockpiles of tanks that needed work to collect at the factories because this lowered morale. Tanks destined for overseas shipment also needed special treatment to prevent damage during transit.[57]

The Ordnance Department took control of the New York Central Railroad shops in Toledo, Ohio, in January 1942 and hired the Electric Auto-Lite Company to operate it as a tank depot. Shortly thereafter, the Ford Motor Company opened tank depots in vacant assembly plants at Chester, Pennsylvania, and at Richmond, California, both with easy access to rail and water transportation. In December 1942, Ordnance replaced the Toledo tank depot with one in Lima, Ohio, managed by the United Motors Service Division of General Motors. There were serious backlogs of unfinished tanks through most of 1942, when there were severe shortages of tracks. By March 1943, this and other shortages were resolved and the tank depots operated effectively for the remainder of the war.[58]

Although the Ordnance Department got a late start in tank procurement, and despite all the missteps, false starts, changing policies, faulty tank designs, the lack of standardization of tank engines, and other problems, many of its own doing, the overall record for tank production was impressive. The American production total of 88,410 tanks in 1940–45 was nearly four times the British total of 24,803 and the German record of 24,360. These comparisons are not entirely fair for reasons other than the much larger size of the American economy. Germany was able to turn out only 988 tanks in 1945 after the Allies crippled Germany's industrial capacity and then occupied the country. Because it was able to meet much of its tank requirements through Lend-Lease, Great Britain manufactured only 2,476 tanks in the first six months of 1944 and none in the final year of the war.[59]

American manufacturers not only supplied the U.S. military with an adequate supply of tanks but also satisfied much of the tank requirements of its allies through Lend-Lease. The United States supplied its Lend-Lease partners with 37,323 tanks (42 percent of American tank production). The British Empire took 27,751 tanks, including 20,071 medium tanks, predominantly M4 Shermans. More than half the tanks used by British forces were American-made. The Soviet Union received 7,172 tanks and the French forces took another 1,406 units.[60]

American-made tanks, despite their flaws and imperfections, received much praise from users of all ranks. British general Bernard L. Montgomery praised all the American tanks, starting with the M3 Stuart light tank. He described the M3 Grants as the first tanks used by the British Eighth Army in North Africa with the capability of destroying the German tanks. The Grants were "a tower of strength during the days when the war went against us in Egypt" and credited the Grant and Sherman tanks with the British victory at El Alamein. Montgomery praised the workers who built the Shermans at the various American tank plants: "I would like them to realize

U.S. Fifth Army M4 Sherman tanks lined up for assault on
German positions near Pistraloma, Italy, October 1944 (*ACWP*).

how these Sherman M4s have dominated the German tanks and driven them from
the battlefield wherever we have met them." In August 1944, a marine private sent
a letter to a friend in Detroit describing his encounter with a Chrysler-built Sherman tank on Tinian Island in the Pacific. He was lying on the ground in a sugarcane
field, wounded by Japanese machine-gun fire, when a tank rolled up next to him.
He crawled to some harder ground, the tank drove right over him, and the tank crew
pulled him up into the tank through the escape hatch and then delivered him to the
medics. In his own words, "tanks are mighty fine things—mighty fine!"[61]

Other Armored Vehicles

The automobile industry and others produced an almost bewildering variety of vehicles for the military during World War II. All trucks, including jeeps, will be treated
in the next chapter, as will amphibious vehicles. Most amphibians were not armored,
including amphibious jeeps and the General Motors "Duck," while the Studebaker
"Weasel" had only very light armor. Amphibious landing vehicles (LTVs) were not
manufactured by automobile companies, so they will be excluded here, as will half-
tracked vehicles, although American industry built 39,328 of them during the war.
Three truck manufacturers—the White Motor Company, Autocar, and the Diamond
T Motor Company—built some of these, but surviving records are too skimpy to

adequately cover the manufacture of these vehicles. Earlier parts of this chapter covered tank destroyers made by auto companies, but there were also scores of other types of "motor carriages for self-propelled weapons" manufactured for which there is little available information, including anti-aircraft guns (19,784 produced) and medium field artillery (6,696 units). The remainder of this chapter will focus instead on armored cars and universal carriers.[62]

The Ford Motor Company was the dominant producer of armored cars, accounting for 12,564 of the 16,438 delivered to the Ordnance Department during the war. Ford developed plans and specifications for a 6 X 6 (six-wheel drive) wheeled armor car in the summer of 1941 and submitted a proposal to make 2,260 of them, dubbed the T17. On the day following Pearl Harbor, Ford received a contract to build two pilot T17s. The Ordnance Department sent Ford a purchase order by letter on 6 February 1942 authorizing the company to manufacture 2,260 T17 armored cars at a cost not to exceed $67,067,800. Ford would build the T17 at its Twin City Branch Assembly plant in St. Paul, Minnesota. The T17 armored car weighed about 25,000 pounds, making it as heavy as a light tank. The Ordnance Department preferred a much lighter vehicle and soon discontinued production of the T17 in favor of the T22 (M8), which will be discussed shortly. In typical government fashion, Ordnance increased its order for the T17 to 3,760 units (more than $114 million) on 26 November 1942 by mail, two days after reducing the contract to 250 units by telegram. Between October 1942 and mid-March 1943, Ford completed only 250 of the T17s at its Twin City plant.[63]

Ford also began design work on a lighter armored car, the T22 (later the M8) in August 1941 when it designed the T17. Ordnance asked Ford to build two pilot T22 light armored cars in November. Ford completed its first T22 pilot model in March 1942, which underwent testing in Dearborn, Aberdeen, and Fort Knox, Kentucky. On 10 July 1942, Ford received a formal contract covering 2,260 T22s, but this grew to cover 11,070 units by the end of July. The vehicle was still undergoing design modifications and both Ford and Chrysler developed competing designs. The Ford design used no chassis frame (Chrysler's did), so the hull served as the frame. Ford's design had a lower profile, always desirable, and used a synchronized transmission, whereas Chrysler's did not. The Ordnance Department ordered Ford to put its design into production, and in the fall of 1943 the Armored Force Board selected the Ford T22, renamed the M8, as the army's standard armored car.[64]

The M8 armored car was a light armored vehicle with 3/8-inch and ¾-inch armor, with six wheels and six-wheel drive. It weighed 14,500 pounds, less than two-thirds the weight of the T17 armored car, and featured a cast steel turret fitted with a 37-mm rifle. This was a high-speed reconnaissance vehicle the British called the

Greyhound because of its maximum speed of 56 mph. Ford simultaneously developed a clone, the M20 (originally the T26 Armored Command Car) Armored Utility Car, which weighed slightly more than 6 tons, was an open-topped vehicle with a square crew compartment instead of a turret, and came with 50-caliber machine gun instead of the 37-mm rifle. The two vehicles were otherwise identical.

Ford made its initial proposal to manufacture 6,622 T26s at the end of May 1942 and the Ordnance Department gave Ford a purchase order by letter on 29 March 1943 authorizing $20 million for 6,622 T26s. Ford started production of the M8 simultaneously at its Twin City and Chicago plants in March 1943. Production of the T26s, renamed the M20, began in Chicago in mid-April. Contracts for both vehicles were canceled on 17 August 1945. Over the life of these contracts, Ford produced 6,397 M8s at the Twin City plant and another 2,127 at the Chicago plant, for a grand total of 8,524 M8s. The Chicago plant also assembled 3,790 M20s, making Ford the dominant manufacturer of light armored vehicles. The total value of Ford's armored car contracts was $151.6 million, the fifth largest for Ford after Liberator bombers, Pratt & Whitney engines, tanks and tank engines, and jeeps.[65]

The final armored vehicle to be considered in this chapter is the Ford-built Universal Carrier, which was produced at Ford's Somerville Branch Assembly plant near Boston. This vehicle was originally designed by the British in the 1930s as a light armored vehicle to transport troops across areas swept by enemy fire. Its light armor, speed, and maneuverability made it an ideal vehicle for this purpose. The Ordnance Department began negotiating with Ford in February 1942 to manufacture the Universal Carrier. At the request of Ordnance, Ford's engineers made major design changes and conducted extensive testing before the company agreed to make it. The redesigned version was a full track-laying, right-hand drive vehicle with light armor, driven by a 100-horsepower Mercury engine. The Ordnance Department sent Ford a letter of intent dated 30 September 1942 authorizing Ford to proceed with the manufacture of 21,000 Universal Carriers. The Somerville plant produced the first unit in March 1943 and turned out only 45 units in the first three months but then increased output dramatically. June production of 290 units jumped to 858 units in November 1943 and peaked at 1,040 units in June 1944. Ordnance reduced the size of the contracts later in 1944, and Somerville turned out only 122 Universal Carriers in May 1945, the last month of production. Ford produced a total of 13,893 Universal Carriers with a contract value of $101,946,000. All of them were sent to British forces under Lend-Lease.[66]

American industry produced a total of 249,083 combat vehicles, virtually all of them armored, during the war. This total includes tanks (88,410), motor carriages for self-propelled weapons (46,706), and other combat vehicles (113,967), which included armored cars, cargo carriers, personnel carriers, and command cars. A relatively small share of self-propelled weapons went to U.S. allies (7,275 units out of 46,706), but the United States provided its allies with 47,629 other combat vehicles described earlier (42 percent of U.S. production). The vast majority of these (40,059) went to the British Empire.[67]

This was an impressive achievement, and these vehicles, particularly tanks, played a vital role in the outcome of the war. Looking at the larger picture, the 2.4 million trucks built during the war, almost entirely by the automobile industry, were more important. World War II was largely a motorized war in which troops and everything needed to sustain them moved by truck. The next chapter will examine the automobile industry's performance in supplying trucks, including jeeps and various amphibious vehicles, to the military.[68]

SIX

Jeeps, Trucks, and Amphibious Vehicles

In stark contrast to the Ordnance Department's decision to use five different engines in Sherman tanks, the Quartermaster Corps, which was responsible for providing the military with trucks, moved decisively toward standardization of truck designs before the onset of World War II, and for good reason. During World War I, American troops in France had more than two hundred different makes of trucks, including many from British, French, Italian, and Spanish manufacturers, along with captured German trucks. Maintaining and repairing this fleet of trucks was nearly impossible. Between the wars, the Quartermaster General tried to standardize truck models within each weight class but was stymied by federal law requiring competitive bidding when purchasing trucks. When the army wanted to buy new trucks, scores of manufacturers would submit bids. A different manufacturer would typically win each of the various contracts, so the army had a mishmash of vehicles between the wars.

In a memorandum dated 19 June 1940 addressed to the assistant secretary of war, Quartermaster General Edmund T. Gregory asked for an end to competitive bidding for truck procurement. His memorandum carried the endorsements of the chiefs of the four using arms: Infantry, Cavalry, Field Artillery, and Coast Artillery. By 1939 the army had settled on five chassis types for general-purpose trucks, based on the load capacity: ½-ton, 1½-ton, 2½-ton, 4-ton, and 7½-ton. In 1940 the army added a ¼-ton chassis, replaced the ½-ton chassis with a ¾-ton chassis, and added three chassis to fill the gap between the 4-ton and the 7½-ton, bringing the total to nine chassis types. Gregory requested authorization to negotiate contracts with only one truck maker for each chassis type. He wanted to start negotiations immediately with the Dodge Division of Chrysler, General Motors, and Mack and to award each of them an exclusive contract for a particular model. The assistant secretary of war approved this new approach, pending congressional approval, but with conditions attached.[1]

The Quartermaster General (QG) was required to ask for written bids for a particular contract and then enter negotiations with some of the bidders before recommending a single manufacturer for the work. Only about fifteen days were allowed between the request for proposals, which was publicly advertised, and the opening of bids. On 2 July 1940, Congress had authorized war contracting "with or without advertising." The Quartermaster Corps (QC) was not required to accept the lowest bid and, after early February 1941, was instructed to discontinue public advertising altogether. It could reject proposals based on its judgment of the manufacturer's production capabilities or engineering competence. The development and production of the jeep, to be discussed shortly, illustrates how this new procurement system worked. The second major change to truck procurement came in mid-July 1942 when Lieutenant General Brehon B. Somervell transferred responsibility for trucks from the QC to the Ordnance Department, which was already responsible for tanks. Having only one army department dealing with the automobile industry made the tank and truck procurement system more efficient. By then, the secretary of war had standardized eight truck chassis for military use, ranging from the ¼-ton, 4 X 4 truck (jeep) to the 6-ton, 6 X 6 truck. The official army designation for trucks indicated the total number of wheels and the driving wheels, so a 4 X 2 has four wheels but only two driving wheels. A 4 X 4 is a four-wheel, four-wheel-drive truck.[2]

The Jeep

In the late 1930s the army was considering a lightweight, fast four-wheel-drive truck that could be used as a command or reconnaissance vehicle.[3] In late May 1940, the QC asked 135 manufacturers to submit proposals for a 4 X 4 ¼-ton vehicle with an 80-inch wheelbase, weighing no more than 1,300 pounds. The companies submitting proposals would need to deliver 70 pilot vehicles within seventy-five days, but the first was due only forty-nine days after the contract was awarded. When the 22 July deadline for proposals came, only two companies expressed interest: the American Bantam Car Company of Butler, Pennsylvania, and the Willys-Overland Com-

Prototype jeep from the American Bantam Car Company, September 1940 (*ACWP*).

pany of Toledo, Ohio. American Bantam was a very small automaker established in 1937 to build an improved American Austin mini car for the U.S. market. American Bantam had experimented earlier with modifying an Austin roadster for use as a military reconnaissance vehicle. A few weeks before Bantam had the signed contract in hand, the company hired engineer Karl J. Probst to manage the design, development, and manufacture of the pilot models. Willys requested an extension of the delivery time limit to 120 days; because of the penalties Willys would have incurred, Bantam had the lowest bid and won the contract. The contract, worth $171,185, went to Bantam despite the estimated weight of the vehicle (1,850 pounds), well above the specified weight limit.[4]

Bantam delivered its first pilot vehicle to Camp Holabird (near Baltimore) on 23 September 1940 and the model underwent extensive testing over the next three weeks, covering 3,500 miles of tough terrain. Willy-Overland and the Ford Motor Company observed the tests, at the invitation of the QC. Satisfied with the tests, the army prepared to buy 1,500 of these light trucks from Bantam. Here, procurement's new face appeared. Major General Edmund B. Gregory was reluctant to give Bantam exclusive control over the supply of these vehicles, mainly because Bantam was a very small firm. Gregory awarded Bantam a contract for 1,500 jeeps in November

1940 and was prepared to award similar contracts to Ford and Willys after they each produced acceptable pilot models. Bantam protested this arrangement, but Gregory argued that it was best to have more than one firm involved, since the jeep was still undergoing design changes.[5]

Ford received a contract for 1,500 jeeps on 20 November 1940, three days before it delivered its first pilot jeep to the Quartermaster Depot at Camp Holabird. After extensive testing of pilot models from Bantam, Willys, and Ford, the QC found defects in all three models but decided that a modified version of the Willys jeep would become the standard design. Ford began turning out the GP model jeep at its River Rouge plant in February 1941 and assembled GPs there through the end of the year. In mid-July 1941, the QC asked for bids from all three companies on a contract for 16,000 jeeps. Although Willys was the lowest bidder (by $640,000), the QC wanted to award the contract to Ford, but the OPM gave Willys the work. Bantam also received no contracts, although the company eventually built trailers for jeeps.

Within months it became clear that Willys was not capable of producing the quantities of jeeps that the army would need. In early October 1941, the QC awarded Ford two contracts, each for 15,000 jeeps, followed by another contract at the end of December for 63,146 additional jeeps. These were to be built exactly the same as the Willys jeep; Willys would provide Ford with a complete set of blueprints, specifications, and parts lists. On 22 January 1941, the Quartermaster Corps Technical Committee recommended standardization of the jeep across all manufacturers.[6]

The first 4,458 jeeps that Ford built were Ford-designed and identified as the GP model. They were powered by a modified Ford tractor engine that developed 42 horsepower. In the fall of 1941, the QC asked Ford to duplicate the Willys model in all respects, including using the more powerful Willys automobile engine, which produced 60 horsepower. Ford offered to increase the bore of its tractor engine and thus its power, but the QC insisted that all jeeps have completely interchangeable parts. The QC also mandated that Willys and Ford use the same axles and transfer cases made by Spicer Manufacturing Corporation and transmissions produced by Borg-Warner. Ford retooled at a cost of $4 million to make the Willys engine and produced its first jeep with that engine, designated as the GPW model, on 2 January 1942. The rest of Ford's large production run of jeeps, some 277,896 in total, were GPW models. Ford built these jeeps under license from Willys, which collected no licensing fees.[7]

One important condition attached to the large contracts Ford received for jeeps starting in October 1941 was a requirement that jeeps be assembled in several Ford branch assembly plants in addition to the Ford River Rouge plant. The QC required

End of the jeep assembly line, Willys-Overland, Toledo, Ohio *(ACWP)*.

the decentralization of jeep assembly to facilitate shipment of finished jeeps from all three coasts. Four well-located branch assembly plants shared assembly of jeeps with Dearborn: Louisville; Chester, Pennsylvania; Dallas; and Richmond, California. Ford's branch plant at Edgewater, New Jersey, assembled jeeps the first four months of 1943 only. By the end of the war, the assembly of the GPW model jeep was distributed as follows: Dallas (93,748 units) and Louisville (93,364) were the largest assemblers, followed by Richmond (49,359), the Rouge plant (21,559), Chester (18,533), and Edgewater (1,333).[8]

Throughout its production of jeeps, the Ford Motor Company had higher production costs than Willys and therefore charged the government more for its jeeps. Spreading assembly among the branch plants led to less efficient operations. The branch plants typically operated at only one-third of their capacity (the River Rouge plant at only one-tenth). Producing a relatively small number of jeeps (277,896 GPWs over four years) prevented Ford from investing in specialized tooling and machinery that could have reduced costs considerably. Ford's manufacturing capacity was 6,000 units a day, in contrast to Willys, which had a capacity of about 500 jeeps per day. The Willys output of 352,215 GPWs allowed the company to operate at near capacity for most of the war. Willys and Ford accounted for the entire production of 647,343 jeeps, including amphibians.[9]

In many respects, the jeep became *the* iconic vehicle of World War II, with an almost mythological reputation of toughness, durability, and versatility. The famous wartime correspondent Ernie Pyle called the jeep "a divine instrument of wartime locomotion" and added: "Good Lord, I don't think we could continue the war without the jeep. It does everything. It goes everywhere. It's as faithful as a dog, as strong as a mule, and as agile as a goat. It constantly carries twice what it was designed for, and still keeps on going. It doesn't even ride so badly after you get used to it."[10]

Trucks

The army purchased 2,382,311 trucks between 1939 and December 1945, ranging in carrying capacity from the ¼-ton jeep to a 20-ton 6 X 4 tractor designed to pull heavy trailers. There were thirty distinct truck types, based on carrying capacity, wheels, and driving wheels, which the army lumped into four major groups: light trucks (¾-ton or under), medium trucks (1½-ton), light-heavy trucks (2½-ton), and heavy-heavy trucks (over 2½-ton). The distribution of trucks delivered to the army broken down by these four categories was as follows: light (988,167), medium (428,196), light-heavy (812,262), and heavy-heavy (153,686). Amphibious vehicles are included in these totals but will be discussed in a separate section at the end of this chapter. The development and production of each of the major trucks will be considered briefly here.[11]

Willys, Ford, and the Dodge Division of the Chrysler Corporation accounted of nearly all of the 988,364 light trucks made for the war effort. Willys and Ford produced 647,343 jeeps, including amphibious versions. Dodge made a ½-ton 4 X 2, a ½-ton 4 X 4, and a ¾-ton 4 X 4 truck, assembling a total of 329,021 of these models in its nearly new (1938) truck plant on Mound Road in Warren, Michigan, just north of Detroit, designed by Albert Kahn. Dodge turned out 1,542 ½-ton 4 X 2 trucks between October 1941 and April 1942. Between January 1941 and June 1942, the Mound Road plant assembled 72,286 ½-ton 4 X 4s in a variety of body styles including open- and closed-cab cargo models, panel trucks, ambulances, and command reconnaissance cars. Dodge accounted for 73,828 of the 91,869 ½-ton trucks the army bought in 1940–42. The most important truck Dodge turned out at the Mound Road plant was the ¾-ton 4 X 4, which replaced the ½-ton 4 X 4. Between April 1942 and August 1945, Dodge assembled 255,193 units and was the sole producer of the ¾-ton trucks the army bought during the war. These came in a wide variety of body styles: cargo, carryall, command car, ambulance, reconnaissance car, and gun motor carriage.[12]

In mid-1940, after Congress authorized the QC to negotiate contracts for each

Chevrolet 4 X 4 truck assembly line, Kansas City plant (*SA/KU*).

class of trucks with an individual producer, the QC named the Chevrolet Division of General Motors the exclusive supplier of medium 1½-ton trucks. Once hostilities broke out and the demand for medium trucks exceeded Chevrolet's production capacity, other manufacturers took on some of the work. The army took delivery of 428,196 1½-ton trucks in three main versions: 4 X 2, 4 X 4, and 6 X 6 cargo. The army bought 217,012 of the 4 X 2s, the most of any single type. Ford produced 77,604 of these, entirely for export, and Dodge turned out 16,216 units. The rest came from Studebaker and REO. The army also bought 167,373 of the 1½-ton 4 X 4 model, and Chevrolet accounted for nearly all of them. The Yellow Truck and Coach Company supplied 9,007 between 1936 and 1943. The 6 X 6 version came exclusively from Dodge, which delivered 43,224 units during the war.[13]

The 2½-ton cargo truck, classified as a light-heavy truck, was easily the most important truck of World War II. The most common 2½-ton trucks were the 2½-ton 6 X 6 (676,433 units) and the 2½-ton 6 X 4 (117,759 units). The 6 X 6 became known as the "workhorse of the army." Each of the three axles had its own differential, so power could be applied to all six wheels on rough terrain and on steep hills. The front axle was typically disengaged on smooth highways, where these "workhorses" often carried loads much above their rated capacity.[14]

Dodge ½-ton 4 X 4 Scout car (*CKH*).

Beginning in 1936, the QC began buying a small number of military trucks from Yellow Truck and Coach, so the two parties had some experience working together before Pearl Harbor. The QC awarded Yellow Truck a contract for 1½-ton 4 X 4 trucks, 187 in total, to be built in April–August 1936. A second contract for 121 more of the same model came in 1937. These were Yellow Coach's first four-wheel-drive trucks for any customers, civilian or military. Yellow Truck built 9,007 of the 1½-ton 4 X 4s for the army between 1936 and 1943, but mainly in 1939–42. Yellow Truck's engineers proposed a 2½-ton 6 X 6 model to the QC, which ordered 240 (1 pilot and 239 production units) to be delivered in May–June 1938. In the words of Russell A. Crist, the production control manager at Yellow Truck and Coach during the war, "By the middle of November 1939, orders for military trucks had broken out on the company's books like a rash on a baby." By early 1941, Yellow Truck had orders on hand for 13,188 of the 2½-ton 6 X 6s. The QC had ordered substantial changes to the model as Yellow Truck brought it into production, including altera-tions in sheet metal and the use of a standard 6-cylinder engine developing 91.5 horsepower. Yellow Truck turned out 8,596 units in 1940; 54,109 in 1941; 112,151 the following year; and a peak output of 131,723 of the 2½-ton 6 X 6s in 1943. What became the GMC Truck and Coach Division of General Motors in 1943 produced a grand total of 528,829 of the 676,433 6 X 6s built over the course of the war.[15]

The QC intended to make the Yellow Truck and Coach the exclusive supplier of 6 X 6 trucks. Yellow Truck and Coach began assembling 6 X 6 trucks for the QC in mid-1940 but faced serious shortages of axles and transfer cases from Timken-Detroit Axle. Yellow Truck opened a second assembly operation in September 1942 at a Chevrolet plant in St. Louis. This truck model was in such high demand that production became a severe bottleneck for the QC. Yellow Truck and Coach could not satisfy the demand, so the QC turned to three additional suppliers to make up the shortage: the Studebaker Corporation of South Bend, Indiana; REO Motors of Lansing; and the International Harvester Company. The Studebaker trucks were not entirely interchangeable with the Yellow Truck versions, mainly because they used engines made by the Hercules Motor Company and Yellow Truck made its engines in-house. This did not result in maintenance problems in the field because all of the Studebaker trucks went to Lend-Lease countries, mainly the Soviet Union, while the GMC Truck versions went to the U.S. Army.[16]

The QC authorized Studebaker to produce its own version of the Yellow Truck 2½-ton truck sometime in early 1941, and Studebaker completed the first trucks, designated as the US6 model, in June 1941. By the end of the year, the automaker had completed 4,724 units but by March 1942 was assembling 4,000 a month. By the end of the war, Studebaker produced 87,742 of the 6 X 4 models, 105,917 of the 6 X 6 versions, and small numbers of other models, for a total of 197,678 trucks. The other manufacturers producing the 6 X 6 were REO Motors (22,204) and International Harvester (roughly 30,000). Yellow Truck turned out 24,910 of the 2½-ton 6 X 4s, accounting, along with Studebaker, for all the 6 X 4 versions. Yellow Truck and Coach produced the lion's share of the 2½-ton 6 X 6 trucks.[17]

Studebaker began producing military trucks with closed cabs but switched over to open cabs in December 1942 at the request of the QC. The company went back to making closed cabs in March 1943 after building roughly 10,000 open-cab versions and then made closed cabs exclusively for the rest of the war. The reason for the switch was simple: the largest customer, the Soviet Union, preferred closed cabs, presumably because of the cold Russian winters. All the closed-cab trucks Studebaker built after March 1943 went to Russia.[18]

Although there were never enough trucks to satisfy the needs of the army, production of light, medium, and light-heavy trucks up to 2½-ton capacity increased at a rapid enough pace in 1941–43 to avoid any serious shortfalls. This was not the case for heavy-heavy trucks (four tons and up). In mid-July 1943, after recognizing the great importance of heavy-heavy trucks in the North African campaigns, the army nearly doubled the planned production for 1944 from 35,000 to 67,000 units. When the new production targets were announced in July 1943, heavy-heavy truck output was only 3,000 units per month. Adding to the challenge was the fact that the WPB simultaneously decided to increase the production of farm implements and heavy-duty trucks for civilian use. The Ordnance Department turned to a score of small-volume specialized producers of heavy equipment to reach the higher targets for 1944. By the end of the war, Autocar, Diamond T, Federal Truck, and White Motors built 4-ton trucks; Autocar, International Harvester, and REO assembled 5-ton trucks; and Brockway and Mack Truck made 6-ton models. These models accounted for nearly three-quarters of all the heavy-heavy truck production during the war. Production of heavy-heavy trucks reached a peak of 50,862 units in 1944, far below the target of 67,000. Over the first six months of 1945, truck manufacturers built nearly 28,000 heavy-heavy trucks.[19]

Amphibians

Once satisfied with the performance of the jeep, the army wanted an amphibious version of it. Ford Motor Company and Firestone experimented with rubberized pontoons to keep the jeep afloat in water but failed to develop a practical design. Several manufacturers proposed amphibious vehicles in 1941 and built pilot models to submit to the QC. In July 1940, inventor Roger W. Hoffheins of Buffalo submitted a design for the "Aqua-Chetah," which had a propeller that could be raised when the vehicle was on land. His firm, the Amphibian Car Corporation, built twelve pilot models for the army. Roderick Stephens, a naval architect with the firm of Sparkman and Stephens, also submitted an amphibian design that the Marmon-Herrington Corporation of Indianapolis turned into pilot models in late 1941. The army rejected these proposals in large part because they were not modifications of the existing jeep. In November 1941, members of the National Defense Research Committee (NDRC), the research arm of the National Defense Advisory Commission (NDAC), approached Ford about designing an amphibious jeep. In mid-December, Ford engineers began developing a pilot model using Stephens's drawings as a starting point and produced a model that was 350 pounds lighter than the Marmon-Herrington design and had a more flexible hull and better seals. On 2 January 1942 the NDRC recommended that Ford receive a contract to build three pilot models at a cost not to exceed $75,000 (later increased to $143,000).[20]

Ford completed the first pilot model on 10 February 1942, tested it extensively, and delivered it to the army on 7 March 1942. Ford delivered a second pilot model on 1 April and a third one on 8 May 1942. The QC awarded Ford a contract on 11 April 1942 to build 5,000 amphibians. By the end of November 1942, Ford had contracts in hand for 12,781 amphibians, including the three pilot models. The first amphibian rolled off Ford's assembly line on 10 September 1942, and six more were completed that first day. Ironically, Ford assembled them in Building B (1918), the first major building erected at the Ford Rouge plant and used by Ford to build

Eagle boats during World War I. The company fulfilled the amphibian contracts for 12,781 units between September 1942 and May 1943 at a total cost to the army of $38,986,000, an average cost of $3,050 per amphibian.[21]

The Ford amphibian, designated as the GPA model, was also called the amphibious reconnaissance car and the "Seep," a contraction of "Sea jeep." It was sometimes called a "jeep in a bathtub" because of its unjeeplike appearance. To reduce costs and to ease assembly and maintenance of the GPA, all of the common parts shared with the GPW model were interchangeable. To convert a standard jeep into one that could float and swim presented Ford's engineers with significant challenges. The amphibious jeep had a lightweight and waterproof hull with a frame independent of the jeep's frame, along with a surf shield, propeller, rudder, and bilge pump. It had an 84-inch wheelbase, four inches longer than the standard jeep, and weighed approximately 800 pounds more (4,460 pounds versus 3,650). New machines allowed for continuous welding of all the seams on the hull, making it waterproof.

Ford's engineers designed special bellows-type watertight seals of synthetic rubber to prevent water leakage through the hull openings where axles, the propeller, and other parts protruded. The original two-blade propeller was replaced by a three-blade version. A power take-off drive installed in the jeep's transfer case provided power to the propeller shaft and to the bilge pump, which had a capacity of 50 gallons per minute. Ford also designed an ingenious system for controlling the rudder with cables linked directly to the steering wheel. To overcome the unique cooling problems the GPA faced when in water, the cooling system was modified in several ways, including the use of a radiator core with greater capacity than that on a GPW. The amphibious jeep also had a power-driven capstan (winch) installed on the forward deck to be used to pull the amphibian in situations where the wheels had little or no traction.[22]

Building the amphibious jeep was much more complicated than building the standard jeep because the amphibian was not at all like a standard car or truck. Because the army wanted as many GPAs as possible for the North African campaign, Ford accelerated the process of tooling-up and finished in under ninety days, the fastest ever for Ford. Detroit-based Murray Corporation supplied the frames for the amphibian, and Ford produced the hulls in the body shop at its Lincoln plant in Detroit and the engines at its Motor Building at the River Rouge plant. Final assembly took place in Building B at the Rouge plant. The completed amphibians then underwent five miles of road tests on a track next to Building B, followed by water testing, with a focus on leaks, in the boat slips at the Rouge plant. After passing inspections conducted by both Ford and the army, the amphibians were prepared for delivery. Those going overseas were knocked-down, protected against rust, and then packed into wooden crates for shipping.[23]

During the same time frame in which Ford developed the amphibious jeep, General Motors developed a much larger and more important amphibious cargo carrier, the 2½-ton 6 X 6 DUKW or "duck." The army recognized that conditions for moving freight in World War II were completely different than those of World War I, when cargo could be off-loaded from ships at ports with piers and heavy cranes. Supplies needed to be delivered to hostile beaches, along with men and motorized vehicles. In late March 1942, the QC asked the NDRC to develop an amphibious cargo carrier based on a 2½-ton truck. The NDRC worked with the New York naval architects Sparkman and Stephens, Inc., and Yellow Truck and Coach to design this amphibious carrier. Ford was also asked to build it but declined because it was not making a 2½-ton truck at the time and did not have the right components available. Yellow Truck and Coach received an order to develop the new vehicle on 21 April 1942 and delivered the first pilot model on 2 June 1942. The War Department sent Yellow Truck and Coach a letter of intent on 26 June 1942 outlining a contract for four pilot models and 1,996 production versions. Following successful testing and several design modifications, the QC approved the vehicle design in October 1942. The first DUKW came off the assembly line on 10 November 1942 at the Yellow Truck and Coach plant in Pontiac, Michigan.[24]

The name for this unique vehicle derived from Yellow Truck and Coach's manufacturing code assigned to it: D for 1942, U for utility, K for front-wheel drive, and W for two rear driving axles. The official designation DUKW quickly turned into "Duck." The DUKW shared a lot of design features with the amphibious jeep, despite its larger size (8 feet 2 inches wide and 31 feet long versus 5 feet 4 inches wide and 15 feet 2 inches long for the amphibious jeep). Once Ford declined the opportunity to bid on the vehicle, Ford shared its jeep drawings with Yellow Truck and Ford's engineers offered assistance as well. Ford also allowed DUKWs to be water-tested in the ship basin at its Rouge plant. The normal fierce competitiveness of the automakers faded away for the duration of the war.[25]

Despite the successful testing of the DUKW, the army did not warm up to the new vehicle right away. Through a bit of good fortune, the DUKW proved its value under extreme conditions. Roderick Stephens was about to demonstrate a DUKW to a group of army officers near Provincetown, Massachusetts, on Cape Cod on 1 December 1942, when the Coast Guard yawl *Rose* on patrol nearby began to break up in a near hurricane-strength storm. Stephens maneuvered the DUKW out to the *Rose* and rescued the crew. There were still skeptics in the army, but when the DUKW proved invaluable in Patton's invasion of Sicily in July 1943, demand for the vehicle increased dramatically. Yellow Truck and Coach opened a second assembly plant in St. Louis in 1944 to produce DUKWs. Production of this amphibian, which started at a modest 263 units in 1942, reached 4,720 units in 1943, jumped sharply

U.S. Third Army DUKW crossing the Danube, April 1945 (*ACWP*).

to 11,386 units in 1944, and then fell off in the last year of the war to 4,778 units. Yellow Truck and Coach was the exclusive supplier of DUKWs and delivered a total of 21,147 units to the army over the course of the war.[26]

The DUKW played an important role during the war. The army used them in every amphibious beach landing in the European and Pacific theaters, where DUKWs moved men, equipment, and materials from ships to the shore. The Army tied two and sometimes four DUKWs together and then lowered tanks, half-tracks, trucks, and fighter aircraft onto the DUKWs for transport to land. Following the Normandy invasion in June 1944, DUKWs transferred goods and vehicles from transport ships to the shore before the dock facilities destroyed by the Germans could be repaired. Between D-Day and 8 May 1945, the Allies unloaded 15.8 million tons of equipment and supplies at French and Belgian ports, with one-fifth of the total moved by DUKWs. They also served an important role in speeding the invasion of Germany, particularly in crossing German rivers where Allied bombs had destroyed the bridges.[27]

The final vehicle considered in this chapter is the "Weasel," a tracked personnel carrier developed by the Studebaker Corporation. The Office of Scientific Research and Development and the Ordnance Department approached Studebaker in early 1942, asking them to design a vehicle that could traverse deep snow and ice. This came on the heels of possible military action against the Japanese in Alaska. Ordnance awarded Studebaker a contract in May 1942, and the automaker quickly and secretly designed a tracked vehicle it tested on a glacier in British Columbia. Initially labeled the T15, it was renamed the M28 Weasel. It was 60 inches wide and 128 inches long, weighed 2.3 tons, and carried only two soldiers. The Ordnance Department replaced it in 1943 with the M29 Weasel, which weighed less (3,725 pounds) but carried four passengers. Neither Weasel was amphibious. A redesigned M29 Weasel, the M29C, was designed to be fully amphibious. Studebaker added flotation cells (tanks) at the front and rear, track aprons to make it more water-worthy, and dual rudders. The tracks propelled the M29C though the water. Studebaker delivered 4,476 M29s and 10,647 M29Cs to the Ordnance Department during the course of the war.[28]

Overall, the automobile industry performed remarkably well in supplying the army with an adequate supply (2,382,311 units) of well-designed, solidly built trucks. After supplying the army with only 32,604 trucks in 1939 and 1940 combined, deliveries jumped to 183,614 units in 1941. With the war officially under way, truck orders and deliveries exploded to 619,835 units in 1942. Production levels then remained at roughly the same level for 1943 (621,502 units) and 1944 (596,963 trucks). As would be expected, output fell by nearly half to 327,893 units in 1945. The truck production targets set by the Ordnance Department were seldom met in full, a reflection of sudden and unrealistic increases in production scheduled by the army.

As was the case with tanks and other combat vehicles, a substantial share (35 percent) of U.S. truck production went to U.S. allies through Lend-Lease. Out of the 836,772 trucks delivered through Lend-Lease, a remarkable 457,561 (55 percent) went to the Soviet Union, including 151,053 medium trucks and 220,662 trucks rated at 2½ tons. The British Empire took 292,174 units (35 percent), including 104,430 jeeps and 97,112 medium trucks. Most of the remaining shipments under Lend-Lease went to the French forces and to China.[29]

The Quartermaster Corps and the Ordnance Department largely achieved the goal of standardizing military trucks: the jeeps produced by Willys and Ford were virtually identical, and the 2½-ton 6 X 6 trucks were nearly identical, although those produced by Studebaker and GMC used different engines. Some GMC-built models used Timken axles and others used axles made in-house by General Motors. Although GMC Truck and Coach built all of the DUKWs, scores of mostly minor design changes along the way meant that parts for DUKWs were not entirely interchangeable. Still, the maintenance nightmare of World War I had been largely eliminated. Perhaps the most remarkable achievement of the military truck program was the rapid development, testing, and production of two entirely new vehicles, the jeep and the DUKW, both of which were very successful on the battlefield.[30]

SEVEN

Guns, Shells, Bullets, and Other War Goods

The automobile industry's production of aircraft engines, aircraft components, complete airplanes, tanks and other armored vehicles, and trucks of all types was the industry's major contribution to the war effort. Automobile manufacturers did not make long-range artillery for the army or navy but did produce a substantial quantity of anti-aircraft guns and machine guns. The industry also manufactured a bewildering variety of war goods ranging from submarine nets to searchlights to gyroscopes to radar units to U-235 gaseous diffusers for the Manhattan Project. The production of many of these weapons and equipment, which had no resemblance to automotive products, demonstrated the automobile industry's resilience and ingenuity in solving production challenges.

Guns, Shells, and Bullets

In his State of the Union address of 6 January 1942, President Roosevelt identified four critical items that the United States needed to focus on in preparing for war: aircraft, tanks, merchant ships, and anti-aircraft guns. He announced targets of 20,000 anti-aircraft guns for 1942 and 35,000 for 1943. Actual production in 1942 was 14,509 units, but industry surpassed the 1943 target and by war's end had produced 49,775 anti-aircraft guns for the army alone. The section will treat only two anti-aircraft guns: the Bofors 40-mm gun, a Swedish-designed gun manufactured by the Chrysler Corporation, and the Oerlikon 20-mm gun, a Swiss-designed weapon made by the Hudson Motor Car Company, the Pontiac Motor Division of General Motors, and others.[1]

In 1940 the Colt Manufacturing Company was the only producer of anti-aircraft guns for the U.S. Army, a 37-mm model, and turned out only 170 during the year. Colt had increased production to 40 guns a month by early 1941 and the Ordnance Department was committed to this weapon until the Chief of Coast Artillery strongly recommended the 40-mm Bofors gun instead. This Swedish-designed gun had proven its value in the Spanish Civil War and at Dunkirk. In the fall of 1940, the U.S. Navy and the Army Ordnance Department independently obtained Bofors guns for testing. The navy opted for a twin-mounted, water-cooled version of the Bofors, and the army preferred a single-mount, air-cooled design. The Chrysler Corporation built both. Chrysler's engineers first examined the Bofors gun on 4 January 1941, and the navy gave the automaker a contract to redesign the gun for mass production. Chrysler had to convert the original specifications from meters to inches and from European to American metallurgical standards. By making the gun parts interchangeable, Chrysler's engineers reduced the assembly time from about 450 hours under the European hand-filing and fitting methods to less than fourteen hours with the modern assembly system. On 5 February 1942, the first mass-production Bofors gun came off the assembly line.[2]

The Bofors anti-aircraft gun was one of Chrysler's major contributions to the war effort. By the end of the war, the company had produced 30,095 single guns and 14,442 pairs, or the equivalent of 58,978 single guns, all assembled at the Plymouth Lynch Road plant in Detroit. The Army Ordnance Department bought a total of 34,116 single-mount Bofors guns from all suppliers and Chrysler accounted for nearly 90 percent of the total. Chrysler also made more than 120,000 Bofors gun barrels, including replacements. The Firestone Tire & Rubber Company built the gun mount and carriage for the Bofors and faced similar challenges to those Chrysler encountered in converting the specifications from meters to inches. Twelve Chrysler plants were involved in the Bofors project, along with more than 2,000 subcontractors.[3]

The other significant anti-aircraft gun manufactured by the automobile industry was the Oerlikon 20-mm automatic cannon, the primary anti-aircraft gun used by the U.S. Navy. A Swiss company, Werkzeug Maschinenfabrik Oerlikon, held the patent for the cannon, originally designed by Reinhold Becker in 1914 and used in a limited way by Germany toward the end of World War I. After Oerlikon modified the design, the cannon could fire 450 rounds per minute and had a range of 2,000 meters against airplanes. In mid-January 1941, Hudson announced it had signed

Bofors gun crew, New Guinea *(ACWP)*.

a contract with the navy to manufacture "parts for guns and torpedoes" at a plant Hudson would build at Nine Mile and Mound roads just north of Detroit. The announcement projected a 400,000-square-foot factory complex on a 113-acre site at a cost of $13 million. It would employ 4,000. In late April 1941, with construction under way, the plant had grown to a million square feet, the site was 135 acres, and the projected cost was $20–30 million. Naval anti-aircraft guns would be the major product manufactured there.[4]

The U.S. Navy announced it was awarding a $14,038,500 contract to Hudson at the end of July 1941 to build complete Oerlikon guns. Events beyond Hudson's control briefly halted construction of the Naval Arsenal in August 1941. In a dispute over pay, 2,000 members of the Building Trades Council of Detroit refused to work one Saturday after discovering that the contractor had cut their overtime pay rate from double-time to time-and-a-half. Their international union had agreed to the reduction on defense projects but failed to notify the local union leaders or the rank and file. They returned to their jobs Monday but would not work overtime until they resolved the issue.[5]

Work at the naval ordnance plant got under way slowly. The first machines began operating on 21 July 1941, but the navy did not require Hudson to deliver the first three "sample guns" until December. By mid-September, the navy had increased the contract to 8,000 guns. At the end of October 1941, Hudson president A. Edward Barit and Rear Admiral W.H.P. Blandy, U.S. Navy Chief of the Bureau of Ordnance, jointly dedicated the U.S. Naval Ordnance plant in Centerline, Michigan. Production began slowly, in part because an outside supplier of gun mounts was behind schedule in its deliveries. Hudson managed to produce only 34 guns in January 1942 but then output climbed quickly to 1,053 guns in April, making Hudson the largest manufacturer of Oerlikon guns in the country. Pleased with Hudson's performance, the navy awarded the automaker contracts for an additional 10,000 guns. Hudson increased production nearly every month in 1942 and over the last four months of the year turned out more than 1,500 a month. Output peaked at 2,330 guns in September 1943, and when Hudson lost this contract at the end of October 1943, it had produced a grand total of 33,201 Oerlikon guns for the navy.[6]

Reports of the effectiveness of these Hudson-built anti-aircraft guns in naval warfare consistently praised their quality and workmanship. Detroit newspapers reported that Rear Admiral W.H.P. Blandy sent congratulatory telegrams to the Hudson Naval Ordnance plant workers in December 1942 and again in May 1943. In a sea battle in the Solomon Islands, a single unnamed American battleship equipped with Oerlikon guns shot down thirty-two Japanese dive-bombers in thirty minutes. Only one bomb hit the battleship, causing minor damage, according to the ship's commander, Captain Thomas Leigh Gatch.[7]

On 5 October 1943, Blandy sent a telegram to the employees of the plant announcing that the navy was ending Hudson's management of the plant and replacing them with the Westinghouse Electric and Manufacturing Company. The management contract was due to expire on 28 October. The navy had notified Hudson of its decision before the company directors met on 20 September, when Hudson president A. E. Barit informed them of this decision. Barit went to Washington to confer with Blandy and to convince him to reverse the decision but was unsuccessful. We will never know the precise reason why the navy made this decision with any degree of confidence. Their "official" reason was the desire to consolidate the operation of the Hudson plant with their two ordnance plants in Canton, Ohio, and Louisville, Kentucky, both run by Westinghouse. According to one report, notices the navy posted in the ordnance plant indicated that the navy was dissatisfied with the rate of production under Hudson management. The loss of this management contract was a major blow to Hudson's prestige as well as its profits.[8]

Several observers suggested that the navy was pleased with the production and

4.7-inch anti-aircraft guns, Fisher Body plant, Grand Rapids, Michigan (*ACWP*).

the cost of the Oerlikon guns but displeased with the other work performed at the naval arsenal. The navy expected Hudson to produce specialized products, such as catapults for launching airplanes, in quantities as small as a dozen. They also expected Hudson to repair damaged ordnance at the plant, in effect serving as a specialized machine shop. Hudson was most comfortable with mass production of standardized products, while the navy often required "one-off" production. The layout of the arsenal, in fifteen scattered buildings, was not Hudson's design. Oerlikon gun production involved only two buildings, but all of the buildings had their own machine shop, making management of machining difficult. The navy also accused Hudson of "labor hoarding," that is, keeping excessive numbers of workers on the payroll as a hedge against unexpected contracts. Perhaps Westinghouse, with its experience in producing customized, "one-off" electrical equipment, was a better "fit" for the navy.[9]

The Pontiac Motor Division of GM was the second significant manufacturer of Oerlikon guns. In spring 1941, Pontiac received a contract from the U.S. Navy to manufacture Oerlikon guns to be used by the U.S. Merchant Marine against enemy aircraft. This weapon was seen as particularly effective against dive-bombers. Pontiac subcontracted 173 of the 195 parts to outside suppliers, including the entire gun mount. Pontiac fabricated the most difficult parts at its plant in Pontiac: the breech casing, trigger casing, and barrel.[10]

These two guns provided the U.S. Navy with most of its firepower against enemy aircraft. Out of a total of 18,239 anti-aircraft guns installed on U.S. Navy vessels in June 1945, 12,561 were 20-mm Oerlikon cannons and 5,140 were 40-mm Bofors guns. Most of the 538 remaining anti-aircraft weapons were .50-caliber machine guns used on submarines. The Oerlikon was the preferred naval anti-aircraft gun throughout most of the war. The Navy purchased more than one billion rounds of 20-mm ammunition after Pearl Harbor. Through September 1944, the Oerlikons were credited with one-third of the identifiable "kills" of enemy aircraft. With the increase in Japanese suicide attacks in the last year of the war, the Navy preferred the longer-range Bofors gun over the Oerlikon.[11]

The Oldsmobile Division of GM, with its main plants in Lansing, was a substantial producer of a variety of cannon, primarily for the Ordnance Department. Olds began by making the 20-mm M2 cannon for aircraft starting in October 1941 and continued through January 1944. Beginning on 12 July 1942 they completed 2,779 37-mm M4 guns for aircraft in less than a year's time. In May 1943–May 1944, Olds also assembled 37-mm M9 cannons, 2,930 in total. Their production achievements also included 75-mm M3 cannon for tanks and 76-mm cannon for tank destroyers. By mid-February 1943, Oldsmobile had completed more than 10,000 cannon at their Lansing works. Although the division also made artillery shells in quantity, it specialized in cannons during the war. Oldsmobile was more of an assembler of guns than a fabricator. The three principal types of guns they made included 473 parts, but Olds made only nine of these in-house and used 155 subcontractors to make the rest. Oldsmobile used fewer than half of the 3,375 machine tools used for gun production in its own factories, with subcontractors accounting the most of the machine tools.[12]

Machine guns were the third substantial weapon the automakers supplied to the Ordnance Department. In January 1942, President Roosevelt announced the production targets for both 1942 and 1943: 330,000 .30-caliber machine guns and 170,000 .50-caliber machine guns. The goal of 500,000 machine guns per year was particularly ambitious because machine gun production in 1941 was only 77,151 units, which was already a large increase over the 8,788 machine guns manufactured in 1940. Machine gun production in the 1930s was limited to two government arsenals, at Springfield, Massachusetts, and at Rock Island, Illinois, and a single private gun maker, the Colt Patent Fire Arms Company of Hartford, Connecticut.[13]

The first automobile company to make machine guns for the Ordnance Department in the 1940s was the Saginaw Steering Gear Division of General Motors, with operations in Saginaw. The Ordnance Department first approached the Saginaw Steering Gear Division about manufacturing machine guns in early 1938. After visiting the Springfield Arsenal and a Colt plant, on 29 March 1938 the division agreed to accept an educational order to build Browning .30-caliber machine guns. The Ordnance Department had no funds at the time, and the educational order was finally placed with Saginaw Steering Gear on 15 June 1940, more than two years after the initial offer. This GM division would make 500 machine guns and then turn over to the Ordnance Department all the blueprints for the gun and the machinery needed to make it.[14]

By mid-September 1940, the Ordnance Department and GM had agreed to a program to mass-produce machine guns. Ordnance awarded GM contracts worth $20 million to equip four plants to make a total of 71,225 machine guns: the Saginaw Steering Gear Division plant in Saginaw (20,004 machine guns); the A. C. Spark Plug Division plant in Flint (14,741 guns); the Frigidaire Division factory in Dayton, Ohio (19,998 units); and the Guide Lamp Division plant in Syracuse, New York (9,097 guns). The contracts to manufacture the machine guns amounted to an additional $61.4 million. By mid-April 1941, production in Saginaw and in Flint was already under way, with assembly to begin at Dayton and Syracuse by mid-summer. The A. C. Spark Plug Division and the Frigidaire Division manufactured .50-caliber Colt machine guns, while the Saginaw Steering Gear and Guide Lamp Division built .30-caliber Browning machine guns. This was a massive undertaking for GM, which had to acquire more than 8,000 machine tools costing more than $28 million to start production.[15]

The Saginaw Steering Gear Division plant was the first to produce machine guns under the contracts granted in September 1940, a reflection of its prior experience with an educational order. The contract called for the plant to produce the first machine gun accepted by the Ordnance Department by December 1941, followed by the production of forty guns in January 1942, eighty in February, and so forth. Construction of a new plant measuring 660 feet long by 361 feet wide began in November 1940. By March 1941 the building was completed, including concrete floors, and machinery was being installed as it arrived on the scene. The official dedication of the gun plant took place on 22 April 1941. In the meantime, on 27 March 1941, Saginaw Steering Gear Division assembled its first machine guns in a nearby storage building, more than nine months earlier than the contract required.[16]

Saginaw Steering Gear Division was the first American manufacturer to produce machine guns in quantity since World War I. The Browning .30-caliber machine gun was not a simple machine. It had 189 individual parts, 153 of which were made in

Saginaw, involving 1,800 distinct operations. Making the bolt, for example, involved 83 hand and machine operations. The production setup required 1,300 machines, 1,165 of which were new. The remaining 135 came from storage at the Rock Island Arsenal but needed to be rebuilt and motorized. The plant also required more than 6,000 tools, fixtures, and jigs for machine gun production. Designing the needed tooling required 62,000 man-hours of engineering labor, while building the tools, fixtures, and jigs consumed another 250,000 man-hours, mostly in the plants of the tool suppliers. By April 1941, when machine guns first came off the line in quantity, the plant employed 800 workers, but by February 1942 the workforce had climbed to 4,000 men and women.[17]

GM's success in mass-producing unfamiliar items like machine guns was remarkable. The corporation completed 24,733 machine guns in 1942, then increased production to 282,169 units in 1942 and 375,408 in 1943. By the end of the war, GM had produced a total of 1.9 million machine guns, roughly 70 percent of total U.S. production of 2,679,819 units. About 61 percent of the machine guns went into aircraft and 36 percent went to the ground forces. GM reduced the unit cost of the .30-caliber machine guns by 84 percent and the unit cost of the .50-caliber model by 76 percent. Most of the savings came from improving the production methods and the machinery used to fabricate machine gun components. Improvements in metalworking methods also reduced the alloy steel requirements for machine guns by 40 percent.[18]

All of the automakers became significant producers of artillery shells and rockets. General Motors was easily the largest producer of various artillery shells, with a wartime production of 119,562,000 shells, or 13 percent of the 942 million artillery or mortar shells purchased by the Ordnance Department. Chrysler made 101,232 incendiary bombs; its Highland Park plant built 4.5-inch rockets, 328,327 in total; and the New Castle, Indiana, plant made 20-mm practice shells (3,000,000), 20-mm projectile balls (19,933,000), 20-mm armor-piercing shot (1,989,801), and armor-piercing cores for .50-caliber machine gun cartridges (222,000,000).[19]

Right after Pearl Harbor, an Army Ordnance officer allegedly asked K. T. Keller, the president of Chrysler Corporation, if his company could make 3–5 billion .45-caliber cartridges at their idled Evansville, Indiana, assembly plant. Keller immediately agreed to do this and the officer asked him why he made up his mind so quickly. Keller replied, "I still can't imagine what a billion is like, so I'd like to make a billion of something and find out." By the end of the war, Chrysler's Evansville factory literally made "bullets by the billion." Before the war, a workforce of 650 assembled 275 Plymouth cars a day there, but employment soared to a peak of 12,650 when it became an ammunition plant.[20]

First drawing of .45-caliber cartridges, Chrysler Evansville (IN) plant (*ACWP*).

Evansville's production included 2,768,688,000 cartridges for .45-caliber weapons (68 percent of the total purchased by the Ordnance Department) and 485,463,000 cartridges for .30-caliber weapons (out of 25 billion purchased). The plant also repacked another 1.5 billion rounds for the Ordnance Department. Chrysler was the only automaker to manufacture small arms ammunition. The Ordnance Department operated eleven additional small arms ammunition plants during the war: the Remington Arms Company operated five of these; the Federal Cartridge Company and the United States Cartridge Company each operated one; the U.S. Rubber Company managed three plants; and Goodyear operated one factory. Remarkably, just as Chrysler prepared for production at its Evansville plant in July 1942, the Ordnance Department ordered the automaker to substitute steel for brass for the cartridges cases so as to conserve brass. Although this last-minute change required Chrysler's engineers to complete a quick analysis of the steel they would need and to retool much of the plant, full-scale production began in October.[21]

Miscellaneous War Goods

The auto industry also produced a wide range of war goods that were not weapons in the usual sense but were nevertheless a vital part of military operations. The automakers made many products that were far afield from their "normal" range of products. One was the Sperry Gyroscope Company gyrocompass used in ships. The U.S. Bureau of Ships asked Chrysler on 5 February 1942 to consider manufacturing the delicate, complicated piece of equipment. In about a week, after examining a sample and the blueprints, Chrysler agreed to make the device. They delivered the first compass on 11 September 1942 and by the end of the contract (February 1945) had produced 5,500 compasses, three times more than Sperry thought possible. Ford Motor Company produced "gun directors," which were aiming devices used to improve the accuracy of anti-aircraft guns. Also designed by the Sperry Gyroscope Company, these were complex mechanisms consisting of more than 11,000 precision parts. Ford manufactured 1,202 gun directors between August 1942 and May 1943, when the machines Ford made became obsolete. Ford also produced 5,360 "rate of climb indicators" in 1943. Not to be outdone by its automotive competitors, General Motors made 301,000 gyroscopes for airplanes, marine instruments, and automatic pilots.[22]

Chrysler made another "exotic" product, an antenna mount for mobile short-range radar units. Chrysler did this work as a subcontractor for General Electric Company, under an agreement signed on 22 September 1942. They completed the first production unit in February 1943 but did not achieve quantity production until May. When the contract ended a year later, in May 1944, the Dodge Main plant had turned out 2,098 sets of radar equipment. The basic radar antenna mount included the radar "dish," the intricate gearing mechanisms used to both elevate and turn the dish, and the pedestal supports. Chrysler also designed a special semitrailer to house the mobile radar unit, but because Dodge's truck plant was already overcommitted, Fruehauf built it.[23]

In addition to building engines used in airplanes, tanks, and trucks, the car companies built a variety of engines for other applications. Chrysler built 21,131 marine engines and 119,814 industrial engines used to power electricity-generating stations, pump water, and operate pipelines. Hudson Motor Car Company built 4,004 Invader gasoline engines for landing craft, under license from the Hall-Scott Motor Company. General Motors assembled diesel engines for trucks and submarines, while Packard built engines for PT boats.[24]

Chrysler produced an interesting mix of goods for the war effort at its Jefferson Avenue plant in Detroit. There, Chrysler made 9,002 steel pontoons and a curious and useful hybrid marine vehicle, the marine tractor, more commonly known as the "sea mule." Chrysler Division president David A. Wallace first proposed this unique design. By modifying one or more pontoons and equipping them with an engine and steering equipment, Chrysler produced an extremely reliable and inexpensive tugboat. Development of the sea mule began in January 1942 and pilot production started in July, with full-scale work under way by October. Chrysler assembled them on-site and launched them into the Detroit River at the back of the factory. The Jefferson plant assembled 8,229 sea mules by the end of the war, in fifteen different types, with engines producing up to 560 horsepower.[25]

The Jefferson plant also manufactured 253 sets of equipment that artificially generated smoke screens used to conceal ships and amphibious troops from the enemy; 20,404 heavy-duty fire pumps, powered by Chrysler industrial engines; 352 air raid sirens; 1,994 special submarine nets; and 1,550 searchlight reflectors. Chrysler designed lightweight submarine netting that would allow enemy submarines to penetrate it but would release flares to pinpoint the submarine's position. The navy also needed parabolic reflectors for its searchlights polished with great accuracy to increase the operating range. Chrysler used its "superfinishing" process to create reflectors that gave the searchlights a range of more than thirty miles.[26]

In addition to manufacturing parts for anti-aircraft guns and several airplanes, Chrysler's Airtemp Division plant in Dayton made a variety of other war goods: 14,370 air-conditioning and refrigeration units, mostly used for food preservation on ships; 17,200 furnaces and 29,589 heaters of other types, including portable tent heaters; 37,932 cookstoves; and 62,192 field ranges for cooking.[27]

Chrysler also played an important role in the development of the atomic bomb. On 2 April 1943, a delegation from the Manhattan Engineer District, the code name for the atomic bomb project, met with the top Chrysler officials in Detroit. They asked Chrysler to manufacture large metal diffusers used in the gaseous diffusion process to separate U-235, the raw material for one type of atomic bomb, from U-238, the main isotope found in uranium. The diffusers had to be made of nickel, the only metal able to resist the uranium hexaflouride gas produced in the diffusion process.

Rather than make the equipment of solid nickel, which would have exhausted the existing national supply, Chrysler instead proposed a process to electroplate nickel onto steel diffusers. Government "experts" claimed that nickel-plated diffusers would not withstand hexaflouride gas. Here, Chrysler's expertise in metallurgy generally and in electroplating came into play. Chrysler's laboratories produced electroplating samples that held up better than "pure" nickel and the Manhattan District instructed Chrysler to start work on this $75 million contract, code-named X-100.

To help guarantee secrecy, the scientists and engineers worked in the upper floors of an empty department store in downtown Detroit, far from the rest of Chrysler's engineers. This project was kept so secret that only eight Chrysler employees knew the product the corporation was making. The manufacturing operations took place at the Plymouth Lynch Road plant in Detroit after Chrysler emptied the building and created a clean manufacturing plant, in part by installing air-conditioning. Chrysler made four types of diffusers, which they shipped to the Oak Ridge, Tennessee, U-235 plant in more than a thousand railroad carloads. To ship these fragile tanks safely, Chrysler designed a new railroad flatcar suspension system.[28]

General Motors War Work

Listing all of the defense products manufactured by the automakers is an impossible task. Earlier parts of this chapter and earlier chapters of this book cover nearly all of the products made by Ford, Chrysler, Packard, Studebaker, Hudson, and Nash. Because there is no single listing of the hundreds of products General Motors manufactured, the coverage of the largest automaker's contributions is less complete than it is for the other automakers. To be sure, the significant GM-built defense products already covered in this book accounted for the bulk, in terms of dollar value, of GM's war work. The corporation delivered nearly $4 billion in war materials through 30 June 1943. Aircraft engines accounted for 22.8 percent of the total value of deliveries and, when combined with aircraft parts (7.3 percent) and complete aircraft (4.4 percent), brought the total of all aircraft products to 34.5 percent of GM's deliveries. Trucks accounted for 17.3 percent of the total, tanks and armored cars another 15.1 percent, and all guns accounted for 12.9 percent of deliveries. General Motors was a substantial producer of diesel engines for marine applications, making up 13.5 percent of the corporation's deliveries of war goods through June 1943. A wide variety of other products accounted for the remainder (6.7 percent) of GM's work.[29]

Each of GM's scores of divisions outside the car and truck divisions made several products, but there is no complete listing of these. At the urging of the government, General Motors and the other defense manufacturers subcontracted a major part of the work. GM decided early in the war to focus on making the most difficult and complex parts of the war goods they were producing and then subcontracting the rest to outside firms. In 1942 alone, GM used 18,735 subcontractors and suppliers. Fewer than half (8,712) had previously worked with GM. In 1942 the Oldsmobile Division made four types of big guns that required 862 parts, but they made only 44 of these themselves. That same year, the Pontiac Division assembled the 40-mm Bofors anti-aircraft gun, which had 464 parts. Pontiac made only 40 of these parts, but these accounted for half of the total cost of the gun. Most GM plants relied on other GM divisions to supply at least some parts and materials. Established connections and communication lines among GM divisions eased the process of identifying potential subcontractors. General Motors did an analysis of the value added by other GM divisions to the manufacture of 22 products in mid-1943, and this ranged from 0 percent in the case of M1 carbines built at the Saginaw Steering Gear plant to 46 percent for the M5 tank built by Cadillac.[30]

There is only scattered evidence of the work of the independent automotive body companies such as Briggs, Budd, and Murray, which consisted mostly of aircraft components. Unfortunately, few records survive detailing the war work of the small independent auto companies and the scores of companies that supplied parts and components to the automakers before the war.

This study has examined the work of the civilian and military officials who planned war production from Washington and from Detroit. The bulk of the analysis has focused on the work of the leaders of the automobile industry, the military services, and the civilian government in designing the defense products needed for the war, building and equipping the factories used for war work, and coordinating production. Design and production engineers from the automobile industry played vital roles in initiating the mass production of aircraft, a wide range of vehicles, and weapons of all types. Wartime workers, who were as unfamiliar with factory work as the production managers were unfamiliar with the new products they made, were a key element in the transformation of the automobile industry into the "arsenal of democracy." The labor demands of the war brought a flood of new workers into the plants making war products, namely women, African Americans, and whites from Appalachia and the South. The "changing face" of the workforce in the auto industry will be the subject of the next chapter.

EIGHT

The New Workers

Rapidly expanding defense production, especially in 1942 and 1943, created the need for an expanded workforce for the automobile and parts makers engaged in war production. Industries outside the automobile industry, especially those engaged in building aircraft, ships, and munitions of all types, also developed an enormous appetite for more workers to staff their plants. Simultaneously, the growing manpower needs of the expanding military forces, satisfied through enlistments and the draft, siphoned off millions of workers from the labor pool. Toward the end of 1942, but especially in 1943, many industries struggled to find enough workers to produce the war goods they were under contract to deliver. Most defense industries, including the automobile industry, met their needs for additional workers by tapping previously underutilized pools of labor: white workers from West Virginia, Kentucky, Tennessee, and the Deep South; African American workers mainly from the South; and women workers primarily from both urban and rural areas in Michigan. The story of how these new workers came to be hired by the auto industry, their experiences working in defense production, and their overall impact on the automobile industry's performance during the war will be the focus of this chapter.

As late as 1940, the U.S. economy was still suffering from the lingering effects of the Great Depression, with 8.1 million unemployed, some 14.6 percent of the civilian labor force. As rearmament got under way in 1940 and 1941, an adequate labor supply was not an issue. Unemployment levels fell to 5.6 million (9.9 percent of the civilian labor force) in 1941, to 2.7 million (4.7 percent) in 1942, and then to only 1.1 million (1.9 percent) in 1943. The civilian labor force grew significantly during these years, from 56.2 million in 1940 to 64.6 million in 1943, even though millions were leaving for the military. Virtually all of this growth was the result of the influx of African Americans and women into the labor force.[1]

In 1940, the four branches of the U.S. military (army, navy, marines, and the coast guard) consisted of 458,368 men and women. This number grew rapidly to 1.8 million in 1941, 3.9 million in 1942, and then 9 million in 1943. Troop strength in 1944 expanded further to 11.5 million and peaked in 1945 at 12.1 million men and women. The military branches had planned even larger armed forces and pushed the War Production Board (WPB) to expand defense production to equip these forces. At the end of September 1942, the Joint Chiefs of Staff approved plans for a military force of 10.9 million by the end of 1943. The WPB argued that these military manpower plans were unrealistic and could not be supported by the war economy. Roosevelt supported the WPB and the military forces projected for 1943 were reduced by nearly 2 million.[2]

The automobile industry and other defense industries solved the problem of severe labor shortages by drawing on untapped pools of labor, mainly white southerners, African Americans, and women. The automobile industry had employed all three groups in limited numbers and in particular types of work before the war, but their numbers exploded from late 1942 on and they began doing types of work they had not done before. Hiring large numbers of new workers brought distinct challenges to the automakers and caused significant adjustment problems for both the new and old employees. White southerners, African Americans, and women faced different experiences upon entering the defense plants. Each group will be considered in separate sections.

A major challenge the automakers faced was training these new workers, most of whom lacked manufacturing experience. They were expected to perform tasks that were often new to the automakers as well, including riveting aluminum aircraft components and making delicate castings in aluminum and other unfamiliar metals. To train both new and existing workers, all of the automakers established two distinct types of programs during the war: those geared to train their own production workers in various specialized skills, and programs to teach military and civilian personnel how to repair and service the products each company was making. Ford initially trained workers at the River Rouge plant for various jobs at Willow Run and then opened an Apprentice School at Willow Run in July 1942. There, Ford trained 120,000 civilian workers to perform assembly operations, welding, riveting, inspections, and other tasks. Nearly 22,000 workers were trained in welding alone. The company trained workers at several other locations to perform tasks related to the production of tanks, tank engines, and aircraft engines, among other products.[3]

Ford and the other companies also established schools to teach military personnel to repair and service their products. Chrysler, for example, graduated 3,700 army tank technicians (mechanics) from a training school established at the Chrysler tank arsenal. Seeing the tank assembled firsthand, having tank components and complete tanks to work on, and using Chrysler personnel as instructors greatly facilitated the training process. Ford operated similar training schools for army personnel who would repair and maintain B-24 bombers, tank engines, aircraft engines, tanks, jeeps, Seeps, and its other war products. The company also built and operated a training facility that was not connected to any of its defense products: the U.S. Navy Service School on the Rouge River next to the Ford Rouge plant in Dearborn. Henry Ford built facilities to house and train 2,000 enlisted navy personnel, which he leased to the navy for $1 a year. There, instructors from the Henry Ford Trade School trained more than 23,300 men to become electricians, machinists, boilermakers, shipfitters, metalsmiths, and molders, and in a variety of other skilled trades.[4]

The Forgotten Minority: White Workers from the Appalachians and the South

Plentiful jobs and high wages in the auto-industry-turned-defense-industry attracted large numbers of immigrants from distressed areas of West Virginia, eastern Kentucky, and Tennessee to Michigan's factory towns. A special report issued by the U.S. Census Bureau in June 1944 covering migration into the Detroit-Willow Run region since 1940 showed 80 percent of the migrants came from outside Michigan and nearly half of these (47.8 percent) came from the Appalachians and the South. The latter figure included both African Americans and whites. A common wartime joke began with the question, "How many states are there in the United States?" The answer was "Forty-six, because Tennessee and Kentucky are now in Michigan." Whites "native" to Michigan often viewed southern whites with contempt and alarm, considering them nearly as undesirable as blacks. Southern white workers often had even more difficulty adjusting to life in a northern industrial city than did African Americans, many of whom received assistance from the Detroit Urban League and the Detroit chapter of the NAACP in finding housing and transportation. There were no comparable organizations to help white southerners. Many white immigrants from these border states came north with virulent racial hostility toward blacks and only added to any racial hostility already in defense plants.[5]

White southerners, including many from Missouri, Arkansas, and other southern states, faced hostility from the established whites living in southeast Michigan. The natives called them "Kaintucks," "Briarhoppers," and "hillbillies" and described them as ignorant, illiterate, and lazy "yokels" who put mail in fire alarm boxes or arrived at work barefoot. Native whites derided white southerners for following their own brand of religion, "storefront" fundamentalist Christianity often led by worker-preachers. They would not rent rooms to southerners or offer them jobs.[6]

Historian Alan Clive argues that the influx of southern whites into the war industry in Michigan added significantly to racial tensions in the factories and elsewhere. An estimated three thousand worker-preachers spread anti-black and anti-Semitic hate messages from the pulpits of storefront churches on Sunday and even from within the factories. Organizations filled with white southerners but not associated with churches, including the Forrest Club, the National Workers League, the Dixie Voters, the Southern Society, and the Mothers of America, spread messages of hate among factory workers. The Ku Klux Klan (KKK) renamed itself the United Sons of America, continued promoting its traditional racist agenda, and apparently had significant support from workers at Packard and Hudson. UAW president R. J. Thomas blamed the KKK for the "hate strike" at Packard in early June 1943, but there is little evidence to support his accusations.[7]

The experiences of white southerners at dozens of defense plants in southeast Michigan are best understood by focusing on those employed at the Ford Willow Run bomber plant. Peak employment at Willow Run reached 42,331 in June 1943, which included 10,000 women and many hired from out of state. In March 1943, Ford received permission from the War Manpower Commission to recruit workers from Tennessee, Kentucky, Iowa, Illinois, and Texas. The automaker produced a recruitment flyer aimed at Kentucky workers that promised a fifty-four-hour work week, with time-and-a-half for hours above forty, equal pay for women, job training, and opportunities for advancement. They even offered to pay workers' transportation expenses to get to Willow Run. The effort worked. In June 1945, Willow Run's employment department compiled a list of the states of origin for workers hired at the plant between 1 March 1943 and 31 May 1945. Local Michigan residents, mainly from southeastern Michigan, accounted for fewer than half (18,628 of 39,249) of the workers, and roughly 10,000 of those had been transferred to Willow Run from other Ford plants. Workers from Kentucky (6,491) and Tennessee (1,971) accounted for more than half of the out-of-state workers. The next five states with the most workers were Illinois (837), Texas (714), West Virginia (450), Arkansas (397), and Missouri (314). Almost none of these workers had previous experience working in manufacturing. African Americans made up only 9 percent of the in-migrants who came to Willow Run in 1940–44 and there is no evidence of racial conflict at the plant or in the community during the war.[8]

During and after the war, Lowell Julliard Carr and James Edson Stermer, a team of sociologists from the University of Michigan, undertook an extensive study of the Willow Run factory, its workers, and the Willow Run community, published in 1952 as *Willow Run: A Study of Industrialization and Cultural Inadequacy*. They examined the extremely high rates of labor turnover and disaffection at the plant and linked those negative developments directly to the severe shortages of housing for plant workers. The employees who decided to live near the bomber plant ended up in trailers, tents, shacks, and shanties in crowded and squalid conditions. The Willow Run community that emerged during the war was plagued with poor schools, juvenile delinquency, crime, and a host of other challenges. In most respects, the lack of housing was the root cause of most of Willow Run's social problems.[9]

Carr and Stermer document the often-heartbreaking lives of white southern workers at Willow Run. An undetermined number made the trip to Willow Run but never went to work because they could not find a place to live. "Rose H." from Owensboro, Kentucky, wrote to Ford management in October 1943 and explained her dilemma: "I am very sorry I dident get to work in your plant. Because I belive I would have liked my work. But Sir I was up their alone and dident know no one. And dident have eny Place to stay. Even for the one night I was up their, so I dident know what else to do. So I came back home. I am verry sorry I caused you all so much trouble." Others complained that they ran out of money before they could start working or became too sick after arriving at Willow Run to start work. Those who lived in trailers, known as "trailorites," were the fortunate ones at Willow Run. The lack of child-care facilities until July 1943 (and then at a school three miles from the plant) meant that parents either stayed at home or left young children home alone all day.[10]

The Army Air Force analysis of the labor situation at Willow Run, issued in August 1946, concluded that worker morale remained low throughout the war and accounted for much of the labor turnover. Ford assumed that high wages would automatically bring high morale, much like the company had assumed thirty years earlier when it offered a $5 a day pay rate at the Highland Park plant. Long work hours, transportation problems, and the lack of housing all contributed to low morale. Workers coming to Willow Run from rural areas with no industrial experience found the bomber plant overwhelming. Throwing together workers from very different cultures and with different values in a giant factory did not help build a coherent workforce.[11]

African Americans in the War Industries

In 1940, African Americans made up 4 percent of the workers in the automobile industry and only 0.2 percent of the workers in the aircraft industry. Roughly 70 percent of black automobile workers were employed in the metropolitan Detroit area and worked primarily for a handful companies: Ford, Chrysler (Dodge), General Motors, and Briggs Manufacturing, which made automobile bodies. The Ford Motor Company averaged 11,000 black employees between 1937 and 1941, roughly 10 percent of its workforce. Ford towered above the other automakers in the Detroit area in this regard, employing about two-thirds of all blacks working in the auto industry. In 1941, Chrysler employed 1,978 African Americans, 2.4 percent of its workforce, almost entirely at its Dodge Main plant in Hamtramck, a small city surrounded by Detroit. GM's 2,800 black employees, scattered among plants in Saginaw, Flint, and Detroit, constituted roughly 3 percent of its workforce. Briggs Manufacturing had nearly 1,300 black employees, roughly 10 percent of its payroll.[12]

The history of black workers in the Detroit auto industry before World War II is worth recounting. The Packard Motor Car Company, heavily committed to war work in World War I (Liberty airplane engines), employed 1,100 blacks in May 1917, the first automaker to hire African Americans in substantial numbers. Ford had only 50 black workers in January 1916 but employed 2,500 in 1920, still only 4 percent of Ford's enormous workforce. By 1926, Ford employed 10,000 blacks, roughly 10 percent of its labor force, a share that remained fairly steady through 1941. Dodge Brothers was one of the earliest Detroit automakers to hire black workers. John Dodge met with John Dancy, the head of the Detroit Urban League, in November 1919 to discuss the possibility of Dodge Brothers hiring African Americans. John Dodge hired black workers over the next year, but there is no record of the numbers involved. By the late 1920s, Dodge was the second largest employer of blacks among the automakers, with about 850 African American employees, but a distant second to Ford. Many large employers such as the Fisher Body Corporation steadfastly refused to hire blacks. Fisher Body had 12,000 employees in Detroit in 1926, but only sixty black workers, all serving as janitors. The company's hiring practices remained largely unchanged over the next two decades.[13]

The automakers who hired black workers, including Ford, initially placed these workers in the most difficult, dirty, unpleasant, and dangerous jobs in their plants, which helped minimize white workers' objections to their presence. African American workers were rarely found in the mainstream production departments, which meant that they were segregated from white workers. Typically black workers labored in the foundries, paint-spraying operations, heat treatment plants, and sanding operations.

They typically were employed as general laborers, hand truck operators, or sweepers, the lowest-paying jobs in the factory, without regard to education or talent. Black workers at Ford had more opportunities than at the other automakers. While more than half of Ford's black employees worked in the foundries, they also worked in assembly operations and in skilled trades, including tool and die making, and were admitted into Ford's apprentice school.[14]

The labor shortages brought by the expansion of war production coupled with the manpower demands of the military service eventually forced all defense producers including the automobile companies to hire blacks in large numbers. Nationally, the share of jobs in the defense industry held by blacks increased from 4.2 percent in July 1942 to 8.6 percent in July 1945. In early 1941 the Detroit-area labor force included 70,000 blacks, about 7 percent of the total, but only 30,000 of them (42 percent) were employed and only half of those employed, roughly 15,000 (21 percent), worked in manufacturing. The employment opportunities for African Americans had changed dramatically by 1945. Blacks made up 14 percent of a much larger Detroit labor force and held 95,000 defense industry jobs (21 percent of the total). Most automakers-turned-defense-contractors, with a few exceptions like Fisher Body, experienced substantial changes in the mix of their workers in terms of race and by gender. The Chrysler Corporation was a typical example. Chrysler's prewar workforce of 82,243 increased by more than 50 percent to 125,481 employees at the wartime peak level in March 1945. Chrysler employed 1,978 black workers in 1940 (2.4 percent of its workforce), but in March 1945 had 18,148 African Americans (14 percent of the total) on its payroll.[15]

African Americans faced exclusion from work in many parts of the defense industry in the early years of the war and, once employed, experienced severe discrimination in terms of jobs, training, and promotions. President Roosevelt, faced with heavy lobbying by black leaders, especially A. Philip Randolph, president of the Brotherhood of Sleeping Car Porters, issued Executive Order 8802 on 25 June 1941 banning employment discrimination based on race, creed, color, or national origin by defense contractors, labor unions, and civilian departments within the federal government. Roosevelt created the Fair Employment Practice Committee (FEPC) to enforce his executive order.

The FEPC received 12,000 complaints of discrimination during the war and settled about 5,000 of them. The commission launched educational campaigns against racial discrimination in the workplace and exposed numerous cases of prejudice. With fewer than 120 employees trying to serve all of wartime industry, its influence was at best marginal. The FEPC had some success in integrating workplaces and reducing discrimination in northern and western states but made very little progress in southern and border states. There were significant advances made against racial discrimination in war industries, but not by the FEPC or other federal civilian agencies. Progress came as a result of policies followed by some labor unions, particularly the UAW, from the actions taken by employers independent of government mandates, and through the intervention of the military services.[16]

In the automobile industry, black workers faced serious hurdles to job equality even after they were initially employed in foundries, paint shops, sanding operations, or in other dangerous, unskilled work. When employers moved black workers into previously all-white departments though promotions or transfers from other plants, white workers in the affected department and throughout the plant frequently would go on strike until the transfers were rescinded. The UAW international union never authorized or supported these "wildcat strikes," routinely referred to as "hate strikes" by the press, but UAW local unions nevertheless often supported these actions. These racially motivated strikes disrupted war production and at least temporarily slowed racial integration in the plants. There were periodic hate strikes in 1941 and 1942, substantially more in 1943, but then they stopped entirely the following year.[17]

White hostility toward black workers was usually the result of deep-seated racism. Several Detroit-area automobile factories had disproportionate shares of recent white immigrants from Kentucky, Tennessee, and the Deep South. Their racism was part of the baggage they brought with them, and the plants in which they worked in large numbers were also the sites of most of the "hate strikes" early in the war. Frequently white workers refused to share bathroom facilities with blacks, and female workers were especially reluctant to share bathrooms with black women because they believed that black women were dirty and carried venereal diseases white women could contract by using the same bathrooms. This issue produced a strike of more than 2,000 white women workers at the U.S. Rubber Company plant in Detroit in March 1943 after the company hired black female machinists. In spring 1944, when the Chevrolet plant in Flint failed to rehire seven white female workers who had refused to work alongside four black women assigned to their department, 1,500 UAW workers walked out.[18]

The fear of sharing bathrooms was not limited to white women. A similar dispute arose at the Point Breeze plant of the Western Electric Company in Baltimore, which produced combat communications equipment for the U.S. Army. When Western Electric eliminated segregated bathrooms in early October 1943, the union—the Point Breeze Employees Association—went on strike. Western Electric's personnel manager also argued that blacks carried much more venereal disease than whites, so sharing common toilets subjected white workers to unnecessary risk. With the strike still in effect after ten weeks, President Roosevelt ordered the army to seize the plant, which it did on 19 December 1943. Western Electric enlarged its bathroom facilities but kept them segregated, left the dining facilities integrated, and offered venereal disease testing to all. The army returned control of the plant on 23 March 1944, ending the dispute.[19]

There were dozens of hate strikes documented in the greater Detroit area alone and probably many more that were so short-lived or involved so few workers that they went unnoticed. The well-documented hate strikes took place primarily at mid-sized automakers, at plants operated by Packard, Hudson, and Timken Axle, or at suppliers' factories. Chrysler experienced several of these disturbances at its plants, but Ford and General Motors had few. The outcome of these strikes was determined by a combination of factors: the attitudes of white and black workers, the positions taken by the UAW local union and the international union, the approach taken by company management to resolve the disputes, and the willingness of the military services to intervene.

The Packard Motor Car Company plant in Detroit was the scene of several of the largest hate strikes in the early years of the war. The plant had all the elements to produce an explosive environment: a workforce made up mostly of Polish Americans and southern whites, both very hostile toward blacks; local union leadership that allegedly had connections with the KKK; and an openly racist personnel manager. The leadership of the Packard UAW Local 190 had pushed Packard management to promote blacks within the plant, but when the company transferred two black metal polishers from automobile production to defense work in October 1941, about 250 white metal polishers protested and staged a sit-down strike. The shop steward returned the men to their old jobs, and their fate touched off a divisive struggle involving the leaders of Local 190, the UAW's national leadership, C. E. Weiss (Packard's personnel manager), and federal officials. Weiss insisted that the local union leadership promise in writing to discipline any of its members who tried to prevent the transfers. The local union leaders eventually agreed, and in mid-March 1942, six months after the controversy first developed, Packard transferred the two black metal polishers to their new jobs.[20]

A similar dispute arose in January 1942 when the management of the U.S. Naval Arsenal in Center Line, Michigan, operated by the Hudson Motor Car Company, promoted two black janitors, who were trained as machinists, to new jobs. Two hundred white workers walked off their jobs in protest and the company returned the black workers to their previous jobs. UAW Local 154 claimed it was powerless to enforce its own international union's constitution or federal law regarding job discrimination. Hudson's Local 154 elected several black workers to its executive board in April and the company, the navy, and the UAW agreed to upgrade blacks to better jobs. Hudson was desperate to find machine operators. On 18 June 1942, the transfer of a handful of blacks to machine jobs touched off a walkout of ten thousand white workers. Secretary of the Navy Frank Knox threatened the striking workers with wholesale firings and blacklisting at other defense plants, while the UAW threatened to discipline the hate strike leaders by expelling them from the union. The white workers returned to their jobs within a day, as did the black machine operators, and Hudson fired four of the ringleaders with the UAW's support. A unified stance against such strikes seemed to end them quickly.[21]

Chrysler experienced two hate strikes in 1942 at several of its Detroit-area plants over the issue of transferring black workers from one plant to another. In early February 1942, Chrysler transferred black dock workers (boxers and loaders) from the Dodge Main plant to the Highland Park plant, which touched off three sit-down strikes at the latter plant. Richard Frankensteen, a UAW vice president in charge of the Chrysler plants, gave the strikers an ultimatum: return to work or be fired. They went back to work. On 2 June 1942, when Chrysler transferred twenty-six black workers to its Dodge truck plant, about 350 white workers walked out and forced the closing of the plant, which employed 3,000. Chrysler, the UAW, and the WPB stood their ground and fired two ringleaders of the walkout. The plant returned to normal the following day, with the black workers at their new jobs.[22]

Timken-Detroit, a large manufacturer of axles, promoted a single black hammerman helper to hammerman on 7 July 1942, touching off a strike of the white workers. Traditionally blacks had worked as helpers in this plant but never as hammermen, a more skilled and higher-paid job. The company withdrew this single promotion and the men returned to work. The UAW international union, the company, and the U.S. government combined to force the UAW local to agree "that all Negroes who were eligible should be upgraded" and that the first black man who had been promoted could remain as a hammerman. Colonel George E. Strong, the Army Air Force contract compliance officer based in Detroit, informed the local union that he intended to enforce Executive Order 8802. The upgrading of a second black worker to the hammerman's position touched off a very brief walkout by a handful of workers.[23]

The most serious hate strikes of the war, but not the last, took place at the Packard plant in Detroit in May and June 1943. Some 2,500 black workers were employed at Packard at the time, mostly in the foundry. On 24 May, Packard upgraded three black men to jobs on the aircraft engine assembly line, which caused several hundred workers to immediately walk off their jobs. UAW Local 190 agreed to withdraw the three men and hold a conference to resolve the issue. In a heated meeting of the union members with R. J. Thomas, the president of the UAW, one worker shouted out, "I'd rather see Hitler and Hirohito win than work beside a nigger on the assembly line!" Black foundry workers at Packard protested their own union's actions and shut down the foundry for three days. The white workers returned to their jobs but walked out again on 3 June 1943 after the three black workers were reinstated in their new jobs. About 90 percent of the Packard workforce, some 25,000 in total, joined the strike.

The UAW and the Army Air Force confronted the leaders of Local 190 and C. E. Weiss, who supported the strike and opposed the promotion of black workers. In a public statement issued on 5 June, Colonel George Strong threatened to fire all striking workers and thus make them eligible for the draft. The following day, he suspended thirty ringleaders to make his point. On 7 June almost everyone returned to work, but this was not the last of the hate strikes at Packard. Segregation within many departments remained the rule, and white workers at Packard briefly struck again in October and November 1944 when the company transferred black workers into previously all-white departments. The last of these walkouts involved 39,000 workers and ended only when the union withdrew the promotions, angering the black workers.[24]

The hate strikes of 1943, especially the ones at Packard, were simply one example of widespread racial animosity that pervaded the Detroit landscape in 1942 and 1943. The wartime expansion of the defense industry brought an influx of tens of thousands of new workers to Detroit, where housing became extremely crowded for blacks and whites alike. In late February and early March 1942, whites rioted to prevent black families from moving into the brand-new Sojourner Truth Housing Project in a mostly white area in north-central Detroit. The rioters succeeded for a while, but the black families finally moved into Sojourner Truth at the end of April with police and military protection. The signature event of Detroit's troubled wartime race relations was the Detroit Race Riot of 20–24 June 1943, which required federal troops to restore order. In the course of the riot, twenty-five blacks and nine whites died, over seven hundred were injured, and the city suffered more than $2 million in property damage. Remarkably, Detroit's defense plants remained calm during the riot.[25]

Black workers did not passively accept their fate when they faced discrimination, abuse, indifference, and hostility from their own union brothers. Black workers at Chrysler's Dodge Main and Dodge Truck plants walked off in July and August 1941 to protest discrimination in promotions and transfers. Black janitors at the Chrysler Highland Park plant struck in early 1943 over discrimination in promotions. More than 3,000 black foundry workers at the Ford Rouge plant staged a three-day wildcat strike in April 1943 to protest Ford's refusal to hire additional black workers. Black workers walked out at Packard in November 1944 to protest the UAW local union's caving in to its white members and returning black workers who had been promoted back to their lower-level jobs.[26]

Among those seeking work in the defense plants during the war, black females faced the most pervasive, virulent, and persistent discrimination, far worse than that faced by black men. They are treated here as African Americans rather than as women because they faced hostility based on their race rather than gender. Automobile companies that hired thousands of white women by 1943 simply refused to hire any black women. White female members of the UAW were as strongly opposed to the introduction of black women into the workplace as anyone. At a UAW Women's Conference held in February 1942, Evelyn Scanlon, representing the women of UAW Local 3 (Dodge Main) but reflecting the views of most women workers, objected to a motion supporting desegregation of the shop floor. Scanlon proclaimed, "I don't think we should consider bringing them (black women) into the shops—if we bring them in even in this crisis we'd always have them to contend with. And you know what that means—we'd be working right beside them, we'd be using the same rest rooms, etc. . . . I'm against it."[27]

A spate of incidents in the first half of 1943 likely reflected an increase in the hiring of black women by defense contractors. In late January 1943, the Hudson Naval Arsenal hired two black women to work in the cafeteria but fired them after white women workers threatened to quit. Sixteen busboys and cafeteria porters, all black, walked out in protest. The personnel manager claimed he fired the women because they "distracted" the other black cafeteria workers from doing their work. On 12 February 1943, Packard promoted three black women to jobs as drill press operators after they completed a training program. White women holding the same jobs walked out and the local union returned the black women to their training school. The UAW brought in the FEPC and the U.S. Army in the person of Colonel Strong to pressure the company to return the black women to their new jobs and Packard obliged. The company, however, forced these women to use a segregated bathroom. The white women then returned to work, but when Packard added four additional black female drill press operators on 18 March 1943, about three thousand white Packard workers walked off their jobs in two different wildcat strikes. The company, the union, and the government refused to cave in to these hate strikes and Packard remained racially tense for much of the rest of the year.[28]

Even when black women found jobs at defense plants, they typically faced severe discrimination in terms of their job assignments and general working conditions. Black women employed at Chrysler's Jefferson Avenue plant in Detroit found that they were to clean men's bathrooms or were required to move barrels of metal shavings weighing two hundred pounds or more. They had been trained to work as elevator operators, but the male elevator operators refused to give up their jobs. Chrysler forced the black women to use a segregated bathroom located a long distance from where they worked and were told to eat their lunch in the bathroom rather than in the cafeteria the rest of the workers used. The black women complained to their local union but received no relief, so they quit their jobs. Six hundred black men went on strike in support of the black women, and Chrysler settled the dispute by rehiring the black women who quit and giving them lighter work to perform.[29]

The Ford Motor Company was probably the most intransigent of all the automakers in refusing to hire black women despite its size and its history of hiring black men. When Ford began to hire workers for the Willow Run bomber plant in early 1942, the company took applications at its employment office at the River Rouge plant. In February, three black women trained as secretaries were refused the opportunity to fill out job applications for secretarial positions. Ford announced that it was not going to hire any black women for the Willow Run plant because they would create "disturbances." The UAW protested, but after Ford held a series of meetings with its white female workers at Willow Run in May 1942, the company claimed that its white women workers refused to work with black women. The FEPC attempted to pressure Harry Bennett, who was in charge of labor relations at Willow Run, to hire black females, but he simply refused. The UAW picketed the employment office at the Rouge plant for much of the summer, and Ford finally hired twenty-five black women to work at its small Ypsilanti parts plant in fall 1942. Under continuous pressure from the UAW, the FEPC, and various black organizations such as the NAACP, Ford hired a handful of black women at Willow Run in December 1942. By September 1943, when 35,000 worked at Willow Run, the plant employed only 420 African American men and 280 African American women, or 2 percent of the total workforce. By the end of the war, the Willow Run plant employed only 735 black workers in total, or 3.5 percent of the labor force.[30]

The UAW Research Department regularly conducted surveys of its local unions to determine how many black workers and women workers were employed. The returns often give round numbers, clearly approximations. It is not clear whether the local unions were supplying numbers they received from plant managers or from their own dues and membership records. The survey coverage varies a good deal, sometimes including the "top 185 war plants in the Detroit area" or "all UAW-CIO shops" and sometimes only the fifty largest plants in Michigan. Summary tables often do not identify the scope of the data collected. Because the surveys are not comparable, the discussion that follows will focus on percentages and not the absolute numbers.

The increase in the number of African American workers in the quickly converting auto industry is evident before Pearl Harbor. Black workers made up only 4 percent of all automobile workers in 1940, but in October 1941 they accounted for 9 percent of the workforce in UAW plants in the greater Detroit area, 11 percent in October 1942, and 12.7 percent in April 1943. The UAW Research Department surveyed twenty-eight large plants in Michigan and Ohio for information on the composition of their workforces as of 30 April 1945. The results showed 189,105 employees, 14.7 percent of whom were black. Unfortunately the surviving survey forms do not include several large factories such as the Ford River Rouge and Willow Run plants, Chrysler-Jefferson Avenue, the Dodge-Chicago factory, and various plants in Indiana.

Broader surveys of 185 plants, which included factories in areas with relatively small black populations, such as Ohio, Indiana, and Michigan factories in Lansing, Flint, and Pontiac, showed smaller shares of black workers. A survey conducted in May 1942 showed blacks made up only 5.6 percent of the workforce in these 185 plants, but the same survey completed in January 1943 showed an increase to 6.8 percent. The employment advances achieved by black workers in defense production based in (former) automobile plants, particularly in the greater Detroit area, were far greater than the progress made in all defense plants nationally. The share of black workers in the workforce in war industries nationally increased dramatically from 4.2 percent in July 1942 to 8.6 percent in July 1945.[31]

The very slow advancement of black women into war industry jobs is evident in the employment statistics. By 1 July 1942, some two hundred defense plants responded to a questionnaire from the UAW Research Department regarding female employment. The responding companies employed 393,159 workers, 24,530 of whom were women (6.2 percent of their workforce). The same companies employed only 115 black women in total, less than one-half of 1 percent of their women workers, but only five on production jobs. A December 1942 survey of fifty plants in Detroit, which employed 63,630 women, revealed that the same plants employed only 1,033 black women (1.6 percent of their female workforce). Fourteen of these factories employed no black women. The UAW surveyed thirty-two Detroit factories in April 1943, when they employed 66,125 women, 2,458 (3.7 percent) of whom were black women. The last detailed UAW survey that has survived was completed in September 1943 and included forty-seven factories in Detroit. The number of African American female employees had increased dramatically to 12,671 (15 percent of all women employed). The trend toward hiring more black women is evident in the national statistics as well. Of all black women employed nationally in April 1940, only 6.5 percent were industrial workers and 60 percent were domestic workers. Four years later, 18 percent of working black women had industrial jobs and 44.6 percent were domestics.[32]

The records of individual companies and plants with regard to hiring African Americans, especially women, varied greatly across the automobile industry. Ford, which led the hiring of black workers in the 1920s and 1930s, made no additional progress during the war and by most measures fell behind Chrysler and many of the smaller manufacturers and suppliers. General Motors also appears to have dragged its feet in integrating its workforce, but this may have been at least partly a function of where its plants were located. In June 1944, the UAW Research Department conducted a survey limited to General Motors plants in part because GM refused to provide the FEPC the statistics it requested regarding female and black employment. The GM local unions reported a total employment of 195,246 at more than a hundred plants across the United States. The figure included 61,753 women or 31.6 percent of the total, which is within the general range of women's share of the labor force found in most automakers' defense plants. A smaller survey of GM plants in Michigan (22) with 83,775 workers reported specifically on black men and black women in their plants. African American men made up 7 percent of total employment in these plants and African American women a mere 1.6 percent, with most of them working in Detroit plants. The survey identified nine GM plants that employed no blacks and an additional eight that employed black men but no black women.[33]

Women Workers in the Defense Industry

At the start of the war, women comprised a much larger potential source of labor for war production than did African Americans. In 1940, 14.2 million women made up 25 percent of the civilian labor force (people working or looking for work) along with 42 million men. That same year, 36 million women of working age were not in the labor force and 1.7 million who were in the labor force were unemployed. By 1944 the employment picture had changed significantly. The number of women in the civilian labor force increased to 18.45 million (34 percent of the total), while those unemployed fell from 1.7 million in March 1940 to only 400,000 by March 1944. Those working in civilian nonagricultural jobs increased from nearly 11 million in March 1941 to 18 million in August 1944. Between 1940 and 1944, the number of women of working age but not in the labor force fell from 36 million to 33.3 million, and 1.5 million women who were already employed elsewhere took jobs in war industries.[34]

Once women entered war industries in large numbers, they were found in almost every area of production, including shipbuilding, munitions manufacturing, and aircraft manufacturing, and in the hundreds of factories that previously made automobiles and automotive components. In the aircraft industry, where most of the work

Packing line for .45-caliber cartridges, Chrysler Evansville (IN) plant (*ACWP*).

was light precision work, such as riveting aluminum fuselage and wing sections, the expansion of female employment was breathtaking. The industry employed only 4,000 women at the end of 1941, but by July 1943 aircraft manufacturers employed 310,000 women. In contrast, the automobile industry before the war already had substantial numbers of women workers. In 1940, when the broadly defined auto industry (automobiles and automobile equipment) had 516,062 employees, 41,299 were women, 8 percent of the total.[35]

The automobile industry had small but significant numbers of female workers from the beginning. In 1910, still the industry's fledgling days, 1,044 of the industry's workforce of 41,516 were women (2.4 percent of the total). A decade later, when employment had leaped to 231,462, there were 15,644 women employed (6.8 percent of the total). In the 1930s, female employment ranged from 5.7 percent to 7.2 percent of the total. Some of the earliest work performed by women included assembly of small parts. The July 1909 issue of *Ford Times* shows six women winding coils with magnet wire for the Model T's flywheel magneto. Six years later, an exhaustive study of production at the Ford Highland Park plant shows dozens of women making fields for Model T flywheel magnetos. The same volume illustrates another area of production where women had an early presence: sewing operations. A 1915 illustration of the upholstery department at the Dodge Brothers plant in Hamtramck shows an all-male workforce, but at the Ford Highland Park plant in 1914, forty-eight women worked in the upholstery department sewing cushions. Women also used their sewing skills in making automobile body tops, which consisted of fabric or leather through the 1920s. The study of Ford's Highland Park operations shows a "Body-Top-Making Department" with at least fifty women operating sewing machines. Ford had enough women working at Highland Park to justify several women's washrooms, including one with fourteen sinks. Women even had a separate factory entrance. Still, women were a tiny minority at the Highland Park plant. Of the 15,000 workers who toiled there in 1914, only 250 were women.[36]

The number of women working in the auto industry expanded greatly in the 1920s. In a 1929 study of labor in the auto industry, Robert Dunn claimed that the Hudson Motor Company, A. C. Spark Plug, and the Ternstedt Manufacturing Company each had more than 1,000 women workers, while Continental Motors, Packard, and Buick employed women by the hundreds. A. C. Spark Plug in Flint employed 700 men and 1,200 women. Many employers preferred to hire women to assemble small parts, believing that they were faster and more dexterous than men in this type of work. Women were found in almost all lines of work except the very heaviest. Cadillac employed 58 women in the core room of its foundry. Large numbers worked for body companies and engaged in sanding, rubbing, and polishing body panels. Women operated large punch presses, lathes, grinders, and heavy-duty cranes. They did inspection work, stock-chasing, and tool crib work. Women also worked on trim and upholstery, especially where sewing was involved.[37]

A U.S. Bureau of Labor Statistics study of labor in the motor vehicle industry conducted in 1925 showed that the jobs women held in the automobile and parts plants varied greatly between companies and regions. Women comprised one-tenth of "top builders" in Indiana, but none plied that trade in neighboring Ohio. A few female punch-press operators were found in Michigan and New Jersey but nowhere else. The 947 "trim bench hands" surveyed were evenly split between men and women. The survey included 3,432 women (2.4 percent of the total workforce) in the auto industry and identified 99 possible occupations. Women were found in two dozen job categories, but nearly one-third of all the women surveyed in 1925 were sewing machine operators. Another 474 women worked as "trim bench hands," 437 as inspectors, and 318 as "final assemblers," accounting for an additional 36 percent of the women workers.[38]

A Bureau of Labor Statistics survey of 448 automobile plants completed in May–June 1940 and published in 1942 provides a detailed picture of women's jobs in the industry on the eve of the war. The survey included 471,270 workers, with 322,941 (68.5 percent) working in automotive assembly or body plants and the remaining 148,329 (31.5 percent) employed in automotive parts factories. The industry employed 35,969 women or 7.6 percent of the total workforce, but 28,041 (78 percent of women workers) were in parts plants and only 7,928 (22 percent) toiled in the assembly and body plants. Nearly one-fifth (18.9 percent) of workers in the part plants were women. The survey showed that they worked in only a handful of job categories. In the auto assembly and body plants, women made up 73 percent of sewing machine operators and nearly half of small-parts assemblers. Most of the rest worked as body assemblers and trimmers. The vast majority of the women working in the parts plants were concentrated in four jobs: small-parts assembly (39.6 percent); inspection (17.3 percent); machining operators (13 percent); and punch-press operators (12.8 percent).[39]

Through the late 1930s, women who wanted to work in industry faced widespread prejudice and "unwritten rules" that affected their employment. Some companies refused to hire married women, which forced them to keep their marriages secret. More commonly, manufacturers would discharge women workers who became pregnant, believing that they could no longer safely work. The employment statistics from the automobile industry suggest little prejudice against women based on marital status alone. The 1940 Population Census showed 15,406 women workers in auto plants, 61 percent of whom were married, 28 percent single, and 11 percent widowed or divorced. A U.S. Department of Labor study of women workers in 1944 showed 215,000 women employed in manufacturing in the Detroit-Willow Run area, more than four times the number (46,800) employed in 1940. The region was defined to include Wayne, Oakland, Macomb, and Washtenaw counties. Married and single women each comprised 45 percent of the female workforce in 1944, while widowed and divorced women accounted for the remaining 10 percent.[40]

The increase in the absolute numbers of married women in the auto industry, as well of their share of the total, meant that more women who had children in their care took defense jobs. In 1944, in the Detroit-Willow Run area, 20 percent of all employed women and 35 percent of married, widowed, or divorced women had children under fourteen living in their households. The majority (61 percent) of these women had one child in their care, 26 percent had two children, and 13 percent had three children or more. Given the numbers of women with children in the defense industries, especially starting in 1943, there was a growing need for child care for working women. The federal government, working with state governments, helped fund a limited number of child-care facilities, but most working mothers relied on child care outside of government-funded child-care centers.[41]

The Works Progress Administration (WPA) provided limited funding for nursery schools though most of the 1930s as a way of providing unemployed poor women with child care so they could find jobs. By December 1942, roughly 2,000 WPA child-care centers were open nationally but were threatened by the elimination of the WPA itself. In early 1943, the Federal Works Agency (FWA) took over the WPA nurseries and operated them with funds supplied under the Lanham Act (October 1940) but kept only 1,150 of them open. The FWA supported a limited number of child-care facilities through grants-in-aid to the states. At the end of June 1944, a total of 1,995 FWA-supported child-care facilities, both nursery schools and centers for older children, enrolled a total of only 108,157 children, mostly in defense industry regions with severe labor shortages.[42]

Fortunately, working mothers in war industries could rely on a host of other child-care options. Women working in war industries in the greater Detroit area in 1944 used the following types of child care: husbands working a different shift (16 percent); older children (2 percent); a relative living in the household (40 percent); a relative outside the household (15 percent); paid help living in the household (8 percent); and neighbors (7 percent). Nursery schools accounted for a mere 2 percent of the child-care service. Most child care was supplied by family, friends, and other trusted individuals.[43]

When the automobile industry converted to war production in 1942, employment declined for men and women alike, from 583,000 in October 1941 to 429,000 in April 1942 as conversion moved forward. The Office of Production Management (OPM), the UAW, and the major auto companies agreed to a Six-Point Transfer Agreement in October 1941 that gave laid-off auto workers preference, based on seniority, for new jobs in the defense plants. Still, the automakers, male union members, and the UAW remained opposed to hiring women workers until all the unemployed men could be reabsorbed by the defense industry. For example, five hundred women auto workers laid off from a Fisher Body plant in Lansing in February 1942 had trouble finding work in other Lansing defense plants. They complained bitterly when the REO Motor Car Company of Lansing hired four hundred women for defense work, but only ninety-five of the new hires were laid-off Fisher Body workers. In June 1941, more than one hundred Michigan auto plants employed 14,675 women, but they had only 11,806 on the payroll a year later.[44]

Both the numbers of women employed in the auto industry and the types of jobs they held changed dramatically in the course of the war. The number of women working in the auto-plants-turned-defense-plants climbed noticeably in late 1942 and early 1943 as manufacturers faced severe labor shortages and used women to fill job openings. The UAW Research Department polled its local unions about women

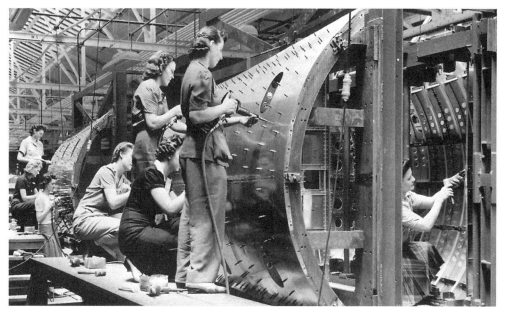

Women assembling Martin B-26 Marauder fuselage sections,
DeSoto plant, Detroit (*CKH*).

factory workers as of 1 July 1942 and 200 locals responded. They reported that there
were 393,159 workers, 24,530 (6.2 percent) of whom were women. Similar surveys
completed in March 1943 by UAW region showed a growing number of women
in the auto plants. Region 1A, which included most of Detroit, reported 132,988
workers, with women making up 18.6 percent of the total. The Region 1 locals that
reported claimed a total of 58,538 workers, 10.3 percent of whom were women.
The timing of the overall increase in women workers in the auto industry, in terms
of raw numbers and the share of all workers, is clearer from industry-wide statistics.
Between October 1940 and April 1942, the auto industry employed 20,600–30,400
women workers (4.8–5.7 percent of the workforce). Female employment leaped to
69,700 workers in October 1942 (12.1 percent of the total) and then grew prodi-
giously over the following year to reach a peak of 203,300 in November 1943, 26
percent of the auto industry workforce. A UAW Research Department survey covering workers in twenty-eight plants as of 30 April 1945 showed women comprising
25.6 percent of the total. The number of women working in all manufacturing in the
greater Detroit area, not just those working in the (former) auto plants, more than
quadrupled from 1940 (46,800) to 1944 (215,000).[45]

Female employment varied widely from company to company and especially
from factory to factory. Women working at the Packard plant in Detroit accounted

for 4.4 percent of the workforce in June 1941, but only 2.7 percent a year later. Over the same time span, the share of women workers in the Ford Highland Park plant increased from 8 to 13 percent. Women workers were generally not found in plants engaged in "heavy" work, such as steel mills, forging plants, and iron, aluminum, and zinc foundries. The Ford Rouge plant, which made iron and steel castings among other things, employed 5,000 women in April 1943, but they made up only 6.6 percent of the workers there. Women typically comprised more than one-third of the workers at plants engaged in assembling aircraft components or complete aircraft but a much smaller proportion at tank and truck assembly plants.

By most measures, 1943 was the pivotal year in the war for the hiring of women. Two Briggs Manufacturing plants in Detroit had only 870 female workers in 1942, or 2 percent of the workforce. By the end of 1943, Briggs had 11,049 women workers, some 45 percent of the total. In June 1942, only 8 percent of the workers at the Ford Willow Run bomber plant were women, but in April 1943, when the plant employed 35,000, women made up 43 percent of the total. Similarly, at the two General Motors Eastern Aircraft Division plants in Linden and Trenton, New Jersey, women accounted for 45 percent of the 21,000 workers. The number of women workers at Fisher Body jumped from 19.8 percent of the workforce in May 1943 to 25.7 percent in November and then to 29.2 percent by the end of June 1944. Factories not involved in aircraft production also experienced dramatic increases in 1943. The Cadillac Motor plant, the Ford Highland Park plant, and Ford's River Rouge plant combined had 300 women employees in spring 1942 but 14,500 in March 1943. The most common "Rosie the Riveter" in World War II was not the burly woman operating a heavy-duty riveting gun at a shipyard but an 110-pound woman operating a lightweight riveting gun assembling aircraft components. In March 1945, when total employment in the automobile industry was 800,000 workers, 334,400 of them worked on aircraft and aircraft components and approximately two-thirds of these workers were women.[46]

The automakers-turned-defense-contractors absorbed much larger numbers of women workers than black workers with much less friction or open conflict. They were able to do so largely by segregating women from men by the jobs they were allowed to perform. Most departments in the war plants employed workers of only one sex. War contractors initially paid women considerably less than men on the grounds that they were doing "women's work," presumably not as physically demanding, dirty, or skilled as "men's work." Company managers had certain preconceptions about what women could or could not do well and about their suitability to perform certain kinds of work. They believed that women were better than men in work that required manual dexterity, especially in manipulating small parts, and

Woman installing wiring harness in B-29 fuselage section, Hudson plant, Detroit (*ACWP*).

at delicate work that required attention to detail, such as assembling bomb sights or gyroscopes. Their fingers were "deft" and "nimble," while their attention to detail and superior eyesight made them excellent inspectors.[47]

Automobile companies had many jobs to fill that had not existed in their plants before the war, such as operating lightweight rivet guns in aircraft assembly work. These jobs were defined as "women's jobs" from the start and were filled almost exclusively by women. Factory managers and production engineers modified manufacturing or assembly processes to make them more suitable for women workers to perform by altering the machinery used or the job itself. Operating the same machine was thus transformed from "men's work" to "women's work" with a stroke of new technology or work processes. Management also changed the definition of which jobs would be performed by women by simply declaring a job as "women's work." In many plants, formerly all-male jobs like that of truck driver became the domain of females. Changes in job classifications became a constant source of friction between company management, the UAW, and male and female workers because of the pay implications.[48]

As the flow of women into the defense industry increased and the demand for their services in a variety of manufacturing jobs grew, the types of work women

Inspecting aircraft engine cylinder heads, unknown location *(ACWP)*.

performed increased dramatically. The Women's Bureau of the U.S. Department of Labor conducted a survey in March 1943 of jobs performed by women working in war production, identifying whether women were "used extensively," "used to some extent," or "used only to a slight extent" in various jobs. According to the survey, women were "used extensively" work that involved drill presses, milling machines, bench lathes, light punch and forming presses, power sewing machines, drill presses, polishing jacks, and other machines used for burring, polishing, and buffing. Women were also commonly engaged in sheet metal forming and riveting; electric arc welding and soldering; electrical parts assembling of all kinds; all types of light assembly work; stenciling and touch-up painting; and inspecting. They also worked in the stock rooms and tool cribs and frequently as clerks. The survey identified only three jobs out of fifty where women were "used only to a slight extent": operating nailing machines, working as shopfitters and loftsmen, and training other workers on the shop floor.[49]

Women moved into many jobs previously performed by men in part because the auto companies redesigned machinery and even the jobs to accommodate women.

Women workers on cartridge trimming machines at Chrysler
Evansville (IN) plant *(ACWP)*.

Production engineers recognized that the average woman did not have the strength
of the average man and had a shorter stature and reach. They reduced the weights
women had to lift by installing conveyor belts, various hoists and other weight-lifting
machines, and automatic lift trucks. A dozen women working in a foundry as mold-
ers were able to equal the production of their male counterparts after machinery was
installed to move the heavy molds. In aircraft assembly plants, revolving jigs enabled
women workers to manipulate large wing sections for riveting. By providing fork-lift
trucks, the auto companies enabled women to work as stock handlers. Many of the
design modifications made to machines resulted in easier and safer work for women
and men alike. The auto companies also reengineered many jobs by subdividing the
work and giving women the "lighter" tasks and the men the rest.[50]

The automobile manufacturers were eager to reclassify old jobs in their factories
previously deemed "men's work" to "women's work" and to label as many new jobs as
possible "women's work" so as to reduce wages. The UAW staunchly fought for equal
pay for equal work for women and African Americans alike but found it more dif-

ficult to defend the principle with regard to women. Company management argued that what might appear to be identical jobs were not because the machinery used or the job itself had been redesigned to accommodate women workers. Women needed "helpers," whereas men did not. Women were not as flexible or as independent as men and needed more supervision. They had higher rates of turnover and absenteeism. The auto companies were more adamant about maintaining wage differentials based on gender early in the war, but the UAW achieved some success in reducing, but not entirely eliminating, these differentials toward the end of the war.[51]

The UAW's advocacy of equal pay for equal work did not stem from its desire for equity for its female members or altruistic motives; it came from the UAW's desire to maintain wage standards in the defense plants. Once the UAW's initial strategy to maintain wage standards by excluding women from war work became untenable, the union sought to minimize the jobs classified as "women's work" to prevent wages from falling. The UAW won an important ruling after it brought a case against General Motors to the National War Labor Board (NWLB) in September 1942 over the issue of equal pay for equal work for men and women. The UAW and GM brought this issue to arbitration with the NWLB, which issued a ruling on 31 July 1943. The board ordered that "wage rates for women shall be the same as for men where they do work of comparable quantity and quality in comparable operations." These decisions did not end the wrangling over wage rates for women in large part because many of the wartime jobs were new to the auto industry. The UAW generally took the view that if a job had ever been done by men, it should be classified as "men's work" forever.[52]

These rulings and the activism of many women workers narrowed the gender gap in wages but did not entirely eliminate it. In many cases, women workers were willing to accept pay raises that fell short of achieving equal pay, even when the work performed was the same as the work of higher-paid men. When the management of GM's Delco-Remy plant in Anderson, Indiana, offered women employees a 10-cent per hour pay raise rather than equal pay with men in 1944, the women accepted the flat rate raise. That same year, the management of the Chevrolet Commercial Body plant in Indianapolis offered to raise hourly wages for women workers from 82 cents to 96 cents; they accepted the offer instead of demanding the male hourly wage of $1.09. Still, the gender gap narrowed over the course of the war. In October 1941, when men earned $1.18 an hour in the automobile industry, women earned $0.80, or 68 percent of what men earned. By August 1944, men's hourly wages had increased to $1.38 and women's to $1.16 (84 percent of men's wages). Taking into consideration that there were many men performing more skilled work than women in many of the plants, including tool and die makers and machinists, the leveling of hourly wages by August 1944 was substantial. Women did not fare as well in the weekly earnings in the auto industry as opposed to their hourly earnings. Women workers' weekly earnings in October 1941 were 65 percent of men's and stood at 78 percent of men's weekly earnings in August 1944. Part of the differential was the result of shorter work weeks and higher absenteeism for women, but this may also have been because unionized women factory workers accepted less-than-equal pay.[53]

The reconversion of the war economy to a civilian economy after the end of hostilities is beyond the scope of this book. The fate of wartime women workers, however, deserves some attention. Most employers, male workers, and the UAW argued that the overwhelming majority of women who had worked in the defense plants wanted to return to their prewar roles of housewives, stay-at-home mothers, students, or single women in search of a husband. Nothing could have been further from the truth. A U.S. Department of Labor survey completed in 1944–45 of wartime women workers and their postwar employment plans showed that the vast majority wanted to continue working outside the home. Of the women working in the Detroit area during the war, 78 percent wanted to continue working in manufacturing and 73 percent wanted to continue working in the same type of job they held during the war.[54]

Automobile workers experienced enormous job losses as demobilization and reconversion began well before V-J Day. Auto industry employment peaked on April 1944 at 746,000 workers, fell to 706,000 a year later, and then to 577,000 in August 1945. Overall employment in the auto industry fell by 40 percent between October 1943 and October 1945, but female employment in the industry declined by 70 percent over the same period. Women workers' share of the auto industry workforce fell from 24.8 percent in April 1944 to 9.5 percent in April 1946. The decline in female employment was even more drastic at some automakers. In November 1943, Ford Motor Company employed 42,000 women, some 22 percent of its workers, but by January 1946 Ford had only 4,900 women on its payroll, a mere 4 percent of its workforce. Many of the layoffs of women were inevitable, given their lower seniority in the plants and the return of servicemen. However, even when they had seniority it was often ignored; one historian argues that management and the UAW conspired to return the auto industry workforce to the way it looked before the war.[55]

The longer-term impact of the massive but temporary use of new workers in the auto industry defense plants during World War II is ambiguous and beyond the scope of this book. The racial and sexual division of labor in the auto industry was at least partially suspended during the war. Tens of thousands of the new workers preferred to remain in the industry, but seniority, racism, and sexism stood in their way. After the war, women's share of the workforce in the auto industry fluctuated between 8.3 and 10.7 percent until 1980, when it jumped to 14 percent. During the war, women showed employers and themselves that they could perform most jobs well, marking what should have been a major turning point in job opportunities for women workers, but it was not. Perhaps the wartime experience planted the seeds for future job advances, but these did not germinate and grow for several decades.[56]

NINE

The Achievement

W hen the United States officially entered World War II following Pearl Harbor, a powerful alliance between the military services and the automobile industry was already in place, resulting in a system for procuring and producing military equipment in significant quantities. President Franklin Roosevelt developed and nurtured this system with the cooperation and assistance of key leaders in the military services, the private sector, and allies within his administration and Congress. He devised a series of innovative strategies to equip America's rapidly expanding military forces in peacetime when the political landscape featured strong isolationist, noninterventionist forces and widespread fears of wartime profiteering by military contractors. His overall political strategy, which continued after Pearl Harbor, was to grant the military and civilian defense contractors far-reaching control over the mobilization of American industry for war production. At the same time Roosevelt minimized the influence of the left wing of the Democratic Party (the New Dealers), organized labor, and Congress.

Converting the economy to war production got off to a rocky start in 1942, with delays in deliveries of war materiel and severe raw materials shortages, but these problems were largely overcome in 1943. Two innovations in the organization of war production helped the civilian authorities, the military services, and the private sector to work together effectively to produce sufficient war goods. The first was the system of procurement contracts initiated and controlled by the military services with minimal civilian oversight. The CPFF contract became the norm, especially for large procurement contracts. The provision for renegotiation of contracts mandated by Congress in April 1942 combined with federal excess profits taxes minimized war profiteering. The DPC financed nearly $10 billion in defense plant construction, which facilitated war production. Starting in December 1940, the DPC also largely controlled the supply and distribution of critical machine tools for the war effort. The mix of machine tools produced and their distribution reflected the priorities set by the military services.

Despite occasional bureaucratic bickering within and between wartime mobilization agencies, including the military services, the wartime planning and procurement system worked reasonably well, although there were mistakes and failures along the way. Harnessing the resources and expertise of the American automobile industry, as well as the great untapped sources of labor, mainly African Americans and women, to manufacture and assemble the needed war materiel helped contribute to the success of the arsenal of democracy.

How successful was this alliance of the military, the civilian federal bureaucracy, and the automobile industry in creating an effective arsenal of democracy? One measure is a comparison of prewar manufacturing capacity with the production of combat munitions during the war. The United States had 32 percent of the world's manufacturing capacity in 1936–38, but in 1942, the first year of full conversion to war production, accounted for only 20 percent of munitions production by the major belligerents. That share jumped to 38 percent in 1943 and to 42 percent in 1944. The British economy was responsible for slightly more than 9 percent of the world's manufacturing capacity in the late 1930s but did not achieve a comparable share of munitions production until 1942, despite its much earlier start in converting its manufacturing to war production. Britain accounted for 11 percent of munitions production in 1943 and 1944, reflecting a more complete conversion.[1]

One might have expected three belligerents controlled by dictators—the Soviet Union, Nazi Germany, and Japan—to have fared better in making war goods than the democracies, especially in light of their earlier rearmament programs. The Soviet Union, with 18.5 percent of the world's manufacturing capacity in 1936–38, accounted for 12–16 percent of weapons production in 1942–44. Nazi Germany, with slightly less than 11 percent of the world's manufacturing capacity in the late 1930s, produced 8.5 percent of weapons manufactured by the belligerents in 1942, 13.5 percent in 1943, and 17 percent in 1944. Finally, the Japanese economy, which had only 3.5 percent of the world's manufacturing capacity in 1936–38, reached 4.5 percent and 6 percent of combat weapons production in 1943 and 1944, respectively.

The German manufacturing achievement, especially in 1943 and 1944, was impressive given the extensive bombing of German industry by the Allies. The American production achievement was primarily the result of its large manufacturing base but also reflected superior worker productivity compared to the other belligerents. In 1944, worker productivity in the war munitions industries of Great Britain and the Soviet Union were only 40 percent of American productivity. Germany achieved a more impressive 48 percent of American productivity but still less than half of the American level. Japan's war industry productivity was a mere 17 percent of that of the United States, reflecting a more labor-intensive manufacturing system.[2]

Historical impressions aside, the Nazi regime did not fully mobilize the German economy for arms production until February 1942, when Hitler put Albert Speer in charge of coordinating and expanding war production. To be sure, the Nazi government began not-so-secret rearmament in violation of the Treaty of Versailles starting in 1933, and arms production increased sharply through the late 1930s. Hitler believed that complete mobilization of the economy for war was unnecessary in the mistaken belief that Germany could avoid fighting a protracted large-scale war. As long as Germany could win swift victories through the limited warfare of Blitzkrieg, there was no need to fully mobilize the economy for war production. Hitler continued to hold this line even after the formal onset of war with Britain and France in September 1939 because of Nazi Germany's quick victories. Hitler was also reluctant to severely curtail civilian goods for fear of losing popular support. He changed this strategy once Germany found itself engaged in serious warfare on several fronts, especially after the invasion of the Soviet Union failed to produce a quick victory.[3]

The Nazi government did not always have complete control over German companies that produced war goods. General Motors–owned Adam Opel A.G., the largest automaker in interwar Europe, resisted doing the bidding of the German government until July 1941, when the Nazis seized the company and ousted GM's management. Daimler-Benz, the premier German automaker, also steadfastly protected some of its independence while producing tanks and aircraft engines for the war effort. Conflicts within the Nazi regime, including disputes about jurisdiction over war production, continued even after Speer took control. Inconsistent and contradictory demands from the Nazi government hampered production at Daimler-Benz and at other manufacturers.[4]

The German Ministry of Armaments and Munitions, managed by Fritz Todt from mid-March 1940 until his death in February 1942, achieved greater centralization of war production, but there was no sense of urgency in its operations. Some historians have characterized the German economy in 1939–41 as a "peacetime economy in war." Speer succeeded Todt and achieved a remarkable increase in arms production, especially in light of the Allied bombing of German industry. Armaments production in July 1944 was more than three times greater than it had been in the first two months of 1942. German aircraft production, which stood at 11,776 planes in 1941, was well below the output of the Soviet Union (15,735), the United States (19,433), and Great Britain (20,094). German industry turned out 39,807 planes in 1944 under adverse conditions, roughly the same as the Soviets (40,300) and considerably more than the British (26,461). Speer achieved this "production miracle" by rationalizing (reducing) the variety of weapons being produced and by imposing centralized control over the entire economy. Recognizing that the war was no longer going to be won by Blitzkrieg, Hitler fully supported Speer's plans and initiatives.[5]

The mobilization of the Japanese economy for war production followed a remarkably parallel trajectory to that of the Nazi economy. Early and easy success in the late 1930s and in the early months of the Pacific war against the United States and Britain left the Japanese government unconvinced that a complete mobilization of the economy was needed. Japanese strategists expected a Nazi victory over the Soviet Union and a long gestation period before the United States could launch counterattacks against Japan. The largest Japanese manufacturers, especially conglomerates such as Mitsubishi, resisted any attempt by the government to centralize economic decisions. Military setbacks in 1942, especially at Midway and Guadalcanal, forced the Japanese government to adopt a different strategy.[6]

Full mobilization and coordination of weapons production was not instituted until November 1943 with the creation of the Munitions Ministry, with Tojo Hideki heading the ministry in addition to his responsibilities as prime minister and war minister. In October, the government had instituted the Munitions Companies Law, which designated important firms as "munitions companies" whose managers were obligated to satisfy government directives or face punishment. All workers in these firms were viewed as military conscripts and were treated accordingly. These companies (six hundred by the end of the war) received preferential treatment in obtaining raw materials. The new government-industry relationship was intended to jump-start arms production, especially aircraft production.[7]

The mobilization program worked, but not soon enough or on a large enough scale to save Japan. Aircraft production increased more than threefold from 8,861 planes in 1942 to 28,180 in 1944, by which time the United States was building 100,000 aircraft. Comparing Japanese and American mobilization of their respective economies is instructive. From 1940 to 1944, total production of the Japanese economy increased by one-quarter, while U.S. output jumped two-thirds. By mid-1944, the destruction of thousands of Japanese merchant vessels by American aircraft and submarines nearly severed the supply lines for vital raw materials for Japanese industry. Japan's industrial production was declining precipitously in the third quarter of 1944, even before significant strategic bombing had begun.[8]

The relatively large size of the U.S. economy and the high levels of productivity of American industry, especially the automobile industry, help explain the enormous production of armaments. In 1941 U.S. GDP was 60 percent of the combined GDP of the United States, Britain, and the Soviet Union. For the war years of 1942–44, the United States accounted for 46 percent of Allied tank production, 51 percent of combat aircraft built, and 55 percent of machine gun production. The American production of weapons, when combined with that of Britain and the Soviet Union, gave the Allies an overwhelming quantitative advantage in weaponry over the Axis Powers of Germany, Italy, and Japan. Focusing on production in 1942–44 provides the best basis for comparison because 1942 was the first year in which the United States, Germany, and Japan fully mobilized their industrial base. Allied superiority in the production of rifles and carbines (22.7 million versus 8.5 million), machine guns (4.2 million versus 1.3 million), tanks (184,000 versus 40,000), and combat aircraft (300,000 versus 115,000) gave the Allies an enormous advantage over the Axis, irrespective of differences in the quality and effectiveness of these weapons.[9]

American industry, especially the automobile industry, received well-deserved recognition for its vital contributions to war production. During the course of the war, the military services and other branches of the federal government developed programs to recognize and reward outstanding war production efforts, part of a general campaign to promote civilian morale on the home front. The most important award was the Army-Navy "E" Award for outstanding achievement in war production. The U.S. Navy initially established the "E" award during the presidency of Theodore Roosevelt (1900–1909) to recognize superior service by naval vessels. A ship that received this award had an "E" flag painted on its gun turrets and the crew wore the flag on their sleeves. The navy later recognized outstanding civilian war production with the award. In the early part of World War II, the army, navy, Maritime Commission, Treasury Department, and other agencies wanted to recognize war production plants. To avoid an "alphabet soup" of overlapping or conflicting awards, the War Department and the Navy Department agreed to a single Army-Navy "E" award to recognize outstanding performance in war production.[10]

The broad criteria for the Army-Navy "E" Award and the selection method were laid out by the army in early July 1942. Nominations for the award would come from army or navy procurement officers or inspectors who would nominate the defense plant at which they were stationed. The criteria included not only the quantity and quality of production but also the number of work stoppages, the health and safety record, conservation of raw materials, and effective management. Each service had an Award Board that would consider the nomination and, once approved, would send it to the other Award Board for their concurrence. A defense plant that won the Army-Navy "E" Award would receive a flag (pennant) that would be flown under the American flag for six months. Each employee would also receive an Army-Navy "E" Award pin to wear. The "E" award was normally presented at a ceremony in which high-level officers of the army or navy, other government officials, and all employees participated. If a defense facility maintained the same record of excellence for six months, it received a Star Award, designated by a white star that would be added to the flag. By the end of the war, 4,283 plants had received the "E" award, eight of which also won six Star Awards.[11]

The plants that received the Army-Navy "E" Award represented approximately 5 percent of defense plants that were eligible nationally. Military officials nominated about 15 percent of the defense plants, but the award boards accepted only one-third of the nominations. Sixty percent of all the award winners won at least one Star Award: 723–776 plants received one, two, or three Star Awards; 820 were recognized with four Star Awards; 206 plants received five; and 8 plants received six Star Awards. The Chrysler Tank Arsenal in Warren was the first recipient of the Army-Navy "E" Award, which was announced on 28 July 1942 and the awards ceremony followed on 10 August 1942. No comprehensive list of the recipients of the Army-Navy "E" Award has survived.[12]

With no cars to sell, the American automakers worried about maintaining connections with their (potential future) customers. All of the automobile companies kept their customers and the general public informed of their wartime contributions through advertising, mainly in national magazines including the *Saturday Evening Post, Life, Look,* and others. They also made conscious efforts to remind the public about the high-quality, economical cars they would produce once again after the war. The advertisements reflected a mixture of the automakers' patriotic pride in their war work and their need to stay in touch with future car buyers. Author Dennis Wrynn compiled hundreds of these wartime advertisements in *Detroit Goes to War,* which will be the basis of the analysis that follows.[13]

Detroit automakers used advertisements to inform readers about their wartime products but also to remind them about their past history and future prospect for supplying high-quality cars. They often combined their prewar advertising slogans with their wartime achievements. Ford cleverly showed an American soldier and his family in a crystal ball, with the slogan "There's a Ford in Your Future." Buick informed their customers about the production of aircraft engines and added the tag line, "When Better War Goods Are Built, Buick Will Build Them." In proudly reminding readers that Packard Motor Car Company made the engines that powered the Curtiss P-40 Warhawk, Packard suggested that readers "Ask the Man Who *FLIES* One" along with their better-known slogan for their cars, "Ask the Man Who Owns One." Plymouth used several variations of its slogan "Plymouth Builds Great Cars" to remind readers of its past history and future promise. Dodge headlined its list of war products with "Dodge Dependability on the Battlefronts." In showing readers the 90-mm anti-aircraft guns it built, the Fisher Body Division of General Motors replaced "Body by Fisher" with "Body Blow by Fisher" and "Armaments by Fisher."[14]

Other automakers took a less subtle approach to their advertising. Nash-Kelvinator shamelessly reminded readers what their "normal" business was. Each ad featured an image of an automobile and a refrigerator at the bottom, with the statement, "In War, Builders of Pratt & Whitney Engines and Hamilton Standard Propellers. In Peace, Nash Automobiles and Kelvinator Refrigerators and Appliances." Their wartime advertisements tended to be more hard-hitting than those of the other automakers, aimed directly at the enemy. Two ads showing aircraft in action with propellers built by Nash-Kelvinator are titled, "Ice Cubes for Japan!" and "Goodbye Mr. Zero." As the war began to wind down, Nash-Kelvinator ads became much less combative and promoted the sales of war bonds and the need to help bring the soldiers home safely. Studebaker ran ads featuring combinations of fathers and sons working together to win the war, with the fathers working at the Studebaker plant and the sons in the military services. Two sons of John Williams, a Studebaker machinist, were shown admiring a B-17 and commenting, "Betcha Dad Worked on Those Engines." Paul Lukevich, a Studebaker mechanic, and son Paul, a marine, were featured in another advertisement, as were Tom Hinkle and his two sons serving in the U.S. Army. All of the fathers built Pratt & Whitney aircraft engines at Studebaker.[15]

The automakers who won the Army-Navy "E" Award included the "E" flag in their advertising. Fisher Body pointed out that it was the first automaker to fly the Navy "E" flag with two stars and the Army-Navy "E" flag. Willys, which won the award for jeep production, included in their advertisements a statement by Undersecretary of War Robert Patterson: "For accomplishing more than seemed reasonable or possible a year ago." Chevrolet ran a separate advertisement, "Three Awards to Three Plants in One Day," proudly pointing out that two of its aircraft engine plants and an axle plant in western New York (Tonawanda and Buffalo) received the award on the same day. In the "Chevrolet" script at the top of the ad, the "V" was enlarged, as in "V" for victory.[16]

The Chrysler Corporation, however, went well beyond the other automakers in celebrating its contributions to the war effort after the end of the war. The company commissioned a series of seven books publicizing its accomplishments that appeared from 1945 through 1949, all written by Wesley W. Stout, a freelance writer who had served as the editor of the *Saturday Evening Post* starting in 1938. Chrysler president K. T. Keller wrote a foreword for each of the seven volumes and was probably the driving force behind this effort.

The first of the books, really a fifty-one-page booklet, was *A War Job "Thought Impossible"* (1945), which described Chrysler's manufacture of 5,500 gyrocompasses for the navy. These were built under license from the Sperry Gyroscope Company at Chrysler's Dodge Main plant in Hamtramck. The gyrocompasses were delicate, precision instruments unlike anything Chrysler had previously manufactured. Neither Sperry nor the navy initially thought Chrysler was capable of turning out these precision instruments in large quantities.[17]

One of the three volumes published in 1946, *The Great Detective,* celebrated another "high-tech" war product entirely unfamiliar to Chrysler. At Dodge Main, the company built radar antenna mounts for short-range radar units under contract with General Electric between September 1942 and May 1944, completing 2,092 in total. The units included the radar dish, the intricate geared mechanisms to elevate and rotate the dish, and the pedestal supports. Chrysler also designed a special semitrailer to house the mobile radar units, which the Freuhauf Corporation manufactured.[18]

Bullets by the Billion told the story of the production of small arms cartridges at Chrysler's former Plymouth assembly plant in Evansville, Indiana. The plant had turned out 275 Plymouths a day with fewer than 700 workers. Chrysler converted the plant into a highly mechanized factory that produced nearly four billion cartridges, mostly for .45-caliber and .30-caliber small arms. The workforce eventually reached 12,560 by drawing workers from a fifty-mile radius extending into northwestern Kentucky and southeastern Illinois. All of the volumes written by Wesley Stout for Chrysler are heavily illustrated with photographs of the plant and the products, but this book is particularly interesting. The majority of the workers shown in the pictures are women, and the few men that are seen appear to be too old for military service. Virtually all the women shown are Caucasian except for the workers in the packing department, virtually all of whom are African American.[19]

The third volume published in 1946, *"TANKS Are Mighty Fine Things,"* praised Chrysler's assembly work at its tank arsenal in Warren. The title was derived from a marine's account of being rescued by a Chrysler tank after he was wounded and pinned down by Japanese fire on Tinian Island in the Pacific. A Sherman tank crew situated their tank directly above him and lifted him into it through an emergency escape hatch on the tank's underside. The tank arsenal was the first defense plant in

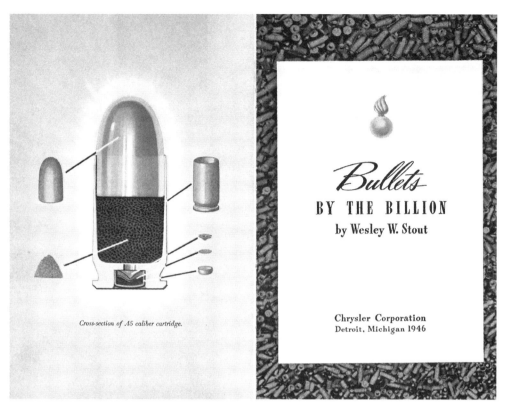

Title page of *Bullets by the Billion (CKH)*.

the nation to win the coveted Army-Navy "E" award for production excellence. The book includes a "colorized" photograph of President Franklin D. Roosevelt's tour of the tank arsenal on 18 September 1942, part of his secret twelve-day cross-country tour of defense plants.[20]

Great Engines and Great Planes was one of two volumes published by Chrysler in 1947. The first third of the volume told the story of the giant Dodge-Chicago plant that built the radial 18-cylinder, air-cooled Wright Cyclone engine for the B-29 Superfortress, described in an earlier chapter. The rest of the book dealt with Chrysler's other significant contributions to aircraft production, including the nose sections for the B-29, center wing sections for the Curtiss-Wright Helldiver, cockpits for the B-17 Flying Fortress, center wing sections and flaps for the B-26 Martin Marauder bomber, and more than ten thousand sets of landing gear and arrester mechanisms (tail hooks) for the carrier-based Corsair fighter plane.[21]

Secret was the second volume published in 1947 and included a statement verifying that the U.S. Army Corps of Engineers had reviewed the volume and approved its publication. The book touted one of Chrysler's wartime products that was kept

First and last; the tank the arsenal first made, the M-3 General Grant and (below) the 45-ton Pershing with 90 mm gun.

"TANKS
are Mighty Fine Things"
by
Wesley W. Stout

Chrysler Corporation
Detroit, Michigan 1946

Title page of *"TANKS Are Mighty Fine Things"* (CKH).

top-secret during and after the war: gaseous diffusion equipment needed to separate U-235, the basic raw material needed for one type of atomic bomb, from uranium. The diffusers needed to be made of nickel, the only metal capable of resisting the hexaflouride gas used in the diffusion process. Making the diffusers of solid nickel would have consumed the world supply of this metal. Chrysler developed a method for nickel-plating the diffusers, each with hundreds of thousands of precisely drilled holes. The company made the diffusers at its Lynch Road assembly plant in Detroit and shipped them by rail to the U-235 plant in Oak Ridge, Tennessee.[22]

Mobilized was the final volume of this set, published in 1949. It was also by far the longest, at 216 pages. Designed to highlight Chrysler's contributions not covered in the first six books, this volume focused on the work of Chrysler Engineering in the war and the work of several Chrysler divisions whose war production was notable. Chrysler Engineering redesigned the Swedish Bofors anti-aircraft guns for mass production, converting the dimensions from metric to inches. Ten plants made parts of the Bofors guns, which were produced for the army and the navy. The Chrysler Division made sea mules (marine tugs), marine engines, industrial engines, searchlights, smoke generators, submarine nets, and dozens of other products. The Dodge Division built over 400,000 army trucks at its truck plant in Warren and rockets at the Dodge Main plant. The Airtemp Division, established to produce large-scale commercial air-conditioners, manufactured portable kitchens, furnaces, and, of course, air-conditioning equipment.[23]

The Chrysler Corporation's commitment to publish this set of seven hardcover books outlining the company's wartime achievements says a great deal about Chrysler's (and K. T. Keller's) pride in their contribution to the war effort. This researcher was not able to discover the quantities the company printed, much less the distribution arrangements. The company's annual reports are mute on this topic. Chrysler also paid for a limited production of a boxed set of handsome leather-bound, gilded versions of the volumes.

To further showcase their contribution to the war effort, in 1947 Chrysler commissioned sixteen artists with battlefield experience to create a series of oil paintings commemorating the war. The artists had complete freedom to portray the war as they saw fit. It is not coincidental that each of the paintings includes a Chrysler-built war product, including M4 Sherman tanks, mobile radar units, Dodge trucks, Chrysler industrial engines, Bofors guns, and various aircraft for which Chrysler supplied components, including the Curtiss-Wright Helldiver, the B-26 Martin Marauder bomber, and the B-29. The company also published these paintings in a paperback grayscale booklet in 1947 and then as a hardcover large format "coffee table" book with full-color illustrations. The original artwork adorned the walls of the executive levels of Chrysler's General Administration Building in Highland Park from 1947 until the early 1950s, when Chrysler donated them to the City of Detroit. They were displayed at the Detroit War Memorial Building on the Detroit riverfront until 1986, when the City of Detroit transferred them to the Detroit Historical Museum. They currently reside in the museum's storage facility.[24]

This is not to suggest that the other automakers did nothing to tout their contributions to the war effort. During the war, most of the scores of divisions of General Motors, which were autonomous in many respects, produced glossy pamphlets in which they featured their war work. The corporation did not, however, publish a more general work treating GM's wartime achievements. It seemed as if Alfred Sloan wanted GM to return to "normal" after the war as quickly as possible. In contrast, the Ford Motor Company made a serious effort to document its war work. When Henry Ford closed his outdoor museum (Greenfield Village) in early 1942, he gave Charles La Croix, an assistant director of the village, the task of compiling Ford's contributions to the war effort. La Croix collected forty-two boxes of materials and wrote an eight-volume summary of Ford's war work. La Croix also collected and catalogued thousands of photographs of war production. Henry Ford died in April 1947 and the Ford Motor Company did not publish these volumes. The rich collection of materials, however, remained well-preserved and available to researchers at the Benson Ford Research Center, part of The Henry Ford in Dearborn.[25]

All of the automobile companies, including suppliers, described their contributions to the war effort in their annual reports. The most significant source for information on the smaller producers are the records of the Automotive Council for War Production (1942–46), housed in the National Automotive History Collection at the Skillman Branch of the Detroit Public Library. Donated by the Automobile Manufacturers Association in the 1950s, this collection fills seventy-seven manuscript boxes and includes nearly four thousand photographs. Researchers interested in learning more about auto industry involvement in the war effort can begin with this collection.

Notes

1. Keith E. Eiler, *Mobilizing America: Robert P. Patterson and the War Effort, 1940–1945* (Ithaca, NY: Cornell University Press, 1997), 43, 44; Donald M. Nelson, *Arsenal of Democracy: The Story of American War Production* (New York: Harcourt, Brace and Company, 1946), 30; Jerome B. Cohen, *Japan's Economy in War and Reconstruction* (Minneapolis: University of Minnesota Press, 1949), 288; Harry C. Thomson and Lida Mayo, *The United States Army in World War II; The Technical Services. The Ordnance Department: Equipment and Supply* (Washington, DC: Department of the Army, 1960), 1–2; Richard J. Overy, *War and Economy in the Third Reich* (New York: Clarendon Press, 1964), 280.

2. Thomson and Mayo, *The Ordnance Department: Equipment and Supply*, 25, 43.

3. U.S. Department of Commerce, Bureau of the Census, *Historical Statistics of the United States, Colonial Times to 1970* (Washington, DC: U.S. GPO, 1975), 716; Alfred P. Sloan Jr., *My Years with General Motors* (Garden City, NY: Doubleday, 1963), 214.

4. Allan Nevins and Frank Ernest Hill, *Ford: Decline and Rebirth, 1933–1962* (New York: Charles Scribner's Sons, 1962), 175–77, 281; David Farber, *Sloan Rules: Alfred P. Sloan and the Triumph of General Motors* (Chicago: University of Chicago Press, 2002), 220–27.

5. Justus D. Doenecke, *Storm on the Horizon: The Challenge to American Intervention, 1939–1941* (Lanham, MD: Rowman & Littlefield, 2000).

6. Ibid., 1–8; Wayne S. Cole, *America First: The Battle against Intervention, 1940–1941* (Madison: University of Wisconsin Press, 1953), 11–14; Wayne S. Cole, *Charles A. Lindbergh and the Battle against American Intervention in World War II* (New York: Harcourt, Brace Jovanovich, 1974), 41–42, 74, 115, 132–33, 142–53.

7. Doenecke, *Storm on the Horizon*, 59–61; Richard M. Ketchum, *The Borrowed Years, 1938–1941: America on Its Way to War* (New York: Random House, 1989), 127–28, 228, 567.

8. Irving Brinton Holley Jr., *Buying Aircraft: Materiel Procurement for the Army Air Forces* (Washington, DC: Department of the Army, 1964), 83.

9. John E. Wiltz, *In Search of Peace: The Senate Munitions Inquiry, 1934–36* (Baton Rouge: Louisiana State University Press, 1963), 122–26; Melvin I. Urofsky, *Big Steel and the Wilson Administration: A Study in Business-Government Relations* (Columbus: Ohio State University Press, 1969), 229–31; Paul A. C. Koistinen, *Planning War, Pursuing Peace: The Political Economy of American Warfare, 1920–1939* (Lawrence: University of Kansas Press, 1998), 253–60. The most

detailed study of World War I profiteering is found in Stuart D. Brandes, *Warhogs: A History of War Profits in America* (Lexington: University Press of Kentucky, 1997).

10. R. Elberton Smith, *The Army and Economic Mobilization: United States Army in World War II* (Washington, DC: Department of the Army, 1991), 63–64; Eiler, *Mobilizing America*, 67, 198.

11. Chrysler Corporation War Records, vol. 22, "General, 1938–1941" and vol. 23, "General, 1942," Chrysler Corporate Archives, Detroit, Michigan (hereafter CCA).

12. Nelson, *Arsenal of Democracy*, 225–26. For more information on this plant, see Saginaw Steering Gear Division, General Motors Corporation, *Out of the Valley to Victory* (Saginaw, MI: Seemann and Peters, 1943), n.p.

13. Samuel I. Rosenman, ed., *The Public Papers and Addresses of Franklin D. Roosevelt, 1940 Volume, War—And Aid to Democracies* (New York: Macmillan, 1941), 202–3, 234; Nelson, *Arsenal of Democracy*, 88–89.

14. Norman Beasley, *Knudsen: A Biography* (New York: McGraw-Hill, 1947), 236; Robert C. Albright, "New Board Will Gear U.S. Industry to Defense Needs: Seven-Member Commission Taps Nation's Vast Resources as Speed Marks U.S. Rearmament," *Washington Post*, 2 June 1940, B3.

15. James J. Flink, "William Signius Knudsen," in George S. May, ed., *Encyclopedia of American Business History and Biography: The Automobile Industry, 1920–1980* (New York: Brucolli Clark Layman, 1989), 265–68.

16. Ibid., 269–78.

17. Beasley, *Knudsen*, 230, 234–37.

18. Ibid., 238, 243–46; William S. Knudsen to Franklin D. Roosevelt, 5 June 1940, box 2, folder 32, series I, Knudsen Collection, National Automotive History Collection, Detroit Public Library, Detroit, Michigan (hereafter NAHC). Beasley erroneously dates this letter 2 June 1940.

19. Eiler, *Mobilizing America*, 486–87.

20. Beasley, *Knudsen*, 248–50, 271–72, 276.

21. Ibid., 251, 259–60.

22. Gerald T. White, *Billions for Defense: Government Financing by the Defense Plant Corporation during World War II* (Tuscaloosa: University of Alabama Press, 1980), 4–10; Paul A. C. Koistinen, *Arsenal of World War II: The Political Economy of American Warfare, 1940–1945* (Lawrence: University of Kansas Press, 2004), 55–57.

23. White, *Billions for Defense*, 11–14.

24. Ibid., 10; Smith, *The Army and Economic Mobilization*, 496.

25. White, *Billions for Defense*, 26, 32–34, 70; Koistinen, *Arsenal of World War II*, 55–57.

26. White, *Billions for Defense*, 29–31, 34.

27. Smith, *The Army and Economic Mobilization*, 497.

28. John B. Rae, *Climb to Greatness: The American Aircraft Industry, 1920–1960* (Cambridge, MA: MIT Press, 1968), 81, 99; Tom Lilly et al., "Conversion to Wartime Production Techniques," in Gene R. Simonson, ed., *The History of the American Aircraft Industry: An Anthology* (Cambridge, MA: MIT Press, 1968), 135–36; Holley, *Buying Aircraft*, 6–7; Jacob A. Vander Meulen, *The Politics of Aircraft: Building an American Military Industry* (Lawrence: University Press of Kansas, 1991), 184–85; Beasley, *Knudsen*, 381.

29. Automobile Manufacturers Association, *Freedom's Arsenal: The Story of the Automotive Council for War Production* (Detroit: Automobile Manufacturers Association, 1950), 1–7; Nelson, *Arsenal of Democracy*, 219.

30. Automobile Manufacturers Association, *Freedom's Arsenal*, 8–12, 15–19.

31. Ibid., 24, 33–34, 39–46; E. L. Warner Jr., "New Plan for Bomber Building Centers on Automobile 'Big Three': Ford, General Motors and Chrysler to Be Made Responsible for Production of Fuselage Parts and Sub-Assemblies," *Automotive Industries* 84 (15 January 1941): 67–69, 96; Holley, *Buying Aircraft*, 306. Holley also provides additional details (304–8) of the challenges faced by the ACAD and its early successes.

32. "500 Planes a Day—A Program for the Utilization of the Automobile Industry for Mass Pro-

duction of Defense Planes, December 23, 1940," in Henry M. Christman, *Walter P. Reuther: Selected Papers* (New York: Pyramid Books, 1964), 1–10; Nelson Lichtenstein, *Labor's War at Home: The CIO in World War II* (New York: Cambridge University Press, 1982), 85–88.

33. Nelson Lichtenstein, *The Most Dangerous Man in Detroit: Walter Reuther and the Fate of American Labor* (New York: Basic Books, 1995), 161–66; Rae, *Climb to Greatness*, 132–33; Holley, *Buying Aircraft*, 310–13; Beasley, *Knudsen*, 286–87.

34. Rosenman, *The Public Papers and Addresses of Franklin D. Roosevelt*, 640, 643.

35. Beasley, *Knudsen*, 299; Eiler, *Mobilizing America*, 52, 80; Koistinen, *Arsenal of World War II*, 48; Automobile Manufacturers Association, *Freedom's Arsenal*, 57–58; Donald H. Riddle, *The Truman Committee: A Study in Congressional Responsibility* (New Brunswick, NJ: Rutgers University Press, 1964), 56–57.

36. Sidney Fraser, *Labor Will Rule: Sidney Hillman and the Rise of American Labor* (New York: The Free Press, 1991), 452–54.

37. Ibid., 454–58, 478–81; Koistinen, *Arsenal of World War II*, 405–6.

38. Fraser, *Labor Will Rule*, 461–69.

39. Beasley, *Knudsen*, 276; Eiler, *Mobilizing America*, 60–61.

40. Beasley, *Knudsen*, 299–301; Eiler, *Mobilizing America*, 81–83.

41. The political struggle to get the Lend-Lease Act approved is detailed in Warren F. Kimball, *The Most Unsordid Act: Lend-Lease, 1939–1941* (Baltimore: Johns Hopkins University Press, 1969). Ketchum (*The Borrowed Years*, 572–82) briefly describes the protagonists.

42. Koistinen, *Arsenal of World War II*, 67, 131, 266; Smith, *The Army and Economic Mobilization*, 499; Michael G. Carew, *Becoming the Arsenal: The American Industrial Mobilization for World War II, 1938–1942* (Lanham, MD: University Press of America, 2010), 206, 225–27.

43. Eiler, *Mobilizing America*, 89; Koistinen, *Arsenal of World War II*, 96–97, 130–31.

44. Koistinen, *Arsenal of World War II*, 133–35; Gregory M. Hooks, *Forging the Military-Industrial Complex: World War II's Battle of the Potomac* (Urbana: University of Illinois Press, 1991), 167–68; I. F. Stone, "Why Knudsen Should Go," *The Nation*, 3 May 1941, pp. 519–20.

45. Bureau of Demobilization, Civilian Production Administration, *Industrial Mobilization for War: History of the War Production Board and Predecessor Agencies, 1940–1945*, vol. 1, *Program and Administration* (Washington, DC: U.S. GPO, 1948), 194–97.

46. Eiler, *Mobilizing America*, 93; Koistinen, *Arsenal of World War II*, 74, 98–99, 182–90; Beasley, *Knudsen*, 320, 323; Nelson *Arsenal of Democracy*, 156, 159, 175.

47. Koistinen, *Arsenal of World War II*, 77–81, 94.

48. Memoranda, Franklin D. Roosevelt to William S. Knudsen, 6 March and 12 March 1941, box 2, folder 44, series I, Knudsen Collection, NAHC; Beasley, *Knudsen*, 256–57.

49. Koistinen, *Arsenal of World War II*, 126, 158, 189–90; Nelson, *Arsenal of Democracy*, 125–27.

50. Riddle, *The Truman Committee*, 15–16, 58–63, 185.

51. Ibid., 64–67.

CHAPTER TWO

1. Automobile Manufacturers Association, *Freedom's Arsenal*, 68–69, 73, 75, 77, 88.

2. Ibid., 84–86, 91–93; Nelson, *Arsenal of Democracy*, 195–96, 276–77; Holley, *Buying Aircraft*, 323.

3. Automobile Manufacturers Association, *Freedom's Arsenal*, 118, 148, 179, 193.

4. Smith, *The Army and Economic Mobilization*, 251; Carew, *Becoming the Arsenal*, 189, 233; Eiler, *Mobilizing America*, 235–36.

5. Eiler, *Mobilizing America*, 235–36; Nelson, *Arsenal of Democracy*, 17–24; Beasley, *Knudsen*, 350–51.

6. "The General Joins the Army," *Time*, 31 July 1944; Beasley, *Knudsen*, 379–80.

7. Eiler, *Mobilizing America*, 283–85; Fraser, *Labor Will Rule*, 486–94.

8. Nelson, *Arsenal of Democracy*, 185–87; Koistinen, *Arsenal of World War II*, 276.

9. "Report on Airplane Program, March 26, 1942, from Mordecai Ezekiel, Consultant, to Robert P. Nathan, Chairman, Planning Committee, War Production Board," box 13, folder VIII, item 5, Donald M. Nelson Papers, Huntington Library, San Marino, California (hereafter Nelson Papers); Memorandum, Robert P. Nathan, Chairman, Planning Committee, War Production Board, to Donald M. Nelson, 27 March 1942, box 11, folder IV, Item 7, Nelson Papers.

10. "Executive Organizational Survey, War Production Board, April 1942," box 10, folder II, item 8, Nelson Papers.

11. John Perry Miller, *Pricing of Military Procurements* (New Haven: Yale University Press, 1949), 52–53; Hooks, *Forging the Military-Industrial Complex*, 103–7, 115–19, 145–46, 170–71; Carew, *Becoming the Arsenal*, 246, 257–58; Nelson, *Arsenal of Democracy*, 198–201.

12. James G. Lacey, *Keep from All Thoughtful Men: How U.S. Economists Won World War II* (Annapolis, MD: Naval Institute Press, 2011), 40, 74–75.

13. John E. Brigante, *The Feasibility Dispute: Determination of War Production Objectives for 1942 and 1943* (Washington, DC: Committee on Public Administration Cases, 1950), 33, 39–41, 80–87, 105; Hooks, *Forging the Military-Industrial Complex*, 114–15, 118.

14. Lacey, *Keep from All Thoughtful Men*, 98–99, 105–6, 113, 183–85.

15. Eiler, *Mobilizing America*, 357–62; Koistinen, *Arsenal of World War II*, 206–7.

16. Eiler, *Mobilizing America*, 364–67; Koistinen, *Arsenal of World War II*, 341; Nelson, *Arsenal of Democracy*, 388–89.

17. Charles E. Wilson to Donald M. Nelson, 29 October 1943; Franklin Roosevelt to Donald M. Nelson, 3 January 1944; Donald M. Nelson to Charles E. Wilson, 15 July 1944 and 25 August 1944, all in box 2, Correspondence, Nelson Papers.

18. *The Reconversion Dispute (Draft)* (Washington, DC: Committee on Public Administration Cases, n.d.), box 12, folder VII, "Reconversion, 1944–1947," Nelson Papers.

19. Albert Z. Carr, "China Notebook, Account of Donald Nelson's Trips to China," box 13, folder IX, Nelson Papers; Nelson, *Arsenal of Democracy*, 413–16.

20. Koistinen, *Arsenal of World War II*, 506–7.

21. Alan Clive, *State of War: Michigan in World War II* (Ann Arbor: University of Michigan Press, 1979), 60; Lichtenstein, *Labor's War at Home*, 154, 159–60, 194–97. Though it was officially known as the National War Labor Board, "National" was quickly dropped in most references to this board. For a more detailed discussion of the no-strike pledge within the UAW, see Martin Glaberman, *Wartime Strikes: The Struggle against the No-Strike Pledge in the UAW during World War II* (Detroit: Bewick Editions, 1980).

22. Eiler, *Mobilizing America*, 291–92, 374; John H. Ohly, *Industrialists in Olive Drab: The Emergency Operation of Private Industries during World War II*, ed. Clayton D. Laurie (Washington, DC: Center for Military History, United States Army, 2000), 313–20.

23. Byron Fairchild and Jonathan Grossman, *The Army and Industrial Manpower* (Washington, DC: Office of the Chief of Military History, Department of the Army, 1959), 172; Koistinen, *Arsenal of Democracy*, 389–90.

24. Miller, *Pricing of Military Procurements*, 52–53, 83–89; Smith, *The Army and Economic Mobilization*, 247.

25. Jacob Vander Meulen, *Building the B-29* (Washington, DC: Smithsonian Institution Press, 1995), 18.

26. Miller, *Pricing of Military Procurements*, 89–91, 126–27, 135–39.

27. Ibid., 170–72; Koistinen, *Arsenal of Democracy*, 434–36. The detailed legal provisions of the renegotiation laws and the administrative rules used in enforcement are laid out in a National Industrial Conference Board booklet, *Practices in Renegotiation of War Contracts* (New York: National Industrial Conference Board, 1943).

28. Miller, *Pricing of Military Procurements*, 279; Smith, *The Army and Economic Mobilization*, 392. Brandes, *Warhogs*, 262–65, cites high salaries earned by defense industry executives, but nothing else, as evidence of high wartime profits.

29. Sloan, *My Years with General Motors*, 214; Charles K. Hyde, *Riding the Roller Coaster: A History of the Chrysler Corporation* (Detroit: Wayne State University Press, 2003), 120; "Percentage of Operating Profits to Sales," box 29, vol. 3, Accession 435, Charles C. La Croix Collection, Benson Ford Research Center (hereafter La Croix Collection, BFRC); Studebaker Corporation, *Annual Report*, 1942–1945, NAHC; Packard Motor Car Company, *Annual Report*, 1942–1945, NAHC; Charles K. Hyde, *Storied Independent Automakers: Nash, Hudson, and American Motors* (Detroit: Wayne State University Press, 2009), 151.

30. Koistinen, *Arsenal of Democracy*, 56; White, *Billions for Defense*, 68–72.

31. White, *Billions for Defense*, 49, 70.

32. Charles K. Hyde, "Assembly-Line Architecture: Albert Kahn and the Evolution of the U.S. Auto Factory, 1905–1940," *IA, The Journal of the Society for Industrial Archeology* 22 (1996): 20–21; Christy Borth, *Masters of Mass Production* (New York: Bobbs-Merrill, 1945), 94, 124.

33. Malcolm W. Bingay, *Detroit Is My Home Town* (New York: Bobbs-Merrill, 1946), 308–9; Grant Hildebrand, *Designing for Industry: The Architecture of Albert Kahn* (Cambridge, MA: MIT Press, 1974), 128–30; Mira Wilkins and Frank Earnest Hill, *American Business Abroad: Ford on Six Continents* (Detroit: Wayne State University Press, 1964), 216–25; Peter G. Filene, *Americans and the Soviet Experiment, 1917–1933* (Cambridge, MA: Harvard University Press, 1967), 119–24; Federico Bucci, *Albert Kahn, Architect of Ford* (New York: Princeton Architectural Press, 1993), 90–96.

34. W. Hawkins Ferry, *The Legacy of Albert Kahn* (Detroit: Wayne State University Press, 1987), 25–26, 127–36; Hyde, "Assembly-Line Architecture," 20–21; Hildebrand, *Designing for Industry*, 183–212; Borth, *Masters of Mass Production*, 123, 124. Information about the breadth of Kahn's defense work came from Albert Kahn Associates' *Job Book*, which is a listing of every job the firm completed, arranged by job number and by date. It is found in the company's corporate office.

35. White, *Billions for Defense*, 69.

36. Bradley Stoughton, *History of the Tools Division, War Production Board* (New York: McGraw-Hill, 1949), 7; White, *Billions for Defense*, 84.

37. "Tooling Program for Conversion of Auto Industry to War Production, Submitted by Walter P. Reuther, January 1942," box 10, folder I, item 5, Nelson Papers.

38. White, *Billions for Defense*, 85–86; Stoughton, *History of the Tools Division*, 2–3, 64–65.

39. White, *Billions for Defense*, 83; Stoughton, *History of the Tools Division*, 81.

40. White, *Billions for Defense*, 63–66.

41. Smith, *The Army and Economic Mobilization*, 7.

CHAPTER THREE

1. Rae, *Climb to Greatness*, 157; Wesley Frank Craven and James Lea Cate, eds., *The Army Air Forces in World War II*, vol. 6, *Men and Planes*, new imprint (Washington, DC: U.S. GPO, 1983), 352.

2. Craven and Cate, *Men and Planes*, 195n.

3. Lilly et al., "Conversion to Wartime Production Techniques," 121–23; Holley, *Buying Aircraft*, 310, 580–82.

4. Holley, *Buying Aircraft*, 580–82; Rae, *Climb to Greatness*, 157.

5. Paul Sonnenburg and William A. Schoneberger, *Allison: Power of Excellence, 1915–1990* (Malibu, CA: Coastline Publishers, 1990), 44–45, 48–51; Maurice D. Hendry, *Cadillac, Standard of the World: The Complete History*, 5th ed. (Kutztown, PA: Automobile Quarterly Publications, 1996), 268; Joseph Geschelin, "Allison Engine Production Demands Special Methods," *Automotive Industries* 84 (1 June 1941): 559; R. M. Hazen, "The Allison Aircraft-Engine Development," *SAE Journal* 49, no. 5 (November 1941): 489. For more on James Allison's life, see Sigur E. Whitaker, *James Allison: A Biography of the Engine Manufacturer and Indianapolis 500 Cofounder* (Jefferson, NC: McFarland and Company, 2011).

6. Sonnenburg and Schoneberger, *Allison: Power of Excellence*, 55, 62; "(Allison) Historical

Dates," folder 77.6.3, Richard P. Scharchburg Archives/Kettering University, Flint, Michigan (hereafter SA/KU); Smith, *The Army and Economic Mobilization*, 496; Allen Orth, "The War Years," 59. The last-mentioned source is an unpublished history of General Motors during World War II, dated 18 September 1956, found in the archives of the General Motors Heritage Center, Sterling Heights, Michigan. The title page has the inscription, "For Mr. Sloan's Book," suggesting that it was to be used as a source of information for Alfred P. Sloan Jr.'s autobiography, eventually published in 1964 as *My Years with General Motors*.

7. Geschelin, "Allison Engine Production Demands Special Methods," 559–61.

8. Michael G. H. Scott, *Packard: The Complete Story* (Blue Ridge Summit, PA: Tab Books, 1985), 142; "Cadillac Motor Car Division, History of World War II," 173–74. The last-mentioned source is a 178-page typescript (undated) found in the General Motors Heritage Center, Sterling Heights, Michigan.

9. "Allison Set for Peak Production," *American Machinist*, 5 March 1942, 165; Hendry, *Cadillac*, 268–70; Orth, "The War Years," 59–60; Holley, *Buying Aircraft*, 562, 581; James E. Knott, "World War II Hero—The Allison V-1710," folder 77.6.7, SA/KU; "Armada of Allison Powered Aircraft," folder 77.6.7, SA/KU; Sonnenburg and Schoneberger, *Allison: Power of Excellence*, 70.

10. K. T. Keller to Secretary of the Treasury Henry Morgenthau Jr., 23 May 1940, vol. 22, "General, 1938–1942," Chrysler War Records, CCA; Beasley, *Knudsen*, 264–67; White, *Billions for Defense*, 29–31; Robert J. Neal, *Master Motor Builders: The Inception, Design, Production, and Uses of the Non-Automotive Engines of the Packard Motor Car Company* (Kent, WA: Aero-Marine History Publishing Company, 2000), 174–75, 345.

11. Robert J. Neal, "By Land, by Air, by Sea—by Packard!" *Automotive History Review*, no. 35 (Winter 1999–2000): 4–10; Neal, *Master Motor Builders*, 44.

12. Packard Motor Car Company, *Thirty-Seventh Annual Report, Year Ending December 31, 1940*, 3, NAHC; Neal, *Master Motor Builders*, 181; Holley, *Buying Aircraft*, 367, 392.

13. Neal, *Master Motor Builders*, 175–76; George Hamlin and Dwight Heinmuller, "In the Nation's Defense: Packard in World War II," in Beverly Rae Kimes, ed., *Packard: A History of the Motor Car and the Company* (New York: E. P. Dutton, 1978), 505–7; "Rolls-Royce Engine Adopted to U.S. Production by Packard Engineers," *Product Engineering* 12 (September 1941): 456–60.

14. "Packard Adds a Plane Engine Plant," *Engineering News-Record* 127 (11 September 1941): 80–83; A. H. Allen, "Packard Converts to Aluminum Castings Production," *Foundry* 71 (April 1943): 136–38; Smith, *The Army and Economic Mobilization*, 496; "Engine-Propeller Report," box 23, folder, Aircraft Engine Photos, Accession 435, La Croix Collection, BFRC.

15. Neal, *Master Motor Builders*, 345–47; Packard Motor Car Company, *Thirty-Seventh Annual Report*, 3.

16. Neal, *Master Motor Builders*, 178–79, 182, 346.

17. Ibid., 234, 346.

18. Box 3, 1:2–4, Accession 435, La Croix Collection, BFRC.; Nevins and Hill, *Ford: Decline and Rebirth*, 178; Smith, *The Army and Economic Mobilization*, 498; Timothy J. O'Callaghan, *Ford in the Service of America: Mass Production for the Military during the World Wars* (Jefferson, NC: McFarland and Company, 2009), 90.

19. Box 3, 1:4–8 and box 5, vol. 1, "Aircraft Engine Plant," n.p., both in Accession 435, La Croix Collection, BFRC.

20. "Plane Engine Plant Sets New Precedents," *Engineering News-Record* 127 (31 July 1941): 48; O'Callaghan, *Ford in the Service of America*, 92, 107–9; Herbert Chase, "Stepping Up Production Pace of Magnesium Castings at Ford," *The Iron Age* 148 (2 October 1941): 32; box 3, 1:25, Accession 435, La Croix Collection, BFRC.

21. Box 3, 1:5, 7, and box 4, 3:7, Accession 435, La Croix Collection, BFRC; O'Callaghan, *Ford in the Service of America*, 157.

22. Box 4, 3:16, 8–21, Accession 435, La Croix Collection, BFRC.

23. O'Callaghan, *Ford in the Service of America*, 93.

24. Ibid., 94; "1944 Engine–Propeller Report," box 4, 3:7, 13, 14, and box 23, folder, Aircraft Engine

Photos, Accession 435, La Croix Collection, BFRC; Joseph Geschelin, "Ford War Plant Facilitated Straight-Line Production," *Automotive and Aviation Industries* 87 (1 December 1942): 18–24, 102, 104.

25. Box 3, 1:9, 29–31, Accession 435, La Croix Collection, BFRC.

26. Donald T. Critchlow, *Studebaker: The Life and Death of an American Corporation* (Bloomington: Indiana University Press, 1996), 118; Craven and Cate, *Men and Planes*, 324; Holley, *Buying Aircraft*, 310; Studebaker Corporation, *Annual Report, 1940*, 2, NAHC; "Engine-Propeller Report," box 23, folder, Aircraft Engine Photos, Accession 435, La Croix Collection, BFRC.

27. Critchlow, *Studebaker*, 118; Joseph Geschelin, "Studebaker Know-How Speeds Flying Fortress Engine Output," *Automotive and Aviation Industries* 88 (1 April 1943): 18–19; Holley, *Buying Aircraft*, 458–59.

28. Fred K. Fox, "Aircraft Engines," *Turning Wheels* 29 (January 1997): 17; Studebaker Corporation, *Annual Report, 1945*, 4, NAHC; Holley, *Buying Aircraft*, 580.

29. Carl Crow, *The City of Flint Grows Up: The Success Story of an American Community* (New York: Harper & Brothers, 1945), 96–99.

30. Ibid., 99–102; Smith, *The Army and Economic Mobilization*, 496.

31. Terry B. Dunham and Larry Gustin, *The Buick: A Complete History*, 6th ed. (Kunztown, PA: Automobile Quarterly Publications, 2002), 236; Crow, *The City of Flint Grows Up*, 100, 124, 164, 165; Orth, "The War Years," 60.

32. Crow, *The City of Flint Grows Up*, 166–67.

33. Ibid., 175–77, 204; "Buick's Cylinder Head Foundry," *Aero Digest* 42 (February 1943): 192; Don Bent, *A Place Called Buick: A History of the GM Powertrain Flint North Site, 1905–2005* (no publication information provided), 102.

34. Crow, *The City of Flint Grows Up*, 175; "Buick Builds 50,000th Engine," *New York Times*, 2 July 1944; "Buick to Build New Engines," *New York Times*, 22 April 1944; *Buick at Its Battle Stations* (Buick Division of General Motors, 1944), 12; Holley, *Buying Aircraft*, 580; Scott, *Packard*, 143–44.

35. Dinner programs, 22 October 1943 and 13 July 1944, in folder, "Buick-GM History: Dinner Programs, 1926–1949," Accession 1974.011.002, SA/KU.

36. M. E. Coyle, comp., "Report of War Production Activities, Chevrolet Motor Division, General Motors Division: Volume for Victory," n.p. This bound, unpublished report is found in the archives of the General Motors Heritage Center, Sterling Heights, Michigan.

37. Ibid.; Smith, *The Army and Economic Mobilization*, 496.

38. "Mass Production of Aluminum Aircraft Forgings at Chevrolet," *Industrial Heating* 10 (October 1943): 1423–42; "Franklin M. Reck, Chevrolet's Streamlined Aluminum Forge," *Aero Digest* 43 (October 1943): 158–62; "Chevrolet Foundry Produces Magnesium Castings for Aircraft Engines," *Industrial Heating* 11 (January 1944): 15–14; "Two Aircraft Engines Built on One Assembly Line," *American Machinist* (1 March 1945): 106–7.

39. The description of Nash-Kelvinator's work on aircraft engines in the next few paragraphs comes mostly from "Introduction," folder, "World War II History," World War II Production Series, box 4, "Nash-Kelvinator War Production, 1942–1945," 8–14, CCA.

40. Ibid.; "Narrative of Navy Program at Nash-Kelvinator, Kenosha, Wisconsin," folder, "World War II History," World War II Production Series, box 4, "Nash-Kelvinator War Production, 1942–1945," 2–3, CCA.

41. "Introduction," 11; "Narrative of Navy Program," 6.

42. "Narrative of Navy Program," 8–10.

43. "Introduction," 12–14; Craven and Cate, *Men and Planes*, 356.

44. Edmund L. (Skip) Eveleth, "The Greatest Wedding of American Industry," Vertical Files, "World War II, Aircraft Engines," BFRC. Eveleth wrote this reminiscence in 1992 at age eighty-three.

45. Ibid.

46. Ibid.

47. The discussion of the Dodge-Chicago plant is an expanded version of my description of this plant that appeared in *Riding the Roller Coaster*, 140–44. The chapter on Chrysler's work during the war was based heavily on Chrysler's War Records, a massive collection of materials found in CCA.

48. Entries of 11 September 1941, 30 December 1941, and 2, 11, 13, and 15 March 1942, Chrysler War Records, vol. 13, *Dodge-Chicago*, 1941, 1942, 1943, CCA; Wesley W. Stout, *Great Engines and Great Planes* (Detroit: Chrysler Corporation, 1947), 18–19.

49. Entries of 27 February 1942, 18, 20, and 30 March 1942, 27 May 1942, and 2 July 1942, Chrysler War Records, vol. 13, *Dodge-Chicago*, 1941, 1942, 1943, CCA; *Dodge-Chicago Plant Division of Chrysler Corporation, for the Manufacture of Aircraft Engines*, letter to the Chrysler stockholders, 14 December 1942, signed by K. T. Keller, Chrysler Corporation vertical files, NAHC. The factory floor space figures are from Craven and Cate, *Men and Planes*, 315.

50. Memoranda from L. L. Colbert, Operations Manager, Dodge-Chicago Plant, 7 and 8 May 1942, 27 June 1942, Chrysler War Records, vol. 13, *Dodge-Chicago*, 1941, 1942, 1943, CCA.

51. Entries of 5 June 1942 and 19 August 1942, Chrysler War Records, vol. 13, *Dodge-Chicago*, 1941, 1942, 1943, CCA; Stout, *Great Engines and Great Planes*, 14–15; "The New Giant of Giants," *Chrysler War Work Magazine* 9 (December 1942): 8; "New Plants of 1943: Dodge-Chicago Division of Chrysler Corporation," *Factory Management and Maintenance* 102 (April 1944): B73.

52. Entries of 15 May 1942, 28 May 1942, and 15 September 1943, Chrysler War Records, vol. 13, *Dodge-Chicago*, 1941, 1942, 1943, CCA; "New Plants of 1943," B72–B74; Stout, *Great Engines and Great Planes*, 13–15.

53. Entries of 4 March, 6 March, 17 March, and 30 March 1942, and report of L. L. Colbert, 29 July 1942, Chrysler War Records, vol. 13, *Dodge-Chicago*, 1941, 1942, 1943, CCA; Carl Breer, *The Birth of Chrysler Corporation and Its Engineering Legacy* (Warrentown, PA: Society of Automotive Engineers, 1995), 188–90.

54. Entries of 10 and 17 August 1942, 23 March 1943, 3 April 1943, and 4 September 1943, Chrysler War Records, vol. 13, *Dodge-Chicago*, 1941, 1942, 1943, CCA; Stout, *Great Engines and Great Planes*, 16.

55. Entries of 15 October 1943 and 1 December 1943, vol. 14, Chrysler War Records, vol. 13, *Dodge-Chicago*, 1941, 1942, 1943; entries of 1 February 1944, 5 June 1944, 31 August 1944, and 6 October 1944, vol. 14, *Dodge-Chicago*, 1944; *Shipments of War Products*, 116, vol. 25, *General*, 1945, 1946, all in CCA.

56. Memorandum of R. H. Hetrick, General Auditor, Dodge-Chicago Plant, 1 August 1944, Chrysler War Records, vol. 14, *Dodge-Chicago*, 1944, CCA.

57. Entries of 2 June 1944, 8 June 1944, 22 July 1944, and 15 December 1944, Chrysler War Records, vol. 14, *Dodge-Chicago*, 1944, CCA; Stout, *Great Engines and Great Planes*, 34.

58. Hetrick memorandum, 1 August 1944; Stout, *Great Engines and Great Planes*, 22–23.

59. Entries of 7 September 1945 and 6 January 1946, Chrysler War Records, vol. 15, *Dodge-Chicago*, 1945, 1946, CCA.

60. Holley, *Buying Aircraft*, 562–63.

61. "Introduction," 4, 5.

62. George Rosen and Charles A. Aneziz, *Thrusting Forward: A History of the Propeller* (Hartford, CT: Hamilton Standard, n.d.), 40–46.

63. "Introduction," 5, 6; "U.S. Buys REO Building for Defense Work: Nash to Build Propellers in Part of Plant," *Lansing (MI) State Journal*, 19 May 1941, 1.

64. "Lansing Plant About Ready: Old REO Factory to Make Bomber Propellers," *Detroit News*, 22 September 1941, 6; Joseph Geschelin, "Propellers in the Making at the Nash-Kelvinator Plant," *Automotive and Aviation Industries* 87 (15 December 1942): 21–25, 72–73; Nomination of Nash-Kelvinator Corporation Propeller Division for the Army-Navy "E" Production Award, 28 January 1943, folder, "World War II History," World War II Production Series, box 4, "Nash-Kelvinator War Production, 1942–1945," CCA.

65. "New Defense Job to Nash-Kelvinator," *Detroit News*, 29 September 1941, 5; "Grand Rapids Plant to Make Propeller," *Detroit News*, 22 December 1942, 35.

66. "Introduction," 6–8; "Popular Names of Military Planes Equipped with Nash-Kelvinator, Hamilton Standard Hydromatic Variable Pitch Quick-Feathering Propellers, June 1, 1943"; and Nash-Kelvinator Corporation Propeller Division, "Salient Milestones in Chronological Order" and "Pertinent Statistics," all in folder, "World War II History," World War II Production Series, box 4, "Nash-Kelvinator War Production, 1942–1945," CCA. For the production records of the various propeller manufacturers and the various types of aircraft, see Holley, *Buying Aircraft*, 562, 576–79.

CHAPTER FOUR

1. Aircraft Industries Association of America, "Aircraft Manufacturing in the United States," in Simonson, ed., *The History of the American Aircraft Industry*; Holley, *Buying Aircraft*, 549, 576–79. Goodyear's achievements are not covered in printed sources except for E. L. Warner, "Goodyear Aircraft's Rapid Growth and Accomplishments through Management Control," *Automotive and Aircraft Industries* 90 (1 February 1944): 32–35, 70, 72, 74, 152, 154.

2. Rae, *Climb to Greatness*, 122, 125; Holley, *Buying Aircraft*, 580.

3. Aircraft Industries Association of America, "Aircraft Manufacturing in the United States," 163, 165; Holley, *Buying Aircraft*, 560.

4. Aircraft Industries Association of America, "Aircraft Manufacturing in the United States," 166–67.

5. Smith, *The Army and Economic Mobilization*, 7, 496; White, *Billions for Defense*, 49.

6. Holley, *Buying Aircraft*, 576–78.

7. O'Callaghan, *Ford in the Service of America*, 180–81; Sloan, *My Years with General Motors*, 381; Hyde, *Riding the Roller Coaster*, 134–35; "Bomber Parts by De Soto and Plymouth," *Automotive Industries* 85 (15 August 1941): 18–19; "De Soto Builds B-29 Components," *Aero Digest*, 1 September 1944, 80–81, 128; Automobile Manufacturers Association, *Freedom's Arsenal*, 193.

8. Holley, *Buying Aircraft*, 332–43, 352. Smith (*The Army and Economic Mobilization*, 235–397) describes similar practices followed by the Ordnance Department and the Quartermaster Corps.

9. Holley, *Buying Aircraft*, 95, 99, 153, 346, 350–52, 463.

10. Ibid., 361–62, 374–75, 390–401.

11. Ibid., 412–15, 422–23, 440–42, 560.

12. Lilly et al., "Conversion to Wartime Production Techniques," 119, 131; Holley, *Buying Aircraft*, 526.

13. G. F. Nordenholt, "Aircraft Are Different: No Other Industry Has Comparable Problems," *Product Engineering* 13 (July 1942): 368–71; Don R. Berlin and Peter F. Rossmann, "Engineering Considerations in the Application of Automobile Methods to Aircraft Production," *SAE Journal* 48 (June 1941): 218–20.

14. Herbert Chase, "Converts Auto-Body Plant . . . ," *Steel* 110 (23 March 1942): 64–67; W. F. Sherman, "Murray Corp. of America Perfects Unique Aircraft Construction Methods," *The Iron Age* 149 (25 June 1942): 33–34; Franklin M. Reck, "Murray Fabricates Aircraft Surfaces on Moving Assembly Lines," *Aero Digest* 42 (March 1943), 207–15; Joseph Geschelin, "Multiplicity of Operations Submit to Automotive Methods at the Murray Plant," *Automotive and Aviation Industries* 89 (15 November 1943): 20–25, 86, 88.

15. Joseph Geschelin, "Conversion for War-Influence of Automotive Mass-Production Methods," *SAE Journal* 50 (July 1942): 276–82.

16. Holley, *Buying Aircraft*, 512–18, 528, 537, 547.

17. Ibid., 528–34.

18. Ibid., 538–47; Mac Short, "Engineering BDV Production of Flying Fortresses," *Automotive and Aviation Industries* 89 (15 October 1943): 17–21, 92–96.

19. Hyde, *Storied Independent Automakers*, 144.

20. Holley, *Buying Aircraft*, 546; Report, Dennis Mulligan, Lt. Colonel, Air Corps, to the Chief, Production Division, Wright Field, 30 December 1942, box 1, Roy D. Chapin Jr. Papers, Bentley Historical Library, University of Michigan; War Records, vol. 25, "Shipments of War Products," 115–16, CCA.

21. Holley, *Buying Aircraft*, 547; Vander Meulen, *Building the B-29*, 7, 20, 27.

22. Vander Meulen, *Building the B-29*, 27, 29, 31; Holley, *Buying Aircraft*, 578; Hyde, *Riding the Roller Coaster*, 132; Hyde, *Storied Independent Automakers*, 146, 148; "Fisher Body Builds B-29 Nacelles," *Aero Digest* (1 November 1944): 90–92, 95, 136; *Fisher Body Craftsmanship Goes to War* (Fisher Body Division of General Motors Corporation, 1945), 4, 8; Frank J. Taylor and Lawton Wright, *Democracy's Air Arsenal* (New York: Duell Sloan and Pearce, 1947), 91; "Shipments of War Products," 115–16.

23. Vander Meulen, *Building the B-29*, 32–35, 54; Beasley, *Knudsen*, 366–72.

24. Hyde, *Riding the Roller Coaster*, 132; Hyde, *Storied Independent Automakers*, 145, 148.

25. Allan Nevins and Frank Earnest Hill, *Ford: Expansion and Challenge, 1915–1933* (New York: Charles Scribner's Sons, 1957), 238–47.

26. Charles E. Sorensen, with Samuel T. Williamson, *My Forty Years with Ford* (New York: Norton, 1956), 276–80.

27. Sorensen, *My Forty Years with Ford*, 280–81; Warren Benjamin Kidder, *Willow Run: Colossus of American Industry* (Lansing, MI: KFT Publishing, 1995), 48, 125.

28. Sorensen, *My Forty Years with Ford*, 281–85; Holley, *Buying Aircraft*, 519, 521.

29. Kidder, *Willow Run*, 65–67; Holley, *Buying Aircraft*, 520–21; O'Callaghan, *Ford in the Service of America*, 47; Chronology for 1942, Accession 435, box 15, vol. 2, La Croix Collection.

30. "Ford Motor Company Willow Run Bomber Plant, Ypsilanti, Michigan, B-24 Construction and Production Analysis," prepared by the Industrial Plans Section, Logistics Planning Division Plans (T-5, Air Materiel Command, Army Air Forces, August 1946), 11–12, Vertical Files, World War II, *B-24 Bomber Construction and Production Analysis*, BFRC.

31. Holley, *Buying Aircraft*, 521–22, 526; Kidder, *Willow Run*, 114–15; Taylor and Wright, *Democracy's Air Arsenal*, 65; O'Callaghan, *Ford in the Service of America*, 48, 53.

32. Holley, *Buying Aircraft*, 522; box 15, 2:26, Accession 435, La Croix Collection, BFRC. For a description of the practice of "lofting" in the aircraft industry, see John C. Widman, "The Automotive Body Engineer in Aircraft," *SAE Journal* 50 (June 1942): 210. I am grateful to Richard K. Anderson Jr. for explaining the lofting process to me.

33. Kidder, *Willow Run*, 9–13, 66–67; Clive, *State of War*, 24.

34. Nevins and Hill, *Ford: Decline and Rebirth*, 213–14; O'Callaghan, *Ford in the Service of America*, 48, 80, 183; Kidder, *Willow Run*, 126–29, 239.

35. Nevins and Hill, *Ford: Decline and Rebirth*, 211; O'Callaghan, *Ford in the Service of America*, 53.

36. Kidder, *Willow Run*, 121–22, 124.

37. Holley, *Buying Aircraft*, 523–24; Nevins and Hill, *Ford: Decline and Rebirth*, 212; Lilly et al., "Conversion to Wartime Production Techniques," 131–32.

38. Sorensen, *My Forty Years with Ford*, 288–89.

39. Nevins and Hill, *Ford: Decline and Rebirth*, 212; Smith, *The Army and Economic Mobilization*, 496.

40. Holley, *Buying Aircraft*, 524–27; O'Callaghan, *Ford in the Service of America*, 55–57; Kidder, *Willow Run*, 136, 240, 241, 271.

41. Kidder, *Willow Run*, 214–15.

42. E. L. Warner Jr., "Decentralization of Willow Run Bomber Plant Results in Volume Output," *Automotive and Aviation Industries* 90 (15 April 1944): 18–20, 85–88; O'Callaghan, *Ford in the Service of America*, 51, 73; Nevins and Hill, *Ford: Decline and Rebirth*, 219, 221; Holley, *Buying Aircraft*, 494n68; Accession 435, box 15, 3:31, La Croix Collection.

43. Charles A. Lindbergh, *The Wartime Journals* (New York: Harcourt Brace Jovanovich, 1970), 608–9, 615–16, 644–45, 661, 737–38. The statement quoted appears on 645.

44. Box 21, 19:40, Accession 435, La Croix Collection, BFRC; Franklin M. Beck, "Willow Run—

Today: A Report on the Present Status of the Ford Bomber Plant," *Aero Digest* 42, no. 4 (April 1943): 244.

45. Nevins and Hill, *Ford: Decline and Rebirth*, 215–16; "Bomber Plant Mancount, 12-19-41," box 15, 1:81, and "Willow Run: Proposed Departmental and Personnel Organization, dated Dec. 5, 1941," box 15, 1:82–85, "Willow Run: Proposed Departmental and Personnel Organization, dated Dec. 5, 1941," both in Accession 435, La Croix Collection, BFRC.

46. Holley, *Buying Aircraft*, 527; O'Callaghan, *Ford in the Service of America*, 72; box 21, 19:33–34, Accession 435, La Croix Collection, BFRC.

47. O'Callaghan, *Ford in the Service of America*, 68, 72; Nevins and Hill, *Ford: Decline and Rebirth*, 218; Rae, *Climb to Greatness*, 151–53; Lowell Julliard Carr and James Edson Stermer, *Willow Run: A Study of Industrialization and Cultural Inadequacy* (New York: Harper & Brothers, 1952), 211.

48. Nevins and Hill, *Ford: Decline and Rebirth*, 164, 215; Clive, *State of War*, 68–69; "B-24 Construction and Production Analysis," 96.

49. Clive, *State of War*, 108–9; O'Callaghan, *Ford in the Service of America*, 73; Carr and Stermer, *Willow Run*, 11n2, 391–94; Kidder, *Willow Run*, 182.

50. Carr and Stermer, *Willow Run*, 87, 245–53; Clive, *State of War*, 110–11; O'Callaghan, *Ford in the Service of America*, 73; Kidder, *Willow Run*, 182.

51. Charles K. Hyde, "Planning a Transportation System for Metropolitan Detroit in the Age of the Automobile: The Triumph of the Expressway," *Michigan Historical Review* 32 (Spring 2006): 81, 84; Clive, *State of War*, 112–13; Nevins and Hill, *Ford: Decline and Rebirth*, 215; Kidder, *Willow Run*, 171.

52. The negative impact of Ford's internal management disputes are delineated in Rae, *Climb to Greatness*, 158; Nevins and Hill, *Ford: Decline and Rebirth*, 228–51; David L. Lewis, *The Public Image of Henry Ford: An American Folk Hero and His Company* (Detroit: Wayne State University Press, 1987), 372–73; and Sorensen, *My Forty Years with Ford*, 301–34.

53. Doris Kearns Goodwin, *No Ordinary Time, Franklin and Eleanor Roosevelt: The Home Front in World War II* (New York: Simon and Schuster, 1994), 363–64; Lewis, *The Public Image of Henry Ford*, 356–57; Sorensen, *My Forty Years with Ford*, 292–97. The Sorensen quotation is found on 296–97.

54. Nevins and Hill, *Ford: Decline and Rebirth*, 192, 213; O'Callaghan, *Ford in the Service of America*, 43, 53–54.

55. Nevins and Hill, *Ford: Decline and Rebirth*, 218–19; Lewis, *The Public Image of Henry Ford*, 349, 359–60.

56. Nevins and Hill, *Ford: Decline and Rebirth*, 225; Sorensen, *My Forty Years with Ford*, 287, 332–33; Lewis, *The Public Image of Henry Ford*, 360.

57. Nevins and Hill, *Ford: Decline and Rebirth*, 259–61; Sorensen, *My Forty Years with Ford*, 329–34.

58. O'Callaghan, *Ford in the Service of America*, 64; Rae, *Climb to Greatness*, 128; Nevins and Hill, *Ford: Decline and Rebirth*, 223–24; Kidder, *Willow Run*, 157; Holley, *Buying Aircraft*, 526–27.

59. Nevins and Hill, *Ford: Decline and Rebirth*, 221; Holley, *Buying Aircraft*, 535–37; O'Callaghan, *Ford in the Service of America*, 64; Kidder, *Willow Run*, 148–58.

60. Nevins and Hill, *Ford: Decline and Rebirth*, 218, 221; O'Callaghan, *Ford in the Service of America*, 68–69, 80; Rae, *Climb to Greatness*, 168.

61. Holley, *Buying Aircraft*, 326; Nevins and Hill, *Ford: Decline and Rebirth*, 218, 224.

62. Holley, *Buying Aircraft*, 327, 565; Lewis, *The Public Image of Henry Ford*, 361.

63. Taylor and Wright, *Democracy's Air Arsenal*, 66–68, 71–72; Joseph Geschelin, "West Coast Airplane Plants," *Automotive Industries* 86 (1 January 1942): 33–39, 76, 78; Joseph Geschelin, "West Coast Airplane Industry," *Automotive Industries* 86 (15 January 1942): 24–31, 65–66; Joseph Geschelin, "Mass Production Methods Used at Bell Plant to Build Airacobras," *Automotive and Aviation Industries* 89 (15 September 1943): 22–26, 88–90.

64. Holley, *Buying Aircraft*, 547, 576–78; William Green, *Famous Bombers of the Second World War*, 2nd rev. ed. (Garden City, NY: Doubleday, 1975), 44, 74, 165–68.

65. Green, *Famous Bombers of the Second World War*, 175, 176; Elizabeth-Anne Wheal, Stephen Pope, and James Taylor, *Meridian Encyclopedia of the Second World War* (New York: Penguin, 1992), 371.

66. B. H. Liddell Hart, *History of the Second World War* (New York: G. P. Putnam's Sons, 1970), 603–5, 611–12; Adam Tooze, *The Wages of Destruction: The Making and Breaking of the Nazi Economy* (New York: Penguin, 2006), 649; Richard J. Overy, *Why the Allies Won* (New York: W. W. Norton, 1995), 122–33; Richard J. Overy, *The Air War, 1939–1945* (New York: Stein and Day, 1982), 120.

67. Robert G. Ferguson, "One Thousand Planes a Day: Ford, Grumman, General Motors and the Arsenal of Democracy," *History and Technology* 21 (June 2005): 157–58; Holley, *Buying Aircraft*, 576–79; Sloan, *My Years with General Motors*, 381.

68. Ferguson, "One Thousand Planes a Day," 158–59; Bill Gunston, *Grumman: Sixty Years of Excellence* (New York: Orion Books, 1988), 8–9, 20; Richard Thruelsen, *The Grumman Story* (New York: Praeger, 1976), 64–65, 80.

69. Gunston, *Grumman*, 24, 33, 35, 36, 40; Thruelsen, *The Grumman Story*, 91, 106, 108, 122, 133.

70. Thruelsen, *The Grumman Story*, 132, 139–41, 144–50.

71. General Motors Corporation, *A History of Eastern Aircraft Division, General Motors Corporation* (New York: Eastern Aircraft Division, 1944), 17–19, 25, 27.

72. Ibid., 24, 39–40; Thruelsen, *The Grumman Story*, 157.

73. General Motors Corporation, *History of Eastern Aircraft Division*, 20, 23, 29–31, 32–35; Thruelsen, *The Grumman Story*, 155–57.

74. General Motors Corporation, *History of Eastern Aircraft Division*, 36, 38, 43, 46; Thruelsen, *The Grumman Story*, 157.

75. General Motors Corporation, *History of Eastern Aircraft Division*, 47, 48; Thruelsen, *The Grumman Story*, 157; Grumman Aircraft Engineering Corporation, *Grumman at War: Grumman Makes Planes for the Men Who Make History* (Bethpage, NY: Grumman Aircraft Engineering Corporation, 1945), 25, 26, 43; Ferguson, "One Thousand Planes a Day," 168; Holley, *Buying Aircraft*, 577.

76. Roy A. Grossnick and William J. Armstrong, *United States Naval Aviation, 1910–1995* (Washington, DC: Naval Historical Center, Department of the Navy, 1997), 117; Liddell Hart, *History of the Second World War*, 349–53; William Green, *Famous Fighters of the Second World War*, 2nd rev. ed. (Garden City, NY: Doubleday, 1975), 247, 250.

77. Nevins and Hill, *Ford: Decline and Rebirth*, 205–6; O'Callaghan, *Ford in the Service of America*, 82–83.

78. Nevins and Hill, *Ford: Decline and Rebirth*, 207; O'Callaghan, *Ford in the Service of America*, 83–84.

79. Box 9, 2:57, 59, 61, Accession 435, La Croix Collection, BFRC; Nevins and Hill, *Ford: Decline and Rebirth*, 207–8; O'Callaghan, *Ford in the Service of America*, 86–87. O'Callaghan's glider production totals (both models) cited in the text are slightly higher (4,289) than the number (4,277) given in box 9, vol. 1, Exhibit G-2, Accession 435, La Croix Collection, BFRC.

80. O'Callaghan, *Ford in the Service of America*, 85–86; box 9, 2:49, Accession 435, La Croix Collection, BFRC, for the Hansen quotation.

81. "Introduction," 23–25; "Contract for Army Helicopters: Big Output Is Proposed, Production to Pass Sikorsky Plants," *Detroit News*, 13 June 1943, sec. 1, p. 12; "Nash Retools for Helicopter: Quantity Production Planned for U.S. Army," *Detroit News*, 15 July 1943, p. 21.

82. "Introduction," 25–26; "Getting Ready to Produce Army Helicopters," *Detroit News*, 16 December 1943, p. 4.

83. "Introduction," 26–28; "Completes Helicopter Tests," *Michigan Manufacturer and Financial Record* 74 (16 September 1944): 11.

84. Riddle, *The Truman Committee*, 122–37.

85. Craven and Cate, *Men and Planes*, 318, 327, 331, 360.

86. Overy, *The Air War*, 164–65; Sir Alec Cairncross, *Planning in Wartime: Aircraft Production in Britain, Germany and the USA* (Oxford: Macmillan, 1991), 174–78.

87. Overy, *The Air War*, 165; Cairncross, *Planning in Wartime*, 122–26, 163.

88. Jerome B. Cohen, *Japan's Economy in War and Reconstruction* (Minneapolis: University of Minnesota Press, 1949), 208–14, 233. For the quotation, see 209.

CHAPTER FIVE

1. Harry C. Thomson and Lida Mayo, *United States Army in World War II, The Ordnance Department: Procurement and Supply* (Washington, DC: Office of the Chief of Military History, Department of the Army, 1960), 242.

2. Michael W. R. Davis, *Detroit's Wartime Industry: Arsenal of Democracy* (Charleston, SC: Arcadia Publishing, 2007), 19; Constance McLaughlin Green, Harry C. Thomson, and Peter C. Roots, *United States Army in World War II, The Ordnance Department: Planning Munitions for War* (Washington, DC: Office of the Chief of Military History, Department of the Army, 1955), 189, 194; Thomson and Mayo, *The Ordnance Department*, 223–24.

3. Thomson and Mayo, *The Ordnance Department*, 225, 242.

4. Frederick A. Stevenson, "From Railroad Cars to Combat Tanks," *Military Engineer* 34 (January 1942): 10–11.

5. Frank J. Oliver, "From Locomotives to Tanks," *Iron Age* 49 (7 May 1942): 64–68.

6. Thomson and Mayo, *The Ordnance Department*, 230–33; Smith, *The Army and Economic Mobilization*, 9; "Tank Production, by Year, by Manufacturer, 1940–1945," provided by TACOM.

7. Thomson and Mayo, *The Ordnance Department*, 242, 250.

8. Ibid., 240; Kevin Thornton and Dale Prentiss, *Tanks and Industry: The Detroit Arsenal, 1940–1954* (Warren, MI: U.S. Army Tank-Automotive and Armaments Command, 1995), 42–43.

9. Beasley, *Knudsen*, 283–84; Hyde, *Riding the Roller Coaster*, 135.

10. Wesley W. Stout, *"TANKS Are Mighty Fine Things"* (Detroit: Chrysler Corporation, 1946), 12–13, 16–18; "Tank Plant Chronology," in box, "Defense 1," and report of R. P. Fohey, 15 August 1940, and miscellaneous materials from the files of E. J. Hunt and B. E. Hutchinson, Chrysler War Records, vol. 44, *Tanks*, 1940, 1941, CCA.

11. Stout, *"TANKS Are Mighty Fine Things,"* 20–21; reports of E. J. Hunt, 4 and 18 October 1940, Chrysler War Records, vol. 44, *Tanks*, 1940, 1941, CCA.

12. Lieutenant Colonel J. K. Christmas, "Our New Medium Tank: A Fast, Heavily Armored Vehicle of Great Fire Power," *Army Ordnance* 22 (July–August 1941): 27–29.

13. "Machinery Being Rapidly Installed at Chrysler's New Tank Arsenal," *Steel* 108 (31 March 1941): 41; "Tanks Ahead of Schedule," *American Machinist* 85 (10 December 1941): 1267–69; "Brand New and Shiny: The Detroit Tank Arsenal of Chrysler Corporation," *Time* 37 (27 January 1942): 19; K. T. Keller, "The Detroit Tank Arsenal: The Chrysler Plant for Mass Production of the Medium Tank," *Army Ordnance* 22 (January–February 1942): 545–46.

14. Memo from E. J. Hunt, 3 October 1941, and construction reports of H. S. Wells, 28 January 1941, 15 April 1941, Chrysler War Records, vol. 44, *Tanks*, 1940, 1941, CCA.

15. Stout, *"TANKS Are Mighty Fine Things,"* 23–26; Thornton and Prentiss, *Tanks and Industry*, 22; "Delivering No. 1 to the United States Army: Chrysler Corporation's First M3 Medium Tank, April 14, 1941," box "Defense 1," CCA.

16. Reports of L. L. Colbert, 31 July and 8 August 1941, Chrysler War Records, vol. 44, *Tanks*, 1940, 1941, CCA; Stout, *"TANKS Are Mighty Fine Things,"* 32–33.

17. David Doyle, *Standard Catalogue of U.S. Military Vehicles*, 2nd ed. (Iola, WI: Krause Publications, 2003), 436–37.

18. Note from Mr. Littel, Detroit Ordnance Department, 14 October 1941, and Chrysler Corporation letter, 17 November 1941, Chrysler War Records, vol. 44, *Tanks*, CCA; Supplements to Tank Contract W-ORD-416, 26 and 27 March 1942, Chrysler War Records, vol. 45, *Tanks*, 1942, CCA; "Shipments of War Products," Chrysler War Records, vol. 25, *General*, 1945, 1946, CCA; Stout, *"TANKS Are Mighty Fine Things,"* 40–41.

19. Liddell Hart, *History of the Second World War*, 298–99; Tooze, *The Wages of Destruction*,

590–91; Elizabeth-Ann Wheal, Stephen Pope, and James Taylor, *The Meridian Encyclopedia of the Second World War* (New York: Penguin, 1992), 8–9.

20. Letter from L. A. Moehring, Comptroller, 20 June 1944, Chrysler War Records, vol. 44, *Tanks*, 1940, 1941, CCA; entries of 17 October 1942 and 16 December 1942, vol. 45, *Tanks*, 1942, CCA; entry of 12 January 1943, vol. 46, *Tanks*, 1943, CCA; Stout, "*TANKS Are Mighty Fine Things*," 34–36. The multibank engine performance specifications are from Doyle, *Standard Catalogue of U.S. Military Vehicles*, 446.

21. Chrysler Corporation Public Relations release, 24 April 1945, Chrysler War Records, vol. 25, *Tanks*, 1945, 1946, CCA; "Roosevelt's Visit to Chrysler," *Detroit News*, 1 October 1942; "Presidential War Tour Makes History for Leak-Proof Security," *Detroit Free Press*, 2 October 1942; "Roosevelt Pays Tribute to the Genius of Chrysler," *Detroit Free Press*, 2 October 1942; "President Saw Production Miracles in Detroit," *Detroit Times*, 2 October 1942.

22. L. A. Moehring, Comptroller, to J. W. Lee II, Public Relations, 20 June 1944, Chrysler War Records, vol. 47, *Tanks*, 1944, CCA; end-of-the-year employment summaries, 31 December 1942, 31 December 1943, 31 December 1944, and 31 December 1945, in Chrysler War Records, vols. 23–25, *General*, 1942–45, CCA; Stout, "*TANKS Are Mighty Fine Things*," 62–63; "How Chrysler Corporation Subcontracts More than 50% of Its War Work" (undated statement found in Chrysler War Records).

23. Summary dated 26 September 1946, Chrysler War Records, vol. 48, *Tanks*, 1945, 1946, CCA; Stout, "*TANKS Are Mighty Fine Things*," 49–50; Automobile Manufacturers Association, *Freedom's Arsenal*, 199, 201.

24. Entries of 1 June, 1 July, 12 September, 17 September, 8 October, and 26 October 1945, Chrysler War Records, vol. 48, *Tanks*, 1945, 1946, CCA.

25. "Fisher Body Tank Program," Accession 1986, box 1, folder 14, pp. 34, 42, 43, SA/KU.

26. Ibid., 39, 43; E. L. Warner Jr., "Changing Over to Tanks," *Automotive and Aviation Industries* 86 (15 April 1942): 17.

27. "All-Welded Tank Built in 47 Days; Fisher Body Sets the Speed Record," *New York Times*, 3 April 1942; "Fisher Body Tank Program," 39, 41 and folder 15, "Fisher Body Tank Program," 35; Thomson and Mayo, *The Ordnance Department*, 242, 257; *Fisher Body Craftsmanship Goes to War* (Fisher Body Division, General Motors Corporation, 1945), 31.

28. Doyle, *Standard Catalogue of U.S. Military Vehicles*, 356; Accession 1986, box 1, Folder 14, 41, 44, 75 and box 1, folder 15, SA/KU.

29. "Tank Program," Accession 1986, box 1, folder 11-1, pp. 63, 68, SA/KU.

30. Orth, "The War Years," 56–57; Edward T. Ragsdale, "New M18 Hellcat Is a Triumph of Engineering Production Know-How and Sub-Contracting," *Automotive and Aviation Industries* 91 (October 1944): 25–26; Doyle, *Standard Catalogue of U.S. Military Vehicles*, 363–64.

31. Doyle, *Standard Catalogue of U.S. Military Vehicles*, 426–29; Orth, "The War Years," 55–56; Thomson and Mayo, *The Ordnance Department*, 250, 251; "Cadillac Motor Car Division, History of World War II," 11, 13. The extensive modifications made by Cadillac engineers to the M3 are spelled out in the latter document on pages 140–51. Annual production statistics for Cadillac by year, plant, and tank model can be found in U.S. Army, Office Chief of Ordnance-Detroit, *Summary Report of Acceptances, Tank-Automotive Materiel, 1940–1945* (September 1945), found in the archives of the US Army TACOM, Life Cycle Management Command.

32. Thomson and Mayo, *The Ordnance Department*, 251; "Cadillac Motor Car Division, History of World War II," 13–14, 20–22, 32–33.

33. "Cadillac Motor Car Division, History of World War II," 22–27, 31, 35.

34. Ibid., 159–60, 177–78; Doyle, *Standard Catalogue of U.S. Military Vehicles*, 429.

35. "Cadillac Motor Car Division, History of World War II," 15, 51, 160–61, 165, 168; Doyle, *Standard Catalogue of U.S. Military Vehicles*, 429.

36. "Cadillac Motor Car Division, History of World War II," 163–65, 168.

37. Thomson and Mayo, *The Ordnance Department*, 252; Doyle, *Standard Catalogue of U.S. Military Vehicles*, 430–31; "Cadillac Motor Car Division, History of World War II," 161, 164, 166–70.

38. "Chronology of Tank Contract," box 12, Tank Manufacture, 1:1–4, Accession 435, La Croix Collection, BFRC.

39. Ibid., 1:3–5.

40. Green, Thomson, and Roots, *The Ordnance Department: Planning Munitions for War*, 374–77; Thomson and Mayo, *The Ordnance Department*, 247–49.

41. Thomson and Mayo, *The Ordnance Department*, 247–49; Accession 435, box 13, Tank Manufacture, 2:42–43, 46–47, 58–59, La Croix Collection.

42. Nevins and Hill, *Ford: Decline and Rebirth*, 193–94; box 12, Tank Manufacture, 1:3–4, Accession 435, La Croix Collection, BFRC.

43. "Exhibit T-1, Contractual Coverage for Tanks and Tank Engines," box 12, Tank Manufacture, vol. 1, and box 13, Tank Manufacture, 2:65, 71, 73, Accession 435, La Croix Collection, BFRC.

44. Box 12, Tank Manufacture, 1:1, 3, Accession 435, La Croix Collection, BFRC; "Exhibit T-1, Contractual Coverage for Tanks and Tank Engines," box 12, volume 1, Accession 435, La Croix Collection, BFRC; O'Callaghan, *Ford in the Service of America*, 127–29, 158.

45. Thomson and Mayo, *The Ordnance Department*, 256–57; O'Callaghan, *Ford in the Service of America*, 129; "Chronology of Tank Contract," box 12, Tank Manufacture, 1:6 and "Termination of Contract W-374-ORD-1213," box 13, 2:82, Accession 435, La Croix Collection, BFRC.

46. Smith, *The Army and Economic Mobilization*, 9.

47. Thomson and Mayo, *The Ordnance Department*, 225–27; Levin H. Campbell Jr., *The Industry-Ordnance Team* (New York: McGraw-Hill, 1946), 235.

48. Smith, *The Army and Economic Mobilization*, 9; Thomson and Mayo, *The Ordnance Department*, 239; Green, Thomson, and Roots, *The Ordnance Department: Planning Munitions for War*, 278–84, 514; Wheal, Pope, and Taylor, *Meridian Encyclopedia of the Second World War*, 432, 471.

49. Thomson and Mayo, *The Ordnance Department*, 259–62; Green, Thomson, and Roots, *The Ordnance Department: Planning Munitions for War*, 278–80, 284; Doyle, *Standard Catalogue of U.S. Military Vehicles*, 446–48.

50. Thomson and Mayo, *The Ordnance Department*, 227, 244–45; William Wagner, *Continental! Its Motors and Its People* (Fallbrook, CA: Aero Publishers, 1983), 87–95; Green, Thomson, and Roots, *The Ordnance Department: Planning Munitions for War*, 202–3, 290–91; Doyle, *Standard Catalogue of U.S. Military Vehicles*, 437, 440.

51. Green, Thomson, and Roots, *The Ordnance Department: Planning Munitions for War*, 294–96; Doyle, *Standard Catalogue of U.S. Military Vehicles*, 436, 442.

52. Green, Thomson, and Roots, *The Ordnance Department: Planning Munitions for War*, 296–98.

53. Ibid., 297–98; Thomson and Mayo, *The Ordnance Department*, 341; Doyle, *Standard Catalogue of U.S. Military Vehicles*, 436; Wagner, *Continental*, 91.

54. Green, Thomson, and Roots, *The Ordnance Department: Planning Munitions for War*, 291–93; Doyle, *Standard Catalogue of U.S. Military Vehicles*, 436–37, 441, 446.

55. Thomson and Mayo, *The Ordnance Department*, 253; Roger Ford, *The Sherman Tank* (Osceola, WI: MBI Publishing Company, 1999), 27, 30.

56. Green, Thomson, and Roots, *The Ordnance Department: Planning Munitions for War*, 298–301; Ford, *The Sherman Tank*, 26.

57. Thomson and Mayo, *The Ordnance Department*, 254–55.

58. Ibid., 254–55. For a detailed examination of the operation of Ford's Richmond, California, tank depot, see Fredric L. Quivik, "The Ford Motor Company's Richmond Assembly Plant, a.k.a. the Richmond Tank Depot" (report prepared for the National Park Service Rosie the Riveter World War II Homefront National Historic Park, Richmond, California, 2 September 2003).

59. Thomson and Mayo, *The Ordnance Department*, 263.

60. Office of the Chief of Military History, Department of the Army, *The United States Army in World War II, Statistics, Lend-Lease*, prepared by Theodore E. Whiting, Carrel I. Tod, and Anne P. Craft, 15 December 1952, p. 25, US Army TACOM Life Cycle Management Command, Warren, Michigan.

61. "England's Tribute to the Builders of American Tanks," *Chrysler War Work Magazine* 10, no. 5 (November 1943): 8–9; P.F.C. Frank Upton to Sgt. William Hendricks, 29 August 1944, vol. 46, *Tanks*, 1944, CCA.

62. Smith, *The Army and Economic Mobilization*, 9; Doyle, *Standard Catalogue of U.S. Military Vehicles*, 329–36, 386–98.

63. Smith, *The Army and Economic Mobilization*, 9; O'Callaghan, *Ford in the Service of America*, 180; box 7, Armored Cars, 1:4–5, 8–9, 30–31, Accession 435, La Croix Collection, BFRC.

64. Box 7, Armored Cars, 1:4–9, box 27, folder, "Armored Car, T22," and L. S. Shedrick (Ford Motor Company) to Colonel J. K. Christmas, War Department, Office of the Chief of Ordnance, n.d., all in Accession 435, La Croix Collection, BFRC.

65. Box 7, Armored Cars, 2:6, 12, 52, 86a, Accession 435, La Croix Collection, BFRC; Doyle, *Standard Catalogue of U.S. Military Vehicles*, 254–56, 265; O'Callaghan, *Ford in the Service of America*, 180.

66. Box 13, Universal Carrier, 1–2, 10–12, Accession 435, La Croix Collection, BFRC; O'Callaghan, *Ford in the Service of America*, 180.

67. Whiting, Tod, and Craft, *The United States Army in World War II*, 25.

68. Smith, *The Army and Economic Mobilization*, 9.

CHAPTER SIX

1. Smith, *The Army and Economic Mobilization*, 252–54; Erna Risch, *United States Army in World War II, the Technical Services, the Quartermaster Corps: Organization, Supply and Services*, I (Washington, DC: United States Army, 1953), 142n69.

2. Smith, *The Army and Economic Mobilization*, 254–55; Thomson and Mayo, *The Ordnance Department*, 282–84; Risch, *The Quartermaster Corps*, 142nn67, 68.

3. There are at least three different but plausible explanations of the name "jeep." For a detailed discussion of this question, see J.-G. Jeudy and M. Tararine, *The Jeep* (New York: Vilo, 1981), 44–46.

4. Jeudy and Tararine, *The Jeep*, 20–23.

5. Ibid., 23–27; Thomson and Mayo, *The Ordnance Department*, 276–77; box 11, Reconnaissance Car, pp. 6, 12, 13, 17, Accession 435, La Croix Collection, BFRC.

6. Thomson and Mayo, *The Ordnance Department*, 277–78; Risch, *The Quartermaster Corps*, 141; box 11, Reconnaissance Car, pp. 13, 14, 23, Accession 435, La Croix Collection, BFRC.

7. Box 11, Reconnaissance Car, pp. 8, 10, 24, 58–59, Accession 435, La Croix Collection, BFRC; O'Callaghan, *Ford in the Service of America*, 180.

8. Box 11, Reconnaissance Car, pp. 24, 62 and box 7, FMC Operations Under GPW Reconnaissance Car Contract, pp. 15, 16, both in Accession 435, La Croix Collection, BFRC.

9. Box 11, Reconnaissance Car, pp. 62, 70, Accession 435, La Croix Collection, BFRC; Smith, *The Army and Economic Mobilization*, 9.

10. Quotations from *Washington Daily News*, 4 June 1943, reproduced in Risch, *The Quartermaster Corps*, 141.

11. Smith, *The Army and Economic Mobilization*, 9. The production of trailers, semi-trailers, motorcycles, automobiles, and other "non-trucks" are excluded from the figures.

12. *War Records*, 25:115, 116, CCA; Doyle, *Standard Catalogue of U.S. Military Vehicles*, 44–48, 55–59; Ferry, *The Legacy of Albert Kahn*, 24, 124–25.

13. Risch, *The Quartermaster Corps*, 143; Doyle, *Standard Catalogue of U.S. Military Vehicles*, 88–100; O'Callaghan, *Ford in the Service of America*, 122; *War Records*, 25:115, 116, CCA.

14. Thomson and Mayo, *The Ordnance Department*, 275.

15. Russell A. Crist, "Truck History," 1 November 1956, pp. 280–84; Donald M. Meyer, "The First Century of GMC Truck History," 13–17. Russell Crist was the longtime production control manager at GMC Truck and Coach Division of the General Motors Corporation, based in Pontiac, Michigan. Both typescript histories are found at the General Motors Heritage Center in Sterling Heights, Michigan.

16. Risch, *The Quartermaster Corps*, 143; Thomson and Mayo, *The Ordnance Department*, 274–75.

17. Doyle, *Standard Catalogue of U.S. Military Vehicles*, 122–26; Clell G. Ballard, "The Studebaker US6: America's Other 2½ Ton Truck," part 1, *Army Motors* (Fall 1996): 13; Ballard, "The Studebaker US6," part 2, *Army Motors* (Spring 1997): 45, 46; Crist, "Truck History," 284.

18. Doyle, *Standard Catalogue of U.S. Military Vehicles*, 122; Ballard, "The Studebaker US6," part 2, pp. 23, 24.

19. Thomson and Mayo, *The Ordnance Department*, 286–96; Smith, *The Army and Economic Mobilization*, 9; Doyle, *Standard Catalogue of U.S. Military Vehicles*, 161–76, 208–12.

20. Colonel E. S. Van Deusen (Office of the Chief of Ordnance-Detroit), "Amphibian Army Truck Developments," *SAE Journal* 52 (September 1944): 18; box 7, Amphibian, pp. 2, 3, 9–11, Accession 435, La Croix Collection, BFRC. The "Timetable" incorrectly identified one of the designers as "Hoffeimer" of Buffalo.

21. Box 7, Amphibian, pp. 4, 5, 41, Accession 435, La Croix Collection, BFRC; O'Callaghan, *Ford in the Service of America*, 180.

22. Box 7, Amphibian, pp. 19–23, Accession 435, La Croix Collection, BFRC.

23. Ibid., pp. 30–35, 41–43.

24. Doyle, *Standard Catalogue of U.S. Military Vehicles*, 119; Thomson and Mayo, *The Ordnance Department*, 284–85; box 7, Amphibian, p. 11, Accession 435, La Croix Collection, BFRC; Crist, "Truck History," 282.

25. Thomson and Mayo, *The Ordnance Department*, 285; Doyle, *Standard Catalogue of U.S. Military Vehicles*, 27, 121; box 7, Amphibian, p. 11, Accession 435, La Croix Collection, BFRC; Davis, *Detroit's Wartime Industry: Arsenal of Democracy*, 74.

26. Thomson and Mayo, *The Ordnance Department*, 285, 286; Crist, "Truck History," 284; Doyle, *Standard Catalogue of U.S. Military Vehicles*, 119.

27. Jean-Michel Boniface and Jean-Gabriel Jeudy, *The GMC 6 X 6 and DUKW: A Universal Truck* (Paris: Berger-Levrault, 1978), 183–89.

28. "Automotive Engineers Develop 'the Weasel,' New Cargo and Troop Carrier, in 34 Days," *Automotive War Production* 2 (August 1944): 2; Joseph Geschelin, "Studebaker Production of M-29C Amphibious Cargo Carriers," *Automotive and Aviation Industry* 91 (1 December 1944): 36; Doyle, *Standard Catalogue of U.S. Military Vehicles*, 343–44.

29. Whiting, Tod, and Craft, *The United States Army in World War II*, 25–26.

30. Thomson and Mayo, *The Ordnance Department*, 295–97.

CHAPTER SEVEN

1. Thomson and Mayo, *The Ordnance Department*, 90; Smith, *The Army and Economic Mobilization*, 11, 141, 142n.

2. Thomson and Mayo, *The Ordnance Department*, 76–78; Green, Thomson, and Roots, *The Ordnance Department: Planning Munitions for War*, 408–10; "Americanizing the Deadly Bofors: Chrysler Reveals Dramatic Story of How It Became World's Largest Producer of Antiaircraft Gun," *Automotive News* 19 (7 February 1944): 24, 27; "Chrysler-Made Guns Bag 32 Japanese Bombers," reported by the Incentive Division, U.S. Navy, Carl Breer Reports, Chrysler War Records, vol. 22, "General, 1938–1941," CCA.

3. Wesley W. Stout, *Mobilized* (Detroit: Chrysler Corporation, 1949), 44, 57; Smith, *The Army and Economic Mobilization*, 11; John R. Miller, "Redesign Speeds Gun Production," *Machine Design* (December 1942): 83–88, 178, 180.

4. Jim Donnelly, "Detroit Goes to War," http://www.hemmings.com/hcc/stories/2005/11/01/hmn_feature18.html; "Hudson Signs New Contract: $13,000,000 Arsenal Will Employ 4,000," *Detroit News*, 11 January 1941, p. 1; "Steel Work Rises for $20,000,000 Arsenal Here," *Detroit News*, sec. 1, p. 9.

5. "Navy Gives Hudson $14,038,500 Order," *Detroit News*, 31 July 1941, p. 16; "Naval Plant

Work Halted by Pay Row," *Detroit News*, 23 August 1941, p. 1; "Workers Back Monday: Naval Plant Construction Halted a Day," *Detroit News*, 24 August 1941, sec. 4, p. 10.

6. Hudson Motor Car Company, Directors' Meetings, 21 July 1941, 19 September 1941, 20 February 1942, and 20 May 1942, CCA; texts of speeches given by A. Edward Barit and Rear Admiral W.H.P. Blandy, at the dedication of the U.S. Naval Ordnance plant, Centerline, Michigan, 28 October 1941, CCA. A monthly summary of production is found with the minutes of the Hudson directors' meetings.

7. "Hudson-Built Guns Score in Pacific," *Detroit News*, 20 December 1942, sec. 1, p. 13; "Sea Victory Credited to Hudson-Built Guns," *Detroit News*, 5 May 1943, p. 10; "Hudson-Built 'Steel Curtains' Protect Fleet," *Detroit News*, 14 February 1943, sec. 4, p. 6.

8. Hudson Motor Car Company, Directors' Meetings, 20 September and 26 October 1943, CCA; "Naval Ordnance Plant to Switch Pilots," *Detroit News*, 7 October 1943, pp. 1, 11; "Hudson Chief, Navy Confer on Plant Loss," *Detroit Times,* 7 October 1943, pp. 1, 3; "A Letter from the Navy," *Detroit Times*, 7 October 1943, p. 4; "Navy Silent on Cause for Change at Arsenal," *Detroit Free Press*, 8 October 1943, p. 21; "Hudson Views Arsenal Loss: Statement on Change Is Devoid of Criticism," *Detroit News*, 10 October 1943, sec. 1, p. 1.

9. "Hudson Co. Loses Reins at Arsenal: Navy Terminates Contract; Gives Job to Westinghouse; Rift Is Reported," *Detroit Free Press*, 7 October 1943, pp. 1, 9; "Inside Story: How Hudson Lost Arsenal," *Detroit Times*, 10 October 1943, pt. 1, p. 2.

10. Charles O. Herb, "Guns to Arm Our Merchant Marine," *Machinery* 48 (January 1942): 107–8; Joseph Geschelin, "Pontiac Concentrates on Oerlikon Anti-Aircraft Guns," *Automotive and Aviation Industries* 87 (1 August 1942): 20–22.

11. Roland Buford and William B. Boyd, *U.S. Navy Bureau of Ordnance in World War II* (Washington, DC: Bureau of Ordnance, Department of the Navy, 1953), 245–46, 266.

12. Helen J. Earley and James R. Wilkinshaw, *Oldsmobile: A War Years Pictorial* (Lansing, MI: Earley Enterprises, 1997), 14–41, 45.

13. Thomson and Mayo, *The Ordnance Department*, 61, 179, 181.

14. Ibid., 157; Saginaw Steering Gear Division, General Motors Corporation, *Out of the Valley to Victory*, n.p.

15. "Day's War Buying Totals $241,722,438: G.M. to Build Plants and Make Machine Guns at a Cost of $61,398,872," *New York Times*, 15 September 1940; "G.M.C. Begins Output of $61,000,000 Guns: First Two of Four Plants Are Busy on .30 and .50 Caliber," *New York Times*, 18 April 1941; Orth, "The War Years," 37–38. The production systems established for .50-caliber machine guns at the A. C. Spark Plug plant and for .30-caliber guns at Saginaw Steering Gear are discussed in great detail in "From Motor Cars to Machine Guns," *American Machinist* (23 July 1941): 702–22.

16. Saginaw Steering Gear Division, General Motors Corporation, *Out of the Valley to Victory*; "Machine Guns—One of General Motors Defense Activities," *Machinery* (April 1941): 138–39.

17. "From Motor Cars to Machine Guns," 713.

18. Orth, "The War Years," 39–40; Smith, *The Army and Economic Mobilization*, 11.

19. General Motors Corporation, *Annual Report for 1945*, 28; Thomson and Mayo, *The Ordnance Department*, 152; Stout, *Mobilized*, 44, 57.

20. Wesley W. Stout, *Bullets by the Billion* (Detroit: Chrysler Corporation, 1946), 1, 2.

21. Thomson and Mayo, *The Ordnance Department*, 201; Smith, *The Army and Economic Mobilization*, 13; Stout, *Bullets by the Billion*, 20–30.

22. Wesley W. Stout, *A War Job "Thought Impossible"* (Detroit: Chrysler Corporation, 1945), 19–31, 34; O'Callaghan, *Ford in the Service of America*, 134–36, 181; General Motors Corporation, *Annual Report for 1945*, 28.

23. Wesley W. Stout, *The Great Detective* (Detroit: Chrysler Corporation, 1946), 51–57.

24. Stout, *Mobilized*, 68–70; Hyde, *Storied Independent Automakers*, 147; General Motors Corporation, *Annual Report for 1945*, 28.

25. Stout, *Mobilized*, 71–74; "New Marine Tractor Beats Tug and Cuts Costs," *Detroit News*, 25

July 1942, p. 4; "Now We Build 'Tugboats,'" *Chrysler War Work Magazine* 9 (February 1943): 8–10; "13 Ships a Day for Chrysler Corporation's 'Dry-Land' Shipyard," *Chrysler War Work Magazine* 10 (March 1944): 12–13.

26. Stout, *Mobilized*, 74–90; "Chrysler Smoke Screen to Protect Our Invading Soldiers," *Chrysler War Work Magazine* 10 (November 1943), 3–4; "Reflectors Made by Chrysler Cast Beam 20 Miles," *Automotive News* 20 (18 December 1944): 4; "Twenty-Mile Tunnels through Darkness," *Chrysler War Work Magazine* 11 (January 1945): 8–9.

27. Stout, *Mobilized*, 193; "Chrysler Airtemp at War," *Chrysler War Work Magazine* 9 (April 1943): 6–7.

28. Wesley W. Stout, *Secret* (Detroit: Chrysler Corporation, 1947), 51–61; James Jones, "The Key to Chrysler's Return to Prosperity," *Ward's Quarterly* 1 (Winter 1965): 58.

29. *Summary of War Operations of General Motors for the Year 1943*, abr. ed. (September 1943). 89. This document is found in the General Motors Heritage Center, Sterling Heights, Michigan.

30. Ibid., 54, 70, 74, 80.

CHAPTER EIGHT

1. U.S. Bureau of the Census, *Historical Statistics of the United States, Colonial Times to 1957* (Washington, DC: U.S. GPO, 1957), 71, 73, 736.

2. Fairchild and Grossman, *The Army and Industrial Manpower*, 46–48, 55.

3. O'Callaghan, *Ford in the Service of America*, 156–58.

4. Stout, *"TANKS Are Mighty Fine Things,"* 102; O'Callaghan, *Ford in the Service of America*, 154–58.

5. Clive, *State of War*, 171, 177–79.

6. Ibid., 138–39, 177–80.

7. Ibid., 138–42; August Meier and Elliot Rudwick, *Black Detroit and the Rise of the UAW* (New York: Oxford University Press, 1979), 110n. Meier and Rudwick argue that the claims that the KKK had taken over Packard Local 190 lack evidence and are at best exaggerated.

8. Holley, *Buying Aircraft*, 527; O'Callaghan, *Ford in the Service of America*, 71–72; box 21, 19:33–34, Accession 435, La Croix Collection, BFRC; Lowell Juilliard Carr and James Edson Stermer, *Willow Run: A Study of Industrialization and Cultural Inadequacy* (New York: Harper & Brothers, 1952), 45n3.

9. Carr and Stermer, *Willow Run*.

10. Ibid., 214–18, 249–53.

11. "B-24 Construction and Production Analysis," 96.

12. Lloyd H. Bailer, "The Automobile Unions and Negro Labor," *Political Science Quarterly* 59 (December 1944): 548–49; Robert C. Weaver, "The Employment of the Negro in War Industries," *Journal of Negro Education* 12 (1943): 389; Meier and Rudwick, *Black Detroit and the Rise of the UAW*, 5–7; Hyde, *Riding the Roller Coaster*, 145.

13. Meier and Rudwick, *Black Detroit and the Rise of the UAW*, 5–9, 18–19; Hyde, *The Dodge Brothers*, 128, 130.

14. Bailer, "The Automobile Unions and Negro Labor," 549; Meier and Rudwick, *Black Detroit and the Rise of the UAW*, 7–9; Robert W. Dunn, *Labor and Automobiles* (New York: International Publishers, 1929), 69.

15. Fairchild and Grossman, *The Army and Industrial Manpower*, 160; Andrew Edmund Kersten, *Race, Jobs, and the War: The FEPC in the Midwest, 1941–1946* (Urbana: University of Illinois Press, 2000), 97, 110; Chrysler Corporation War Records, vols. 23–25, "General, 1942–1946," CCA.

16. Kersten, *Race, Jobs, and the War*, 1–3.

17. The most detailed discussion of auto industry hate strikes is found in Meier and Rudwick, *Black Detroit and the Rise of the UAW*, 119–36, 162–74.

18. Karen Tucker Anderson, "Last Hired, First Fired: Black Women Workers during World War

II," *Journal of American History* 69 (June 1982): 86; Eileen Boris, "'You Wouldn't Want One of 'em Dancing with Your Wife': Racialized Bodies on the Job in World War II," *American Quarterly* 50 (March 1998): 86, 94–95.

19. Fairchild and Grossman, *The Army and Industrial Manpower*, 161–64.

20. Meier and Rudwick, *Black Detroit and the Rise of the UAW*, 127–30.

21. Bailer, "The Automobile Unions and Negro Labor," 569–70; Meier and Rudwick, *Black Detroit and the Rise of the UAW*, 132–33.

22. Bailer, "The Automobile Unions and Negro Labor," 569; Meier and Rudwick, *Black Detroit and the Rise of the UAW*, 131–32.

23. Bailer, "The Automobile Unions and Negro Labor," 570; Meier and Rudwick, *Black Detroit and the Rise of the UAW*, 112, 134.

24. Bailer, "The Automobile Unions and Negro Labor," 570–71; Kersten, *Race, Jobs, and the War*, 105; Meier and Rudwick, *Black Detroit and the Rise of the UAW*, 167–72, 214.

25. Meier and Rudwick, *Black Detroit and the Rise of the UAW*, 176–83; Kersten, *Race, Jobs, and the War*, 105–6.

26. Meier and Rudwick, *Black Detroit and the Rise of the UAW*, 120–21, 155, 163, 214.

27. Megan Taylor Shockley, *"We, Too, Are Americans": African American Women in Detroit and Richmond, 1940–54* (Urbana: University of Illinois Press, 2004), 65.

28. Ibid., 90; Meier and Rudwick, *Black Detroit and the Rise of the UAW*, 166–67; Marguerite Brown, "'Because of My Race': Gender, Race, and Black Women Workers in Detroit during World War II" (Master's thesis, Wayne State University, 1994), 84.

29. Shockley, *"We, Too, Are Americans,"* 91.

30. Brown, "'Because of My Race,'" 38–45; Meier and Rudwick, *Black Detroit and the Rise of the UAW*, 136–38, 147–54.

31. "Discrimination against Negroes in Employment, 1942–1947," United Auto Workers Research Department Collection, box 9, folder 24, Walter P. Reuther Library of Labor and Urban Affairs, Wayne State University, Detroit, Michigan (hereafter WPRL); "Reconversion, 1944–45," box 22, folder 15, WPRL; Fairchild and Grossman, *The Army and Industrial Manpower*, 160.

32. "Discrimination against Negroes in Employment, 1942–1947," and box 11, folder 8, "Women's Questionnaire," WPRL; International Labour Office, *The War and Women's Employment: The Experience of the United Kingdom and the United States* (Montreal: International Labour Office, 1946), 184.

33. "Men and Women in GM Plants, June 1944," box 19, folder 9, WPRL.

34. Fairchild and Grossman, *The Army and Industrial Manpower*, 172; U.S. Bureau of the Census, *Historical Statistics of the United States, Colonial Times to 1957*, 71–72; International Labour Office, *The War and Women's Employment*, 166–67.

35. Fairchild and Grossman, *The Army and Industrial Manpower*, 169, 173; Thelma McKelvey, U.S. Bureau of Labor Statistics, "Women in War Production: Report to the House Committee Investigating National Defense Migration" (Washington, DC: U.S. GPO, 1942), 5. For a detailed discussion of the jobs women held in the wartime aircraft industry, see Chester W. Gregory, *Women in Defense Work during World War II: An Analysis of the Labor Problem and Women's Rights* (Jericho, NY: Exposition Press, 1974), 67–79.

36. Ruth Milkman, *Gender at Work: The Dynamics of Job Segregation by Sex during World War II* (Urbana: University of Illinois Press, 1987), 13; *Ford Times*, 1 April 1909, pp. 8–9; Horace Lucien Arnold and Fay Leone Faurote, *Ford Methods and the Ford Shops* (New York: Engineering Magazine Company, 1915), 1, 21, 58, 372–73, 398–401; Hyde, *The Dodge Brothers*, 108.

37. Dunn, *Labor and Automobiles*, 73–74.

38. U.S. Bureau of Labor Statistics, Bulletin No. 438, *Wages and Hours of Labor in the Motor Vehicle Industry: 1925* (Washington, DC: U.S. GPO, 1927), 2–4, 26–36.

39. Harold R. Hosea and George E. Votara, *Wage Structure of the Motor Vehicle Industry*, U.S. Bureau of Labor Statistics, Bulletin No. 706 (Washington, DC: U.S. GPO, 1942), 1–2, 24, 35, 39.

40. Nancy F. Gabin, *Feminism in the Labor Movement: Women and the United Auto Workers,*

1935–1970 (Ithaca, NY: Cornell University Press, 1990), 36, 80; Milkman, *Gender at Work*, 26; Helen Baker, *Women in War Industries* (Princeton, NJ: Industrial Relations Section, Department of Economics and Social Institutions, Princeton University, 1942), 14; International Labour Office, *The War and Women's Employment*, 230; U.S. Department of Labor, Women's Bureau, Bulletin No. 209, *Women Workers in Ten Production Areas and Their Postwar Employment Plans* (Washington, DC: U.S. GPO, 1946), 27, 36, 45.

41. U.S. Department of Labor, *Women Workers in Ten Production Areas*, 55.
42. Howard Dratch, "The Politics of Child Care in the 1940s," *Science and Society* 38 (1974): 175–76; International Labour Office, *The War and Women's Employment*, 233–35.
43. U.S. Department of Labor, *Women Workers in Ten Production Areas*, 56.
44. Gabin, *Feminism in the Labor Movement*, 54–57; Milkman, *Gender at Work*, 67–68.
45. "Women and Negroes, UAW Regions 1–1D," box 9, folders 8 and 9, and "Reconversion, 1944–45," box 22, folder 15, both in WPRL; Milkman, *Gender at Work*, 51; Gabin, *Feminism in the Labor Movement*, 57; U.S. Department of Labor, *Women Workers in Ten Production Areas*, 36.
46. "Discrimination against Negroes in Employment, 1942–1947," Box 11, Folder 5; "Employment, Wartime, 1942–45," box 11, folder 9; "Women and Negroes, UAW Regions 1–1D," April 1943; box 19, "Men and Women in GM plants, June, 1944"; box 32, folders 10 and 12, "Women, Employment Survey, June 1942," all in WPRL; Accession 1986, box 1, folder 4, "Fisher Body Employment," 112, SA/KU; D'Ann Campbell, *Women at War with America: Private Lives in a Patriotic Era* (Cambridge, MA: Harvard University Press, 1984), 113; Gabin, *Feminism in the Labor Movement*, 59.
47. Milkman, *Gender at Work*, 59; Gabin, *Feminism in the Labor Movement*, 60–61.
48. The most thorough study of these issues is Milkman, *Gender at Work*, esp. 70–77.
49. U.S. Department of Labor, Women's Bureau, *Choosing Women for War Industry Jobs*, March 1943, summarized in International Labor Organization, *The War and Women's Employment*, 193–94.
50. "Provisions in Plants for Physical Differences Enable Women to Handle Variety of War Jobs," *Automotive War Production* 2 (September 1943): 7; Campbell, *Women at War with America*, 124–25; Gabin, *Feminism in the Labor Movement*, 60–61; Milkman, *Gender at Work*, 60.
51. Baker, *Women in War Industries*, 44.
52. Gabin, *Feminism in the Labor Movement*, 61–63; Milkman, *Gender at Work*, 74–77.
53. Gabin, *Feminism in the Labor Movement*, 78; International Labour Organization, *The War and Women's Employment*, 202–3, 209–10.
54. U.S. Department of Labor, *Women Workers in Ten War Production Areas*, 31.
55. Milkman, *Gender at Work*, 112–16.
56. Ibid., 1–3, 155.

CHAPTER NINE

1. Koistinen, *Arsenal of World War II*, 499.
2. Ibid.
3. The most comprehensive discussions of the mobilization of the Nazi economy can be found in Tooze, *The Wages of Destruction*; Overy, *War and Economy in the Third Reich*.
4. Henry Ashby Turner Jr., *General Motors and the Nazis: The Struggle for Control of Opel, Europe's Biggest Carmaker* (New Haven: Yale University Press, 2005), 98–103, 132; Neil Gregor, *Daimler-Benz in the Third Reich* (New Haven: Yale University Press, 1998), 92–100, 134–40.
5. Alan S. Milward, *The German Economy at War* (London: University of London Press, 1965), 58–73; Werner Abelshauser, "Germany: Guns, Butter, and Economic Miracles," in Mark Harrison, ed., *The Economics of World War II: Six Great Powers in International Comparison* (Cambridge: Cambridge University Press, 2000), 151–57; Cairncross, *Planning in Wartime*, 163.
6. Richard Rice, "Economic Mobilization in Wartime Japan: Business, Bureaucracy, and Military in Conflict," *Journal of Asian Studies* 38 (1979): 691–92; Nakamura Takafusa, "The Japanese

Economy as a 'Planned Economy,'" in Erich Pauer, ed., *Japan's War Economy* (New York: Routledge, 1999), 14–15; Jerome B. Cohen, *Japan's Economy in War and Reconstruction* (Minneapolis: University of Minnesota Press, 1949), 49–52, 57.

7. Rice, "Economic Mobilization in Wartime Japan," 691–92; Takafusa, "The Japanese Economy," 18–19; Cohen, *Japan's Economy in War and Reconstruction*, 74–84.

8. Cohen, *Japan's Economy in War and Reconstruction*, 53, 58, 210.

9. Tooze, *The Wages of Destruction*, 641; Harrison, *The Economics of World War II*, 17. Calculations of the GDP of different countries are at best only estimates because of the challenges of comparing different currencies and accounting systems.

10. Tiffany B. Dziurman, "Awarding Excellence," *Michigan History Magazine* 78 (July/August 1994): 22.

11. U.S. War Department, *Compilation of War Department General Orders, Bulletins, and Circulars* (Washington, DC: U.S. GPO, 1943), 147; http://www.history.navy.mil/library/online/e_award.htm.

12. Dziurman, "Awarding Excellence," 22; http://www.history.navy.mil/library/omline/e_award.htm; Stout, *"TANKS Are Mighty Fine Things,"* 135.

13. V. Dennis Wrynn, *America Goes to War: The American Automobile Industry in World War II* (Osceola, WI: Motorbooks International, 1993).

14. Ibid., 36, 47, 52, 57, 85, 88, 95.

15. Ibid., 62, 68, 93, 110, and 121 for Nash-Kelvinator advertisements and pp. 38, 66, 98, 105, 116, and 134 for Studebaker advertisements.

16. Ibid., 36, 37, 92.

17. Stout, *A War Job "Thought Impossible."*

18. Stout, *The Great Detective*.

19. Stout, *Bullets by the Billion*.

20. Stout, *"TANKS Are Mighty Fine Things."*

21. Wesley W. Stout, *Great Engines and Great Planes* (Detroit: Chrysler Corporation, 1947).

22. Stout, *Secret*.

23. Stout, *Mobilized*.

24. *Significant War Scenes by Battlefront Artists, 1941–1945: A Collection of Reflective Paintings in Which Sixteen Artists Interpret War as They Saw It around the World* (Detroit: Chrysler Corporation, 1947, 1951) and Detroit Historical Museum Property Inventory, Accession 1986.014.

25. The General Motors divisional pamphlets are found at the General Motors Heritage Center in Sterling Heights, Michigan. For a discussion of Charles La Croix's work, see O'Callaghan, *Ford in the Service of America*, 1, 2. The Charles C. La Croix Collection comprises Accession 435 of the BFRC.

Index